WEIMAR GERMANY: WRITERS AND POLITICS

WEIMAR GERMANY: WRITERS AND POLITICS

ESSAYS BY

M. Swales
University College, London
R. Gray
Emmanuel College, Cambridge
H. Ridley
University College, Dublin
D. Horrocks
University of Keele
A. F. Bance
University of St. Andrews
M. E. Humble
University of St. Andrews
A. V. Subiotto
University of Birmingham
J. J. White
King's College, London
P. V. Brady
Birkbeck College, London
S. Parkes
Sheffield Polytechnic
R. Speirs
University of Birmingham
J. M. Ritchie
University of Sheffield

T. M.

WEIMAR GERMANY: WRITERS AND POLITICS

EDITED BY

A. F. BANCE

1982

SCOTTISH ACADEMIC PRESS

EDINBURGH

Published by
Scottish Academic Press Ltd,
33 Montgomery Street
Edinburgh EH7 5JX

SBN 0 7073 0291 9

Printed in Great Britain by
Clark Constable Ltd
Edinburgh

Contents

	Page
Preface	vi
In Defence of Weimar: Thomas Mann and the Politics of Republicanism M. SWALES	1
Hermann Hesse: The Prose and the Politics R. GRAY	14
Irrationalism, Art and Violence: Ernst Jünger and Gottfried Benn H. RIDLEY	26
The Novel as History — Hermann Broch's Trilogy *Die Schlafwandler* D. HORROCKS	38
Alfred Döblin's *Berlin Alexanderplatz* and Literary Modernism A. F. BANCE	53
Lion Feuchtwanger's *Erfolg*: The Problems of a Weimar Realist M. E. HUMBLE	65
Kleiner Mann — was nun? and *Love on the Dole*: Two Novels of the Depression A. V. SUBIOTTO	77
The cult of 'Functional Poetry' during the Weimar Period J. J. WHITE	91
Playing to the Audience — Agitprop Theatricals 1926–1933 P. V. BRADY	110
Ödön von Horváth S. PARKES	121
Brecht's Plays of the Weimar Period R. SPEIRS	138
Johst's *Schlageter* and the End of the Weimar Republic J. M. RITCHIE	153
Walter Benjamin — Towards a new Marxist Aesthetic H. RIDLEY	168

Preface

One difficulty which students of the Weimar period do not seem to face is that of establishing 'relevance'. The case is very likely to be the opposite: the temptation is to present the inter-war years in Germany in generalizing, popularizing or even sensational terms which do little service to the cause of understanding a fascinating but elusive period. Complexity is a true part of the fascination and, for that matter, the relevance of the time — relevance in the less facile sense of a salutary reminder of the multiplicity of political and intellectual pressures bearing down upon the most productive spirits of an age.

Part of the object of this collection of essays is to draw attention to, and to restore, the particular complexities surrounding writers so well assimilated into 'world literature' as to have acquired independent existence outside the Weimar context. And a number of contributors to this volume confront prior assumptions which make Weimar so deceptively accessible to our own age. As Hugh Ridley puts it, the true relevance of Weimar is 'neither that of the collector nor that of the antiquarian historian but a relevance which comes from the Weimar Republic's struggle to overcome problems which we have yet to solve, trying out intellectual and cultural forms which our own age sees in no sharper focus'.

Chief among the problems the Republic had to face, however, was one less familiar in the older democracies: the political problem of reaction to its own existence. That edge to political life, the unceasing questioning of the Republic's very basis in legality, led *de facto* to a politicizing of the literature of the period, since no writer could avoid the political categorization of his work. Least of all could there be an escape into the traditional a-political stance of the vatic German *Dichter* (an untranslatable term: poet, writer, prophet); for, as Ronald Gray suggests with reference to Hermann Hesse, dividing spirit and matter has its repercussions in the political sphere, if only by serving to increase passive indifferentism. In Weimar the question arises time and again, as to the relationship of the sphere of art to that of politics and social change. At opposite poles of response to the question stand Hermann Broch, with his apparent downgrading of empirical facts for the sake of assessing the values that lie behind them; and the functionalism (akin to the aims of the Bauhaus movement in applied art and architecture) of *Agitprop* street theatre refining its dramatic 'theory' only under the pressure of practice, or the *Gebrauchslyrik* (functional poetry) which, at its best, serves as a 're-awakening of poetry's moral concern for the iniquities of trivial day-to-day experience and for the predicament of contemporary urban existence' (John White).

It is salutary to return to the struggle with the actuality of facts and be jolted out of our almost irresistible assumptions of historical inevitability (a problem adumbrated by writers as diverse as Broch and Benjamin) about the course of Weimar developments. As Ronald Speirs makes clear, Brecht for example does *not* progress smoothly from Expressionism through *Neue Sachlichkeit* (New Objectivity) to specific political commitment during the twenties. (It is an incidental virtue of a collection of essays by various hands that the reader is offered a good selection of glosses on such a term as the mode-word *Neue Sachlichkeit*). It is easy to see Brecht as the apprentice to Piscator — though even that view needs careful scrutiny — but it is just as important, and less self-evident, to recognize the parallels between Brecht and apparently very different figures such as Benn, Jünger and Spengler; the common denominator being Nietzsche.

To overcome the legacy of cultural despair and irrationalism represented above all by that dominating intellect was, in the German context (as Martin Swales points out) a political task which Thomas Mann *conceived* as political and which his audience received as such. The task of overcoming the German legacy of Olympian oblivion to practical politics was not, after all, to be accomplished at so low a price as the progressive *Neue Sachlichkeit* writers sometimes imagined. Despite himself, a writer of greater stature, Alfred Döblin, although anxious to achieve in his novel *Berlin Alexanderplatz* a straight political appeal, found himself grappling unsuccessfully but gloriously with preoccupations which were not only traditional German ones, but overlapped with the chief concerns of the wider Modernist movement, one of whose begetters was of course Nietzsche.

A lesser writer, Lion Feuchtwanger, is useful in offering in his novel *Erfolg* (Success) a checklist of 'typical' Weimar themes, while content to operate, in not untypical Weimar fashion, with an unresolved conflict of active and passive principles, evinced in the East-West dichotomy which 'reflects the general cultural situation in Germany at a time when the aggressiveness of the Wilhelmine era was giving way to a quest for alternative approaches to reality' (Malcolm Humble). Some of these alternative approaches, however, were as aggressive in the sphere of art as the Second Reich had been in that of politics. Ernst Jünger (but also the more contemplative Hermann Broch, in *Huguenau*) reacted to cultural pessimism with an attempt to wipe the slate clean, in the nihilistic belief that only out of destruction could a new spirit arise.

Parallel to the politicizing of art was the dangerous aestheticizing of politics by some artists, as a response to the intractability of a once grand utopian scheme, the Republic of Weimar, increasingly dragged down into the fragmented trivialities of political bickering. An unmistakably German phenomenon, Weimar was doomed not to find the middle way, but to fall into two extremes, each nurturing the other: the extremes of uninspired day-to-day expediency, and heady cultural discourse inherited from the old belief in the claim of *Geist* (spirit, intellect) to transcend reality. Expressionism was one notorious bridge — as Hamish Ritchie demonstrates in relation to Johst's play *Schlageter* — from art to the aestheticized politics of National Socialism, with its propaganda vocabulary of 'spiritual strenuousness, personal authenticity, and cultural redemption' (Martin Swales). The tragedy was that the middle ground, the way of the liberal, social-critical *Neue Sachlichkeit* authors, of a social analyst like Horváth or Fallada, of the well-intentioned writers of Functional Poetry, was a territory that offered a bare subsistence in Weimar, and could only be held at the expense of the kind of charge levelled by Walter Benjamin, and by Brecht, even at the most radical representatives of the New Objectivity movement, that the capitalistic conditions of these writers' production and of the consumption of their works turned their radical intention into counter-revolutionary effect.

They were by no means the last victims of the polarizing of politics, whose outcome was the monopolizing of German life by the 'Great Irrationalism' which isolated *every* German writer of talent, whatever Weimar faction he subscribed to; and which left him no freedom, however dangerous or democratic the freedoms he had claimed in the realm of the spirit.

This volume seeks to span the range and complexity of Weimar literary production, with a modest stake in the enterprise which engaged the energies of Walter Benjamin: 'to discover and create streams in history, to rechannel the past in the cause of the present'. While aiming to interest scholars and specialists, the collection also has in mind the requirements of that possibly mythical person, the interested lay reader, and to that end the quotations have been rendered in English, though references to the original German editions have also been supplied. This volume appears against great financial odds, and thanks are due to various bodies for the grants they have generously provided: these include the University of St. Andrews, the Carnegie Trust for the Universities of Scotland, and the University of Birmingham.

To my wife Sandra I owe a great debt of gratitude for her editorial help in the preparation of the typescript for press: and I owe thanks also to Mr Douglas Grant of the Scottish Academic Press for his unfailing courtesy and his assistance in bringing this book about.

A. F. Bance, St. Andrews
September 1981

In Defence of Weimar:
Thomas Mann and the Politics of Republicanism

Martin Swales

In a recent article[1] Keith Bullivant has examined the whole question of Thomas Mann's famous — and much debated — conversion to republicanism in the 1920s. He makes the point that, while most commentators have accepted that some such conversion did take place, there is considerable disagreement as to the precise nature of the change of heart (and mind) which it entailed. Bullivant stresses the fact that Mann himself was unmistakably loath to repudiate the *Betrachtungen eines Unpolitischen* (Reflections of an Unpolitical Man); and he makes this fact the corner-stone of his own interpretation, which is to the effect that Mann never ceased to be the apologist for bourgeois culture, for that complex, ironic, German notion of 'Humanität' (humanity) which was so much a sophisticated cultural avatar that it is difficult to be sure what precise political concomitants (and commitments) are implied. Hence, Bullivant argues, in spite of appearances to the contrary, Mann's 'allegiance to his ideal and his unpolitical stance remain constant'. (CSWR 29) And he continues: 'It might well be argued that the tragedy of the Weimar Republic derives in part from the fact that Thomas Mann and, most important, those who identified with him, thought that the sort of ideas he was articulating *were* political. This thus helped to foster a political vacuum in the centre which could be exploited by extremists.' (CSWR 29) Not that Bullivant disputes Mann's concern to come to the assistance of the hard-pressed Republic: but he underlines the 'aestheticization and despecification of the social institution he was claiming to recommend to his public'. (CSWR 29) This leads to what he describes as the 'astounding rhetorical opacity' (CSWR 34) of so many of Mann's political statements. A particular case in point is the advocacy of socialism. Bullivant suggests that it is only 'the growth in strength of right-wing ideologies in the period' (CSWR 31) which makes it seem as though Mann was moving to the left: rather, he was remaining true to his familiar ideological stance. From this it follows that his 'so-called political conversion had little or nothing to do with socialism *pur sang* but everything to do with the defence of bourgeois culture'. (CSWR 31)

I have quoted Bullivant's arguments at length because they raise a number of vital issues in respect of Mann's attitude to politics in the 1920s. And I want to begin by dealing in principle with Bullivant's charges. To begin with an obvious point: Thomas Mann was first and foremost a creative writer — and a prestigious one. He was not a political scientist. That he discussed politics within the framework of artistic and cultural concerns is, therefore, to be expected. Moreover, — and this, in my view, is the essential point — in the climate of Weimar Germany the discourse of politics was heavily imbued with philosophical and cultural vocabularies. And this was especially (but by no means exclusively) true of the extreme Right. Time and time again the attack on the Weimar

Republic was mounted not in specific (institutional) terms, not at the level of legislation, of policy or administrative programme, but rather in terms which asserted the cultural and spiritual unacceptability of republican government to the deepest instincts of the German soul. Only if one remembers this does one see just how eloquently political (in context) Mann's speeches and essays were. Of course, it is legitimate for a critic to say that, judged by the criteria of a different society, of a different social and intellectual climate, Mann's republicanism seems curiously rarefied and spiritualized. What is not legitimate is for the charge to be levelled that Mann was steadfastly deluding himself that he was talking about politics whereas he was in reality merely engaging in a cultural-cum-philosophical debate. If the Mann of the 1920s was not talking politics, then neither was the Mann of the *Gedanken im Kriege* (Thoughts in Wartime), *Friedrich und die große Koalition* (Frederick and the Great Coalition), *Betrachtungen eines Unpolitischen*, neither were Lagarde nor Langbehn nor Moeller van den Bruck nor Quabbe nor Rosenberg. There is the curious implication in Bullivant's article that the propounders of the conservative revolution *were* talking the language of (cultural) politics: whereas the Mann of the republican tracts was *confusing* culture and politics. Surely what Mann was trying to do was to make sure that the conservative, reactionary voices did not have a monopoly of all the best cultural tunes (and, in Weimar Germany, cultural tunes were the best political tunes). In a very precise sense, then, Mann was taking issue with a particular kind of heady cultural-cum-political debate — by challenging precisely the link which his adversaries were making between German culture and one particular political ideology. This is hardly to be accounted obtuseness. Indeed, quite the reverse: Mann had correctly identified the particular discourse which so malevolently threatened the Republic; and he tried to mobilize that same kind of discourse in defence of the Republic. As I hope to show later, Mann's contemporaries did understand, quite clearly, what he was after.

Of course it remains true that Mann could not jump over his own shadow: he could not shed his persona as the writer who was strenuously concerned with the demands and implications of the German cultural tradition, nor could he jump over the shadow of his own age, his own society. If so much of the political debate in the Germany of the 1920s was concerned with the *geistig* (spiritual) validation (or repudiation) of particular political forms and institutions, Mann was, with every fibre of his being, part of that ambience. The commitments he made may not have been politics *pur sang* (judged by the standards of present-day political debate), but they were attuned to the kinds of political commitment that were being articulated all around him: if there was, to borrow Fritz Stern's famous title, such a thing as the 'politics of cultural despair' in Weimar Germany, then surely there was also such a thing as the 'politics of cultural hope'. That was the main thrust of Mann's advocacy.

Moreover, we should not forget that statements which strike us now as vague or imprecise could acquire a quite particular import given the context in which they were made. A number of moments from Mann's life in the years between 1918 and 1936 well illustrate that he was anything but innocent of the extent to which (historical) timing was all-important. One could begin with the *Betrachtungen eines Unpolitischen*. In one sense, this huge essay is an extraordinary, tortuous, complex piece of cultural polemic, a defence of German 'Humanität' (humanity) and irony against the demands of partisan, progressive cosmopolitanism. But it is crucially important to remember the date of its appearance — 1918. The timing makes it a highly polemical political statement. For it became a cardinal document of anti-republican sentiment. The Weimar Republic came into being under inauspicious circumstances: it was widely seen as the product of the military defeat of cherished German aspirations. In consequence, the republican form of government was decried as something that was alien to the true spiritual nature of Germany, as something modern and inauthentic that had been as much imposed on a vanquished nation as were the reparations decreed by the Treaty of Versailles. To this kind of animus — an animus fuelled by the 'Dolchstoßlegende' (stab-in-the-back myth) — Mann's *Betrachtungen* added the authority of sophisticated cultural argument. The stance of the 'unpolitical man' was, in fact, anything but unpolitical: the historical timing made sure of that.

A similar instance of timing is to be found in the matter of the honorary doctorate which was conferred on Mann by the University of Bonn. Now in one sense it is, of course, hardly surprising that a university should elect to honour a great writer. But this doctorate was awarded in 1919, and the timing made clear that it was Mann the defender of embattled German spirituality who was being honoured. Moreover, it was profoundly important that the university in question was at the time situated in the occupied Rhineland, and its geographical position clearly identified it with the doomed national cause. Not quite 20 years later, in 1936, Mann's honorary doctorate was taken away from him: the ostensible cause was his 'Ausbürgerung' (de-naturalization). But once again, in context, the decision was alive with political significance, a political significance of which both Thomas Mann and the University of Bonn were well aware.[2] In this context it is pertinent to recall a passage from Mann's diaries for the years 1935–6. In 1935 Mann ruminates on the fact that another university — Harvard — has offered him an honorary doctorate. Once again, this might seem to be a purely academic matter. But Mann knew that Harvard had declined the possibility of a scholarship endowed by the German government. The offer had been made by Ernst Hanfstängl who was Germany's 'Auslandspressechef' (head of the Reich's International Press Office). Harvard's response had meant that the Hitler government declined to be present at the jubilee celebrations in Harvard. Mann comments about the Harvard doctorate as follows: 'In the foreground there is the consideration of the effect this will have in Germany. The university in question has refused the Hanfstängl scholarship. The honour being offered to me doubtless has also a political purpose.'[3] Mann was, it seems to me, being neither paranoid nor self-aggrandizing when he detected 'also a political purpose' in the matter of these honorary doctorates.

Indeed, it is worth noting that Mann's career as a public figure seems to partake of that task of culturally representing Germany which he undertook in his fiction. Now this notion of cultural representativeness might sound like the hubris of the high-bourgeois artist. But there is more to it than that: for in the Weimar Republic politics were manifestly intertwined with cultural and artistic concerns. One obvious example of this is Thomas Mann's lecture on Wagner and the vituperative response which it provoked. In fact, it was this cultural — but not *merely* cultural — furore that was to begin his exile from Germany.

While he was out of the country delivering the Wagner lecture in a number of European cities, his house and possessions in Munich were confiscated. In 1933 there appeared in his home town — in the *Münchner Neueste Nachrichten* — a repudiation of the Wagner lecture, which left nothing to be desired in respect of the clarity with which it spelt out the political significance of the cultural issue. Indeed, the very first sentence of the 'Protest der Richard-Wagner-Stadt München' (Protest by Munich, the city of Wagner) makes clear that the signatories to this letter are clearly aware of the significant timing of their statement: 'Now that the national regeneration of Germany has acquired firm contours, it cannot be regarded as an irrelevancy if we appeal to the public in our attempt to defend the memory of the great German master against calumny.'⁴ The protest against Mann's view of Wagner comes after Hitler's appointment as Chancellor, after the 'Reichstag' fire, after the banning of the Communist and social-democratic press. The year, it must be remembered, 1933, is the year of the 'Ermächtigungsgesetz' (enabling law). And if we then ask what all this has to do with Wagner, the answer soon becomes clear: 'We sense in Wagner the musical-dramatic expression of deepest German sentiments which we will not allow to be disparaged by aestheticizing snobbery as happens with such conceit and extravagance in Mr Thomas Mann's commemorative addresses on Wagner.' (TMUZ 199) Wagner, then, is symptomatic of that profound German feeling which has become manifest in the 'national regeneration'. And Thomas Mann is seen as the spokesman for that Western, liberal, democratic ideology which is such a profound offence to the most urgent promptings of the German spiritual and national selfhood. The 'Protest der Richard-Wagner-Stadt' continues: 'Mr Mann, who found himself in the unfortunate position of having lost his early national convictions once the Republic was set up and of having exchanged them for a cosmopolitan-democratic viewpoint, has not drawn the salutary conclusion of embarrassed reticence, but has made much of his role as representative of the German spirit abroad.' (TMUZ 199) The reproach here — in spite of what Bullivant maintains — is not that Mann is unpolitical, rhetorically opaque, irredeemably bourgeois: the reproach is that he is being intensely, publicly political (not only in Germany but abroad), and that his politics are an offence to the 'national regeneration'. Reading Mann's Wagner essay now, it is difficult to see it as a pro-republican statement in any obvious sense: but, in its historical context, it amounted to something close to that. And this emerges clearly in the exchange of letters which appeared in the *Münchner Neueste Nachrichten* for June 1933. Peter Suhrkamp wrote to the paper and asked why, at a time of such political sensitivity, it should be thought right 'to involve the utterly politicized public realm in this totally unpolitical question — and to involve it in a way that can only be interpreted politically.' (TMUZ 204) Siegmund von Hausegger (one of the signatories of the original *Protest*) replies: 'I cannot agree with you in your contention that the question of Richard Wagner is totally unpolitical. In times of a reshaping of all values, such as the present, politics demand to be understood in the sense of a specifically constituted *Weltanschauung*.' (TMUZ 205) There is, it should be noted, nothing resigned about the tone of Hausegger's letter: he writes not in a spirit of unwilling acquiescence in the headily politicized mood of the times; rather, he welcomes the profound spiritual upheaval as precisely one in which politics takes on the full stature of a debate about 'Weltanschauungen'. And Hausegger was by no means the only one.

Two further instances of the whole question of historical timing must suffice. I have in mind some observations in Mann's diary which show how particularly sensitive he was to the historical context in which statements became public property. There is the wry comment he makes on a phrase employed by C. G. Jung. Jung had lamented the 'soulless rationalism' which, in his view, militated against the adequate investigation and comprehension of the significance of neurosis. Mann comments: 'The scorn for "soulless rationalism" has negative implications for the simple reason that it implies a full-steam-ahead onslaught on rationalism, whereas the time has long come for people to resist this tendency with all their might.'[5] The key phrase here, it seems to me, is 'whereas the time has long come' — in which Mann expresses a precise — and urgent — sense that certain, in themselves intellectually respectable, arguments become questionable because, in context, they acquire a dubious socio-political resonance which must, at all costs, be countermanded. Precisely this awareness informs his reaction to Hofmannsthal's speech 'Das Schrifttum als geistiger Raum der Nation' (Literature as the spiritual Home of the Nation), which was delivered in 1927. Mann comments on the key notion of the 'conservative revolution' 'to which the late Hugo von Hofmannsthal offered his assent without any concern for the form in which the enraged petty-bourgeois masses in Germany would put it into practice.'[6] He reflects that such dangers were probably less apparent in Vienna (where Hofmannsthal lived). But the speech was republished in 1933 by the S. Fischer Verlag as a separate volume, and Mann comments sadly: 'But his speech must strike people as both prophecy and confirmation; a Jewish publisher prints it, because this is the only kind of material that can be published, and thereby contributes to the spiritual reinforcement and "historical" legitimation of horrors which threaten the whole world.'[7] It is difficult to ignore the political and historical perceptiveness of such a remark, one which has everything to do with Mann's being supremely well attuned to the cultural-political discourse that was so characteristic of (particularly) conservative circles in the Weimar Republic.

When one views Mann in context, two things become clear: first, that he did make an impact on his audience because of (and not in spite of) the fact that he mobilized cultural concerns in the service of political discussion and debate; second, that his constantly reiterated defence of reason, rationality (of, for example, the value of the 'Schriftsteller' (writer) in answer to the German reverence for the 'Dichter' (poet)) was an important — and admirable — attempt to stem the rising tide of irrationalism whose dangers he rightly and clearly identified. A number of factors need to be documented. The first — and most obvious — has already been mentioned: without any doubt Mann's contemporaries understood the nature of the political stand he was adopting. Otto Werner, writing in October 1922, regrets both the fact — and the nature — of his political commitment: 'If, once upon a time, you conceived of the bourgeois who strayed into art as a tragic figure, so now you, on the platform, have yourself become a bourgeois who strayed into politics and fell for democracy.' (TMUZ 105) There was, in other words, no shortage of voices urging Mann to return to the realm of art whence he came. More savage are those who denounce him for lacking the profound and mysterious oneness with the deeper wellsprings of his own nation. Again and again these critics attack him for his blighting, inauthentic intellectualism. Curt Hotzel, for example, reacts as follows to the *Appell an die Vernunft* (A Call to Reason): 'Thomas Mann, with his position and ideology of morbid spirituality, of commitment to cosmopolitan intellectualism, with his alienation from any attachment to the people and the soil, simply cannot understand these profound, dark, religious — and therefore pagan and unbourgeois — currents.' (TMUZ 178) From this it would appear that Mann's 'Bürgerlichkeit' is synonymous with cosmopolitan intellectualism: the combination is, to put it mildly, a curious one, but then any stick was welcome with which Germany's greatest living author could be beaten and discredited. A month later Hotzel returns to the attack, describing Mann as the 'worshipper of senile reason, of cold, sober rationality.' (TMUZ 180) What rumbles implicitly behind this onslaught is the favourite Nazi opposition of on the one hand, 'the sound common sense of the people' and on the other 'subversive criticism'. Mann was, it seems, particularly sensitive about the charges of cold, cerebral intellectualism. And it is clear that he constantly tried to assert his indebtedness to — and embeddedness in — the complex spiritual heritage of the German nation. Keith Bullivant, therefore, has a point when he observes that Mann, at times, could speak in terms 'redolent of "Blood and Soil" literature'. (CSWR 33) Certainly, on frequent occasions, he employed the rhetoric of the 'third way', the 'middle way' that was to be the German answer to the choice between capitalism and communism. George L. Mosse has cogently shown[8] the extent to which such an invocation of the third way was part and parcel of the ideology of the conservative revolutionaries and fed into the Nazi programme for a bourgeois revolution which would assert the corporate oneness of socialism without in any way changing the existing patterns of ownership of either land or means of production. What Mosse's book shows is precisely *how* seductive such an appeal was to the German middle classes. Mann tried to capitalize on this seduction, but to channel it into a different political direction. That he sought to capture this crucial ideological ground in the service of another set of political commitments than those which it was commonly held to underwrite is not, I think, to be accounted folly or imperception. Moreover, his audiences did not misunderstand, did not confuse him with the conservative revolutionaries.

Certainly, what so many reactions to Mann in the 1920s and 1930s make clear is that the public had no doubt as to his insistence on political commitment. Friedrich von der Leyen, who reproaches him with overlooking 'the decisive significance which the invocation of race, breeding, and blood, of the German and teutonic heritage could have for imaginative literature,' (TMUZ 193) concedes — albeit in a tone of fastidious regret — that Mann has grown more overtly political since 1918: 'But Thomas Mann, who calls himself unpolitical, has, since the *Betrachtungen eines Unpolitischen*, placed his essays and addresses squarely at the centre of the political battles of the day: in the process, because his challenged antagonists did not remain silent, the essays have become more nervous and energetic, more relevant and sharp in formal terms, yet at the same time they have become more short-sighted, violent, and self-conscious.' (TMUZ 192) Whatever is in dispute here, it is not the fact that Mann has firmly and polemically entered the political arena. What is also not in dispute is the urgency and force of Mann's voice — the fact that he has to be answered. Ludwig

Brehm, writing in the *Völkischer Beobachter*, is not alone in regretting that Mann is no longer on the side of the angels (Georg Quabbe was another, who dedicated one of his writings 'to the memory of the unpolitical observer'). Resentment is voiced that Mann 'with baffling speed and dexterity has formed a firm friendship with a system of political democracy whose inauthentic and un-German degeneration has never been more sharply and cogently condemned than by him in his time.' (TMUZ 195) The reproach here, *pace* Bullivant, is not that Mann is failing to be political: but it is that he has got his allegiances all wrong. One specific allegiance Mann proclaimed was to socialism (in the early 1930s). This Bullivant disparages, referring to Mann's 'astounding rhetorical opacity', (CSWR 34) and describing the *Rede vor Arbeitern in Wien* (Speech to the Viennese Workers) as 'a most difficult speech that must have caused its audience some trouble.' (CSWR 34) Now admittedly, Mann was hardly an ideal WEA lecturer. But it is noteworthy that Adolf Grimme, in a letter to Mann of November 1932, writes to thank him for the *Wiener Rede*, and asks him to participate in a large demonstration to be organized by the 'sozialistischer Kulturbund' (socialist cultural league) in early 1933. Grimme makes clear that what he expects from Mann is not that he make the case for socialism in terms of the nuts and bolts of practical, economic, and institutional policies, but rather that he should affirm the spiritual and cultural claim for socialism: 'For the immanent tendency of socialism is nothing but humanism transferred from the realm of the purely ideal into that of total reality; it is, as it were, the real-idealistic phase of the German idea of "Humanität".' (TMUZ 197) No doubt this is not, in Bullivant's phrase, 'socialism *pur sang*' either: but it is a version of (typically Weimar) cultural politics, one which is a clear attempt to wrest the initiative from the conservative Right.

J. P. Stern has shown in his recent study, *Hitler: The Führer and the People*, how so much Nazi propaganda was couched in a particular kind of discourse, one in which the political was largely informed by a heady vocabulary of spiritual strenuousness, personal authenticity, and cultural redemption. And it is important to note that a great deal of what passed for political debate in the short-lived existence of the Weimar Republic was curiously devoid of a modest and practical consideration of political aims and means. The legacy of Expressionism was anything but helpful in this respect: over and over again political aspirations were framed in terms of some vatic transfiguration of banal reality: redemption ('Erlösung') rather than legislation assumes a central place in the political vocabulary. As Kurt Sontheimer puts it, 'The Weimar Republic experienced a veritable onslaught of *Geist* on political and social reality, such as scarcely any other phase of German history witnessed. Seldom has the claim of *Geist* to transcend reality been made with such arrogance, with such pitiless radicalism.'[9] Certainly Thomas Mann belonged in the company of 'die Geistigen' (men of the spirit): but two factors distinguish his political utterances from those of so many of his contemporaries. First, he saw clearly that such heady cultural discourse did entail certain commitments or stances within the sphere of practical politics; second, he recognized that the cultural underwriting of politics was dangerously dominated by the conservative ideologists. His tireless invocation of the German cultural past was an attempt to break that domination. Sontheimer comments: 'behind it there was, admittedly, the real experience that the threat to German *Geist* now came from the side of Romantic-conservative thought.'[10] The central ideological thrust of this kind of conservative thinking has been superbly analyzed by Fritz Stern in his famous study *The Politics of Cultural Despair*. Of Lagarde he writes: 'no sharp distinction between his religious and political thought can be drawn: he sought to recapture in the political realm what had been lost in the religious.'[11] Moreover, we should not forget the widespread popularity of this kind of thinking in the last years of imperial Germany (a popularity that was intensified rather than weakened by the collapse in 1918). Langbehn's *Rembrandt als Erzieher* (Rembrandt as Educator) was, unbelievably, a best seller. Stern shows that it owed its enormous success to its hectoring, redemptive urgency. Stern writes: 'to be acceptable to Langbehn, politics had to be ennobled by unpolitical ideals, enveloped by a mystique at once deprecating the present and glorifying the future.'[12] This curious investing of politics with a spuriously regenerative afflatus was part and parcel of the Weimar ethos. It was an ethos that, precisely because of its lack of focus, was sustained and fuelled by all manner of scholars, thinkers, journalists. Peter Gay notes, for example, that a philosopher of the impenetrability of Martin Heidegger could acquire a certain popular following: 'whatever the precise philosophical import of *Sein und Zeit* [Being and Time] and of the writings that surrounded it, Heidegger's work amounted to a denigration of Weimar, that creature of reason.'[13] In this sense, Heidegger's work is much more than a purely academic performance. Moreover, its popularity seems to be linked with what Fritz Ringer has characterized as the central ideology of the German academic community between 1920 and 1933. He points out the extent to which a curiously all-purpose version of 'Lebensphilosophie' (life philosophy), of vitalistic holism took possession of the academic life of the German 'mandarin' culture:

> Synthesis, the whole, understanding, viewing: the slogans were always the same. Biologists and physicians were meant to study the whole organism; pedagogues and psychologists the whole man. In sociology and economics, it was the whole community. In every discipline, scholars made war upon individualism, naturalism, mechanism, and the like.[14]

Not, of course, that we should take this to mean that all were tarred with the same brush. Voices were raised from the academic community in condemnation of the rising tide of irrationalism and rabid conservatism. In 1932 Ernst Robert Curtius published a brief volume entitled *Deutscher Geist in Gefahr*. Curtius makes clear his loathing both of communism and of the prevailing currents of nationalism in Germany. But he also affirms the glory of Germany's spiritual profundity — what he calls 'a philosophical proclivity for the essential and primal being of all things.'[15] And, as representatives of this profundity, he mentions — and praises — Heidegger and Scheler. It is, of course, impossible to read *Deutscher Geist in Gefahr* (The Spirit of Germany in Danger) without sensing how urgently and passionately Curtius feels the magnitude of Germany's crisis in the early 1930s. But, in political terms, his warning voice is nowhere near as clear and cogent as Thomas Mann's. Above all, one registers the real difference when one reads the following sentence from Curtius: 'the nation state, democracy, and social reform were the three political lodestars of the nineteenth century. The middle one of these three has been achieved — and is a disappointment.'[16] For all the rhetorical sophistication of Mann's defence of republican democracy, the fact that the affirmation was made and repeated time and time again is important — and admirable. And, taken in context, it shows very considerable political judgment, a judgment that could, on occasion, be missing even in those writers and intellectuals who would seem to be much more concerned with the nuts and bolts of day-to-day political events. Gordon Craig has commented on Tucholsky's *Deutschland Deutschland über alles*, applauding its splendid satirical verve, but stressing the fact that it contains 'a number of cheap onslaughts on republican leaders that showed a staggering naïvety about the foreign and domestic problems with which they had to cope.'[17]

Thomas Mann has often been seen as the archetypal 'Vernunftrepublikaner', as belonging to that 'ideal type' of the grudging, anything but wholehearted supporter of the Weimar Republic. Certainly the Republic was remarkably ill-endowed with passionate, convinced supporters. Yet it would seem to me proper to include Mann in that number. For his whole attempt from the early 1920s on was to insist that the case for republican democracy was more than just arid reasonableness, more than just 'making the best of a bad job.' The urgency with which he marshals cultural arguments in defence of Weimar has precisely to do with his concern to commend it to the deepest needs and dictates of the German cultural psyche. Mann tried to defend both reason and rationality against the swelling chorus of vitalist voices: but he also tried to give the Republic that sorely-needed cultural, spiritual, in a word, *geistig* validation that alone could give it the cachet of respectability. And it is noteworthy that he passes up few attempts to maintain his campaign. Even seemingly innocuous occasions could be made grist to his mill: the *Rede zur Gründung der Sektion für Dichtkunst der Preußischen Akademie* (Address at the Foundation of the literary Section of the Prussian Academy) is made, by implication, to serve the needs of the present political debate. Moreover, we should not forget how consistently and frequently Mann maintained his openly avowed concern with politics — even after the Weimar years. One thinks of his denunciations of the Cold War mentality, of McCarthyism, of his insisting on visiting *both* Goethe cities (Frankfurt am Main and Weimar) in 1949. It is difficult to think of another twentieth-century writer of his stature who was so consistently concerned with politics. When one compares him with, say, the Auden, Isherwood, Spender generation in England it is difficult to maintain the stereotype that Mann was essentially the 'unpolitical German'.

In conclusion, I should like to comment briefly on Mann's fictional and creative work in the context of his political concerns. Clearly he was, as he never tired of asserting, a 'bürgerlich' (bourgeois) writer. Yet what his fiction from *Der Zauberberg* onwards suggests is that the 'Bürger' is not just some identikit opposite to the 'Künstler' (artist), but *also* the citizen of a particular society. And when Mann mobilized German bourgeois culture in support of the Weimar Republic, it was precisely in order to assert that that culture found its proper self-realization in a particular kind of (democratic) society. Writers are often prone to assert that their duty as writers is to write, that it is their duty as *citizens* which demands that they care about politics. For Thomas Mann, the writer — in a peculiar and insistent way — was also the 'Bürger'. Not, of course, that this made him any less indebted to a particular kind of literary and intellectual

tradition, one which accorded great importance to the life of the mind, to philosophical and conceptual experience as a vital agency within reality. And just as
he was prepared in his political speeches to use his prestige as a writer (and his
country's respect for culture) in defence of Weimar, so his creative work bears
the marks of the political allegiance. *Der Zauberberg* (The Magic Mountain) is,
of course, in one sense a profoundly German novel, indebted in an unnerving
and complex way to the tradition of the 'Bildungsroman' (novel of education)[18].
It is not, by any standards, an 'easy read'. Yet in the first year alone some 50,000
copies were sold. While it can hardly be seen as a work expressing an unambiguous message, it does clearly imply a critique of the 'magic mountain' of the
mind, one which has allowed Hans Castorp (and, by implication, his whole
generation) to dream 'about the spiritual shadows of things in his reflective way —
in fact out of the arrogant propensity to take shadows for things, but to see in
things merely shadows.'[19] And yet, of course, it is a novel which lovingly chron-
icles the doings on that magic mountain, which is loath to withdraw its allegiance
to *Geist* as the motor force within the workings of reality. If our eager young
hero, Hans Castorp, does progress at all, it is not to a clear-cut avowal of the
importance of political and social reality, but rather to a spiritual synthesis of
the warring ideologies that surround him. One high point within his quest is to
be found in the chapter 'Schnee' (Snow) although, tantalizingly, even that moment
proves insubstantial and in many ways short-lived. Castorp, in his dream, per-
ceives a vision of perfect humanity, one in which the true nature of man is
revealed in his position as 'Lord of the Contradictions'.[20] The dream is of a
mediterranean (classical) landscape in which a people of physical beauty and
serenely contained social formality live out their lives, knowing of, but not
disturbed by, the dark horrors of the temple sacrifice. Now all this sounds not
only very rarefied but also somewhat ham-fisted in an allegorical way. And
certainly to modern readers it would seem to partake of that 'rhetorical opacity'
of which Bullivant speaks. But, once again, it is important to note that, in
(historical) context, Mann was being much clearer than may now be realized.
When Castorp first sees the vision, Mann writes: 'On holiday travels he had
scarcely even tasted the south, he knew the rough, pale sea and held fast to it
with childlike, awkward feelings, but he had never reached the Mediterranean,
Naples, Sicily or Greece. Even so he *remembered*. Yes, strangely, it was a renewal
of acquaintance that he was now celebrating.'[21] Castorp remembers the classical
landscape, then, because it is part of the cultural heritage of which his spiritual
identity, as a young German, partakes. And that cultural heritage teaches Castorp
not only to think — but to love — the friendlier thoughts about man's humanity.
Here Mann is seeking to answer the argument of the conservative, reactionary
forces in Weimar Germany which asserts that such humane thoughts are a
modern, utilitarian product, and as such devoid of profound and long-standing
historical and cultural legitimation. In a letter of 1 January 1924 to the American
periodical *The Dial* Mann reports to transatlantic readers his enthusiastic welcome for the recent German translation of Walt Whitman: Whitman's advocacy
of democracy is 'nothing but what one could, in a classicizing, old-fashioned
way, call "Humanität".'[22] And Mann goes on to link the appearance of the
Whitman translation with the publication of Ernst Troeltsch's short pamphlet
Naturrecht und Humanität in der Weltpolitik (Natural Law and Humanity in

World Politics). This essay propagates, in Mann's words, 'the historical necessity that German thinking should once again approach the Western European tradition, indissolubly linked as it is with specific religious and ideological elements — while leaving open the possibility of all the criticisms that need to be made of the betrayal and hypocritical misuse of the ancient and Christian idea of "Humanität" '. (TMS 43) If Germany, then, were to join this older Western European tradition, she would find a framework that would sustain and support the humane thoughts about man's moral — and social — destiny. Such thoughts would be older than mere 'Aufklärung' (Enlightenment) optimism: for they are 'the cosmopolitan and unifying thinking of European "Humanität" with its concept of natural law, thinking born from that stoic and medieval linking of justice, morality, and the common good which we have learnt so deeply to despise as utilitarian enlightenment.' (TMS 43) And these insights, Mann suggests, are important for the whole German nation: they have been stirring in certain individuals in Germany, even in those 'who have known a long and thorough sojourn in the magic mountain of Romantic aestheticism.' (TMS 43)

The date of Mann's letter to *The Dial* is January 1924: in that same year *Der Zauberberg* was to appear. Mann's enthusiasm for Troeltsch's essay says, I think, much about the intended allegorical significance of the dream vision in 'Schnee'. For in it, Castorp 'remembers' something that is as old as Western European culture itself. Not, of course, that this memory is able to break the spell of that 'magic mountain of Romantic ideas': it will take the War to do that. But the critique is voiced: culture is manipulated in the service of what is, in context, a political argument. To which it may well be objected that all this is pretty high-falutin' stuff, an arcane cultural debate which has little to do with the real disposition of power and influence in the Republic. But Mann's letter to *The Dial* contains references not only to *Der Zauberberg* but also to *Betrachtungen eines Unpolitischen* and *Von deutscher Republik* (On the German Republic). And all three texts were, as a matter of historical fact, the object of urgent and widespread debate and reaction. For this reason it is surely not hubris on Mann's part when he offers his American readers an analysis of the political mood of Germany that is heavily couched in cultural terms: nor is it the self-delusion of the cultured man when he claims that a defence of the Weimar Republic in more than party-political terms has profoundly to do with the spiritual health of the German nation:

> If one speaks in Germany of 'democracy', one's interlocutors tend to think of nothing more than a form of government, the republic, and to meet one with arguments against this form of constitution which are always ready at hand and which one knows all too well oneself— to the point of being surfeited with them. But little is achieved, the contradictory voice is weak, it is only party-political: whereas one is not talking party politics when one advocates democracy. Rather, in conscious self-correction, one is pleading for certain spiritual necessities, and the German, for the sake of his inner health, will need to come to terms with them. (TMS 42)

One could, of course, argue that the political volatility of the Weimar Republic had precisely to do with the fact that its political discourse was so compounded with aesthetic, cultural, philosophical — *geistig* — values and concepts. Of this questionable ethos Mann undeniably was part. But it should not be forgotten that, within that ethos, his role was a profoundly creditable one. Nor should it be forgotten that he subsequently wrote a novel in which this particular cultural-cum-political temper of the age was explored and criticized with a perception and anguish that has never been equalled. I am thinking, of course, of *Doktor Faustus*, of (for example) the unforgettable portrait of the conservative-revolutionary Kridwiß circle:

> It was an old and a new, a revolutionary and a regressive world in which certain values linked with the idea of the individual — we might say truth, freedom, right, reason — were utterly weakened and rejected, or rather took on a meaning utterly different from that of the last few centuries. They were plucked out of the pale realm of theory, were bloodily relativized, were related to the much higher authority of power, domination, the tyranny of faith. But not in a reactionary way, not in a way that reinstated what had been the case yesterday or the day before, but in a way that approximated to the innovatory displacement of humanity back into theocratic and medieval circumstances and conditions. There it was: reaction and progress, the old and the new, past and future became one, and the political right coincided more and more with the left.[23]

And, compounding this heady metaphysical–cum–political afflatus, there is, in the Kridwiß habitués, a baying with the hounds of historical inevitability. Zeitblom paraphrases their eagerness to rise to the challenge of the times in the following terms. 'It is coming, it is coming, and when it is here, it will find us rising to the demands of the moment. It is interesting, it is even good — simply because it is the coming thing.'[24] It might, of course, be objected that this is too facile a caricature, too much a literary construct to have any precise reference to the political scene of the 1920s in Germany. But this is not true. In 1925 Karl Rauch wrote an article entitled 'Die Jungen mit Josef Ponten gegen Thomas Mann' (Youth on the side of Josef Ponten against Thomas Mann). In it he applauded Ponten's attack on Mann for his vindication of the 'Schriftsteller' (seemingly a matter of purely literary-cum-aesthetic concern). Rauch writes: 'Such assertions, in which the rising German blood finds its first breakthrough in answer to intellectual civilization, must be made visible and fruitful in the service of what is coming and gathering on all sides.' (TMUZ 119) This — even down to the notion of the 'breakthrough' — could have come from *Doktor Faustus*. But it did not: it came from that characteristic Weimar ambience which Mann understood so well. To his eternal credit, his understanding encompassed critique and, in no small measure, courage.

NOTES

1. Keith Bullivant, 'Thomas Mann and Politics in the Weimar Republic' in *Culture and Society in the Weimar Republic* (edited by Keith Bullivant), Manchester, 1977, pp. 24ff. Subsequently referred to as CSWR

2. See the very full documentation provided in Paul Egon Hubinger, *Thomas Mann, die Universität Bonn und die Zeitgeschichte*. München/Wien, 1974, pp. 69ff.

3. Thomas Mann, *Tagebücher 1935–6* (edited by Peter de Mendelssohn), Frankfurt am Main, 1978, p. 58.

4. Quoted in Klaus Schröter, *Thomas Mann im Urteil seiner Zeit*, Hamburg 1969, p. 199. For ease of reference I have on frequent occasions cited this compilation of reactions to Thomas Mann in the 1920s and 1930s. Subsequently referred to as TMUZ.

5. Mann, *Tagebücher 1935–6*, p. 57.

6. Thomas Mann, *Tagebücher 1933–4* (edited by Peter de Mendelssohn), Frankfurt am Main, 1977, p. 194.

7. Ibid., p. 194.

8. George L. Mosse, *The Crisis of German Ideology: Intellectual Origins of the Third Reich*, London, 1964, pp. 280 ff.

9. Kurt Sontheimer, *Antidemokratisches Denken in der Weimarer Republik*, Munich, 1964, p. 391.

10. Kurt Sontheimer, *Thomas Mann und die Deutschen*, Munich, 1961, p. 60.

11. Fritz Stern, *The Politics of Cultural Despair*, Berkeley and London, 1961, p. 53.

12. Ibid., p. 137.

13. Peter Gay, *Weimar Culture*, Harmondsworth, 1974, p. 86.

14. Fritz Ringer, *The Decline of the German Mandarins: The German Academic Community 1890–1933*, Cambridge, Mass., 1969, p. 387.

15. E. R. Curtius, *Deutscher Geist in Gefahr*, Stuttgart/Berlin, 1932, p. 28.

16. Ibid., p. 37.

17. Gordon A. Craig, *Germany 1866–1945*, Oxford, 1978, p. 486.

18. See my study *The German Bildungsroman from Wieland to Hesse*, Princeton, 1978, pp. 105ff.

19. *Der Zauberberg*, Fischer Bücherei, Frankfurt am Main, 1975, p. 750.

20. Ibid., p. 523.

21. Ibid., p. 517.

22. Thomas Mann, 'German Letters' in *Thomas-Mann-Studien*, Vol. 3 (*Dokumente und Untersuchungen*), edited by Hans Wysling, Berne and Munich, 1974, p. 42. Subsequently referred to as TMS.

23. Thomas Mann, *Doktor Faustus*, Fischer Bücherei, Frankfurt am Main, 1975, p. 368.

24. Ibid., p. 371.

Hermann Hesse: The Prose and the Politics
Ronald Gray

Any account of Hermann Hesse that relates him to his times must acknowledge his success beyond his times. He has achieved it three times over, in the years immediately before 1914, after 1918, and again in the 1960s, with an audience not only in Germany but across the world. The award of the Nobel Prize in 1946 marked the first step to fresh recognition. By the early 1960s he had been acclaimed in the USA as a major writer. By 1980 at least three British paperback series were competing for publication, quoting the highest praise from newspaper critics like Bernard Levin and Philip Toynbee, newspapers and journals like *The Listener, The Financial Times, The Observer, The Sunday Times*. The 'blurbs' are not always accurate. The biography on the flyleaf of the Penguin *Glass Bead Game* says 'the Nazis abhorred and suppressed his books', which is less than half true. A quotation from *The Guardian*, which speaks of Hesse as an 'uncompromising pacifist', is also misleading. But the reputation these words establish has gone on building up for almost a decade and is now firm: the bibliographies have appeared, the standard biographies are written, and what is more surprising, a pop-music group, 'Steppenwolf', has named itself after one of his novels. No other German writer ever enjoyed popularity as broadly based as that.

There has been one critical attack on Hesse as a poet, by Karlheinz Deschner,[1] but that was passed over by most people as improper, though some still try to distinguish between the Hesse who has had, in Kurt Rothmann's words, an effect akin to that of *Werther*,[2] and 'hippy Hesse'. The attention paid by Deschner to what Rothmann calls 'long tried linguistic means' was as unwelcome in German universities as it would be in those of any other country. The absence of courses in practical criticism in modern language faculties leads attention away from the writing to what is called the thought, or, where stylistics or structuralism is substituted for criticism, to questions requiring only a technical knowledge or a quasi-mathematical formula. Otherwise there would be no reason to take Hesse seriously enough to go into details, to spell the whole thing out. The poverty of his writing, as much as its success, is significant.

A glance at Hesse's vocabulary reveals the euphemism in Rothmann's ambiguous, perhaps demurring phrase. Hesse does not use 'long tried' ('erprobt') expressions in the sense of 'long tried and found apposite'. He prefers words like 'schön', 'süss', 'hold', 'wunderbar', 'teuflisch', 'höllisch', 'schrecklich', vague gesturings rather than precise or evocative terms. His concern is all with the symbol, never with the enactment, the linguistic expression, which he overrode in the effort at creating the kind of totality his mysticism required. There is Demian, for instance, that superior friend, guide, and leader-figure, who recreated Hesse's reputation in the early 1920s (the novel was published in 1919, the year when the Weimar Republic was founded). To make an impression, Demian has to be more than an ordinary man, and to make him so Hesse resorts to some crude devices.

14

Even as a boy, it appears, Demian was able to quell any schoolmaster by staring him out of countenance. He had, in fact, an extraordinary look:

I saw Demian's face, and I saw not only that his face was not that of a boy, but of a man; I saw more, I thought I saw or sensed that it was not the face of a man either, but something else. It was as though there was something in it of a woman's face, and for a moment indeed the face seemed neither manlike nor boyish, neither old nor young, but somehow millennial, somehow timeless, stamped by other periods than those we live in. Animals might look like that, or trees, or stars — I did not know that at the time, I did not feel precisely what I am now, as an adult, saying about it, but something similar. Perhaps he was handsome, perhaps I liked him, perhaps he repelled me, even that could not be decided. I saw only that he was different from us, he was like an animal, or like a spirit, or like a picture, I do not know what he was like, but he was different, incredibly different from us all.[3]

The attempts at making this cosmic figure believable, the repetition of 'somehow', 'perhaps', the protestations of an incapacity to say what Demian really was, end with an anti-climax when it appears that above all he was just different. And there is a naïveté, not only in the idea of a man looking simultaneously like so many incompatible things, but in the apologetic tone in which it is presented. Hesse is pleading hard for belief in this hero.

The plea is needed, since Demian is to stand in the novel as the possessor of a mysterious wisdom, ultimately derived in a debased form from Nietzsche, with which he impresses the impressionable narrator, Sinclair. Being both animal and man, Demian calls up memories of Nietzsche's 'blonde beast': the book is in some ways a 'Bildungsroman' (novel of education) in which Sinclair learns to be hard and ruthless, as wilful as his guru.

There is dispute about what Nietzsche meant by the 'blonde beast', whether he admired it or saw it as a sign of decadence. So far as Demian is concerned the Nietzschean message takes the form of a reinterpretation of the story of Cain and Abel: Cain, as he presents him, was a man with a certain impressiveness, 'a spirited boldness in his look', which others resented, and which they condemned as an evil assertiveness, the 'mark of Cain'. The parallel with Nietzsche's 'Master' and 'Slave' is clear enough. Where Nietzsche prefers not to go into details, however, Demian rushes in. The murder of Abel is unimportant:

I was very astonished, [says Sinclair.] 'And so you think all that about the killing wasn't true at all,' I [Sinclair] asked, spellbound. 'Oh yes. Of course it's true. The strong man had killed a weak man. Whether he was really his brother, one may reasonably doubt. It isn't important, after all, all men are brothers. So — a strong man killed a weak one. Perhaps it was an act of heroism, perhaps it wasn't. But at all events the other weak men were now very frightened, they complained a good deal, and if anyone asked why don't you kill him yourselves? they didn't say "Because we are cowards", they said "We can't. He has a mark on his forehead. God has placed a mark on him." That's how the whole yarn must have started.' (GW 5, 32)

This rough and ready defence of murder preoccupies Sinclair for some time. When next he hears a parson preaching on the Cain and Abel story he feels deep in his bones that the parson has told the story wrongly (p. 54). Swinging away again, he confides that he could not go all the way with Demian: 'a good deal was too blunt, as was the business about Cain' (p. 60). But Demian wavers equally. At one point he says it is necessary to worship the whole universe, good and evil together: 'so we must have, alongside divine service, a diabolical service' (p. 61). At other time he gives preference to the diabolical, as when he maintains that the unrepentant thief at the Crucifixion was the more admirable because he remained faithful to the devil, his servant (p. 61). At other times again he is emphatically against killing: 'Certainly you aren't to kill or rape girls and murder them, no. But you haven't yet got to the point where you can see what "allowed" and "forbidden" really mean'. On the other hand, another of Sinclair's mentors, Pistorius, who at one point becomes fused with Demian in Sinclair's imagination (p. 117), tells him that 'in certain circumstances' one may kill a man simply because one finds him repulsive (p. 111).

At all events, Sinclair, who has little wish to kill or rape anyway, decides to worship the devil-god Abraxas, which involves much the same kind of contradictoriness as he saw in the face of Demian:

> Bliss and horror, man and woman intermixed, the most sacred and the most gruesome entwined with one another, deep guilt darting through tenderest innocence — thus ran my dream of love, and thus was Abraxas. Love was . . . angelic image and Satan, man and woman in one, human being and beast, highest good and extreme of evil. My destiny, it seemed, was to live this, to taste it was my Fate. (pp. 94–5)

No more account of the impossibilities is taken than was taken in the description of Demian — 'so Abraxas was the God who was devil as well as God' is all that Sinclair has to say, after which he wavers for a long time, vaguely trying to make out what he intends to do. By the end of the novel, decision is forced on him: the war of 1914–18 has begun, and he is bound to take part. Demian receives a commissioned rank; Sinclair sees how all men, or rather all who are fighting for the Fatherland, are brothers; he admires the 'holy ecstasy' with which they accept their fate, and when he reaches the front he realizes increasingly how close the soldiers are to the ideals of Demian and Abraxas:

> 'Many, very many of them had, not only during attacks, but at all times the firm, distant look, somewhat as though they were possessed, that knows naught of aims, and which signifies complete surrender to the monstrous and uncanny. Whatever these men might believe or think — they were ready, they were useable, the future would shape itself out of them.

For a moment, it looks as though this heady language is about to be qualified — very few German soldiers can have really felt like this:

> And the more fixedly the world seemed bent on war and heroism, honour and other ancient ideals, the more distant and improbable every voice apparently calling for humanity sounded, all that was merely superficial, just as the question about the external and political aims of the war remained superficial. (p. 160)

Sinclair appears for the duration of this passage to be critical of the world's ideals of war and heroism. What Hesse has in mind, however, is an altogether different ideal:

> In the depths something was stirring. Something like a new humanity. For I could see many, and many a one of them died at my side — who had intuitively felt that hatred and fury, killing and destruction were not connected with their objects. No, the objects, like the aims, were purely a matter of chance. The primeval feelings, however savage they might be, were not directed at the enemy: the blood-spilling in which they were engaged was only the radiation from within, from the soul split within itself, which wanted to rage and kill, destroy and die, in order to be born again. (p. 160)

The great success of *Demian* in the years after 1919, when it was first published, is understandable, if it was read as a defence of German soldiers' behaviour in terms of a mystical withdrawal from their actual deeds. The novel had, according to Thomas Mann (in the introduction to the first American edition of 1947), an electrifying influence. Hesse 'with uncanny accuracy had struck the nerve of the times and called forth grateful rapture from a whole youthful generation who believed that an interpreter of their innermost life had risen in their midst'. If that is true, Hesse must have appeared to the post-war generation not as a militarist, yet not as a pacifist either, but rather as the successful contriver of a philosophical justification which would take warfare out of the sphere of practical morality.

In *Demian*, Hesse is far from being the uncompromising pacifist spoken of by the *Guardian* reviewer. Nor was his pacifism uncompromising at the beginning of the 1914 war, when he not only volunteered for service but left the safety of Switzerland to answer his call-up (only to be rejected, as he may have foreseen, on the grounds of bad eyesight). It is true that he wrote the pacifistic essay 'O Freunde, nicht diese Töne' ('Friends, this is not the way'), appealing for 'justice, moderation, decency and brotherhood', and containing many similar appeals, utterly opposed to the war. But he also wrote the poem 'Bhagavad Gita', revised in the same month, September 1914, which treats the destruction of war as ultimately unimportant:

> Krieg und Friede, beide gelten gleich,
> Denn kein Tod berührt des Geistes Reich.[4]
>
> (War and peace are both equally valid,
> for no death can touch the realm of the spirit.)

This is close to what Sinclair says at greater length in the final pages of *Demian*.

Later in 1914, Hesse wrote a poem linking death for the Fatherland more closely with the ideal of non-attachment:

> Zu schönem Spiel und liebem Tand
> Ist jetzt nicht Zeit.
> Die Brüder stehn fürs Vaterland
> Zum Tod bereit.

Doch Zeit ist heut und jeden Tag
Zu höchstem Spiel
Daß man sein Leben geben mag
Für fernes Ziel.

Und anders wird zum Sieg kein Streit,
Kein Tun zur Tat,
Als daß die Seele weltbefreit
Den Tod umfaht.[5]

(This is no time for sweet play and loving trifles.
Your brothers stand ready to die for the Fatherland.
But today, and every day, it is time for the highest
venture, to give one's life for a distant goal. And
in no other way can battle become victory or any
activity become a (real) deed, unless the soul, freed
from the world, embraces death.)

Though Hesse continued to write pacifist articles throughout the war, his person-ally ambivalent attitude to all merely human affairs remained present.

During the 1920s, he remained aloof from politics, as he was to do throughout the rest of his life, though he made public his opposition to antisemitism and was generally accounted, though living in Switzerland as he had done since before the war, on the side of the liberals. After his resumption of Swiss citizenship in 1923, his political writing during the life of the Weimar Republic came virtually to an end, though he wrote hundreds of private letters about political matters. One other novel, apart from the work for which he received the Nobel Prize, needs attention, however, not only because it was even more popular than *Demian*, but because it reveals where he stood as the Nazis came to the brink of achieving power.

The impulse to write *Der Steppenwolf* (published in 1930) may have come from a realization that being a superior mortal like Demian was not everyone's lot. To put it briefly, *Steppenwolf* states that, while Demian and similar supermen are superior in their total acceptance of the world in all its good and evil, smaller men like Harry Haller can still get by, provided they have a sense of humour. Where *Demian* puts the case for Cain, *Steppenwolf* puts it for Abel.

In narrative technique *Steppenwolf* is more complicated, yet the naïveté of the earlier novel remains. The narrator who introduces Haller is as guileless as Sinclair and as much inclined to see great genius in him as Sinclair was in Demian. To all outward appearance, Haller is a scholarly recluse who spends most of his time in his room, reading obscure works of literature. For the narrator, he is a genius of suffering, a man with a terrible capacity for suffering, though we do not hear what he suffers for, or from. He is also a man of great depth of pene-tration. On one occasion the narrator and Haller go to a lecture by a famous philosopher, who disappoints his audience by his flattery of them — a simple case of disingenuousness, it seems. For the narrator it is the occasion for a panegyric. On hearing the flattery, Haller gave the narrator 'an unforgettable and terrible look, about whose meaning one could write a whole volume'; a look more sad than ironical, hopelessly sad, desperate, and laying bare the pretentiousness, the vanity, the superficiality, not only of the speaker but of the audience, not only the audience, but the whole age in which it lived, and not only the age but the whole of mankind:

> the look of the Steppenwolf (Haller) penetrated our whole age . . . it went to the heart of all humanity, in a single second it spoke eloquently all the doubt of a thinker, of one who perhaps had knowledge, the doubt about the dignity, the meaning of human life in general. That look said 'See what monkeys we are! See, that is Man!' — and all fame, all wisdom, all achievements of the spirit, all efforts at sublimity, greatness and permanence in human affairs collapsed and became a monkey's tricks.[6]

This devastating glance is only one half of the contradictory opposites with which the book plays. The narrator is persuaded by Haller that nothing human is of any value whatsoever; it only needs one stern look from such a man to bowl him over with *Weltschmerz*. The idea of the Tractate, on the other hand — an inserted account of Haller from a different point of view — is that everything human should be 'affirmed' ('bejaht'), a word often used by Nietzsche in the sense of accepting gladly. The narrator and the Tractate are thus convenient ways of expressing extreme opposite standpoints. A schematized pattern begins to emerge, so cut and dried as to offer little hope for a novel.

The Tractate seems to be presented as an authoritative pronouncement about Haller, diagnosing his spiritual problems and stating the cure. Since the rest of the novel takes Haller through the phases of just such a cure, the Tractate must be intended to be regarded with some seriousness. There are, to begin with, some general statements about the polar opposition which Haller thinks he has in his constitution, the Wolf and the Man, and these receive a certain amount of abstract definition. The Wolf is wild, uncontrollable, bestial, chaotic, dangerous, dia-bolical. He has a fancy for drinking blood and chasing female wolves, and he has a great capacity for suffering, though we are left ignorant of what this amounts to, especially the blood-drinking, which is not one of Haller's habits. The other side of Haller is 'Man', and this is noble, wise, tender, serves God, and has a great capacity for happiness. This side is not straightforwardly good. The picture is complicated since, according to the Tractate, a large part of what Haller calls 'Man' is merely mediocre, the convention-obeying citizen who is cowardly, stupid and trivial, and who hides away from all personal responsibility behind democratic institutions. (The Republic was often attacked in such terms.) This aspect is in fact very visible in Haller, though the Wolf is hard to detect. The essential point is that there are not two sides, but at least three, the debauchee, sometimes also called the criminal; the noble human being, also called the saint, and the neutral, unthinking, unaspiring 'Bürger', bourgeois man.

It is true that the Tractate castigates Haller for trying to place different aspects of himself into these categories. However, since it continues to use them itself, there is no choice but to go on with them. The point of the separation is to make it possible to instruct Harry that he needs to 'affirm' all sides of his personality, and the means of doing this, he now learns, is through humour, which is essentially 'bürgerlich' (bourgeois). The Tractate takes for granted that Harry should contra-dictorily regard both the saint and the debauchee as needing to be 'affirmed'. It is even more surprising in wanting to include the 'Bürger' in the same affirmation. But that is clearly what it says:

> Humour alone, that splendid invention of those who have been confined in their summons to greatness, those almost tragic, highly gifted figures, humour alone (perhaps the achievement that shows man's genius and particularity at its very best) can achieve that impossible task, spreading over and uniting all regions of the human condition with the radiations of its prisms. (GW 7, 238)

The metaphor is inapt: there is nothing gained by speaking of prisms here. But then the whole passage is an assertion that makes no attempt to show why or how humour 'unites' anything at all. One can, given a certain mood, laugh at everything in sight, but that does nothing more by way of uniting than looking, or crying. How 'humour' is particularly connected with the 'Bürger' remains unexplained. The whole passage is a series of shifting meanings, slurrings of associations, driftings from one contradiction to another, and the conclusion turns out to be, as the Tractate acknowledges in the final sentence of the passage, only a well-worn cliché, an 'often formulated requirement'.

One phrase stands out, when one thinks of the political climate in which *Steppenwolf* appeared: 'To live in the world as though it were not the world, to observe the law and yet stand above it' is one form of wisdom advocated in the Tractate. 1930 was the year in which the Nazis first became a sizeable party in the Reichstag. Within three years, the claim would be made that every German was obliged to give total obedience to the State, and one reason for the Nazis' success was the readiness of a large part of the population to give this. When the Tractate speaks, then, of respecting the law yet standing above it, it could be expressing the very attitude of the conforming 'Bürger' at his most impotent. The implication is that law in general is always to be respected. By dissociating practical action from private criticism, dividing spirit and matter, so to speak, the Tractate may have served to increase passive indifferentism in 1933. The brief anti-democratic references in the Tractate point the same way.

Nothing is ever affirmed in Hesse's work without being also denied, and though he continued to make political pronouncements, they were never as clear-cut as Mann's or Brecht's. Where Mann felt impelled to defend, after his own ironical fashion, the new republic of Weimar, Hesse had less and less use for it or for any other practical matter. He simply was not interested in the mundane concerns of a Germany that happened at one time to be a republic, at another to be entering a tyranny — not that he was unmoved, but that he still believed in transcending the opposites of good and evil. 'World betterment' was a fashion, communism 'rather comical', 'democracy or monarchy, federal republic or federation of republics are all the same to us; what interests us is not the what but the how.'[7] His aloofness continued after 1933 till the end of his life.

The statement, in one of the paperbacks, about Hesse's political positions is as misleading as the one which spoke of him as an uncompromising pacifist. It is not true that the Nazis abhorred and suppressed his books. Though they did not exactly promote his sales, twenty of his works were published during the period of Nazi rule, with a print number totalling 481,000 (swollen by a printing of 320,000 of two minor titles, but still an impressive figure, implying large royalties). Indeed from 1937 he was given official protection against attacks made on him by individual Nazis: a confidential circular to the trade journal for publishers from the Reichsschrifttumskammer, Berlin, dated 27 May, 'expressly states' the view, agreed with Josef Goebbels and the Party Commission for the Protection of National Socialist Literature, that he is not to be attacked and the distribution of his works is not to be hindered. There are conflicting accounts about how strictly this was observed, and to obtain the clearest possible picture of Hesse's motives, Volker Michels' collection of the Political Writings is essential.[8] While there is no question of Hesse's favouring Hitler's regime, however, it is clear that he presented no serious danger either. There were episodes in his books like the machine-gunning in *Steppenwolf*, which could even have been interpreted in a sense acceptable to promoters of violence. But while that could be said of some of Hesse's contemporaries also, no writer of repute except Gottfried Benn remained on such terms with the Nazis, and Benn was soon disillusioned.

In 1942 *The Glass Bead Game* was completed, and the strangest part of Hesse's relationship with Nazism began. For several months he had efforts made to publish the book in Berlin; meeting refusal, he agreed to its publication in Switzerland, and here the deliberate refusal to take sides presents the acutest problem. No other reputable German-speaking author would have dreamt of seeking publication in Germany at that late date, or considered it worthwhile or even decent to do so. Hesse, who had never concealed his disapproval of antisemitism, had written nothing in the novel that a Nazi censor would have been likely to delete. *The Glass Bead Game* could not in any way be construed as an attack on the regime, though it might, by its peaceable atmosphere, have offered a contrast to the Germany of that time, and perhaps for that very reason seemed to its author suitable for publication. The audience he could reach in Germany and Austria was far greater than the audience Mann could reach, publishing his German-language editions in Stockholm through a Jewish publisher with whom Hesse no longer had dealings.[9] Seeing that the novel contained nothing in the least degree favourable to any Nazi policy, Hesse may well have seen no harm in attempting to reach that audience.

But what had *The Glass Bead Game* to offer? Its aloofness from political issues at that time was not necessarily in its favour. It did, however, debate the issue of quietism, and the merits of single-minded devotion to the arts and sciences, at great length, and for this reason alone is a contribution to the question of morally responsible behaviour before and during the Nazi tyranny.

At one level among many the novel, though set in the distant future, is a discussion of the position of a writer like Hesse himself. Should he go on with his search for pure truth, his devotion to music, the quest for an absolute synthesis of all knowledge, or should he return from a monastic seclusion to oppose all that was taking place in his native country? The preoccupation with the problem cannot be doubted, though ten or eleven years — 1931 to 1942 — may seem a long time, in the face of monstrosities of real life which mounted in intensity every month, to arrive at an ending as nugatory as this one proves to be.

The themes of *The Glass Bead Game* do not differ essentially from those of any of Hesse's major works. As always the basic plan concerns a pair of polar opposites which continually revolve about one another, while beyond lies the One which subsumes them and knows no distinctions. The new invention is the game itself, devised originally by students of music who developed a frame modelled on the construction of the abacus, with several dozen wires on which could be strung glass beads of various sizes, shapes and colours. The wires corresponded to the lines of the musical stave, the beads to the time-values of the notes, so that with them musical quotations could be transposed or developed or set in counterpoint to one another. Next, the game was taken over by mathematicians, and later still was applied to classical philology and logic, developing into a universal language through which players could express values and set these in an interrelationship, an arrangement and summing up of the whole of knowledge at a given time, 'symmetrically and synoptically, around a central idea'.

It is difficult to imagine how the game could be playable. To start from a given astronomical configuration, or from the theme of a Bach fugue, or from a sentence out of Leibniz or the Upanishads, and then to elaborate the initial motif or 'enrich its expressiveness by allusions to kindred concepts' sounds impressive, all the more so when it is called an approach to the Mind of God, but it is not at all clear how a parallel can be drawn between a piece of classical music and 'some law of nature'. The fiction can be accepted, at best, as representing purely intellectual or spiritual pursuits in contrast to practical and especially political ones.

A greater difficulty arises from the fact that the whole novel is concerned with whether the central character, Joseph Knecht, does right in continuing to play the game in one of the monastic communities where it is the chief occupation, or whether he should renounce his erudite pleasures, remembering that outside 'in the filth of the world poor harried people live real lives and do real work'. This question, raised by a friend, Plinio Designori, meets at first with a negative answer. At length, however, Knecht decides to give up his supreme position as Magister Ludi and writes a letter of resignation to the supreme council, which is not accepted. The council merely repeat to Knecht what he has been in the habit of saying to Designori, and Knecht never engages in argument with them. The question of the necessity for the artist or intellectual to become engagé, or to allow issues of real life to colour his work, is thus never broached. Everything is left vague; not even the simplest instance of the functioning of the game is offered, so that the debate on the propriety of continuing with it remains insoluble. The complete disparity of the game and reality adds to a sense of irrelevance. No alternative is offered between total commitment to playing with the beads, and abandoning the community of game-players: the compromises whereby in real life writers in fact give part of their time to their vocation, part to their political or social allegiances, are given no consideration.

The quality of the novel is shown by its style, which is for the greater part that of the narrator, a man living still later than the future times of Joseph Knecht. Given that the community of game-players is a community of wise men, and that Knecht himself is the greatest among them in his own day, one would expect their way of using words to reflect this. The narrator, however, expresses the impersonality which is a valued element among the game-players not through an unsentimental straightforwardness or a clean, spare unaffectedness but through an arch officialese which might almost be taken for mockery. He is repetitive and verbose, indirect and coy, pedantically meticulous. The opening paragraph sets the tone:

It is our intention to preserve in these pages what scant biographical material we have been able to collect concerning Joseph Knecht, or Ludi Magister Josephus III, as he is called in the Archives of the Glass Bead Game. We are not unaware that this endeavour runs, or seems to run, somewhat counter to the prevailing laws and usages of our intellectual life. For, after all, obliteration of individuality, the maximum integration of the individual into the hierarchy of the educators and scholars, has ever been one of our ruling principles. And in the course of our long tradition this principle has been observed with such thoroughness that today it is exceedingly difficult, and in many cases completely impossible, to obtain biographical and psychological information on various persons who have served the hierarchy in exemplary fashion. In very many cases it is no longer even possible to determine their original names. The hierarchic organization cherishes the ideal of anonymity, and comes very close to the realization of that ideal. This fact remains one of the abiding characteristics of intellectual life in our Province.[10]

It is as though the narrator had set out to concoct a parody of 'Professoren-deutsch' (academic language). The litotes of 'we are not unaware', followed by the qualifications, 'runs, *or seems to run, somewhat* counter', and the addition of 'prevailing' to the 'laws *and* usages' — all these trimmings call for some patience at the outset. For 'life', the narrator prefers 'biographical material' or 'biographical and psychological information', and for 'distinguished members', 'various persons who have served the hierarchy in exemplary fashion'. The trans-lators improve slightly on the original by lopping off the prelude to the simple statement that the organization prizes anonymity, which reads in the original 'It simply is one of the characteristics of the intellectual life of our province that its hierarchical organisation . . .'. And yet, despite the supposedly scanty details, the reader sees at a glance that some nine hundred pages on the life of Joseph Knecht have been assembled.

Very little is ever said without twofold or threefold repetition. 'For he was not happy, calm, and balanced', the narrator writes of Designori, 'he was not confi-dent and secure. On the contrary he was plagued by uncertainty, doubts and guilts.' Designori's marriage was not unhappy in any crude sense, but still it was full of 'tensions, complications and resistances'. It did not give him 'that tran-quillity, that happiness, that innocence and good conscience he so badly missed'. It required 'a great deal of circumspection and self-control', in fact it 'cost him much effort'. His son became a focal point of 'struggle and intrigue' as well as of 'courting and jealousy', until the boy, not only 'pampered' but also 'excessively loved', inclined 'more and more to his mother's side' as well as becoming 'her partisan' (GW 9, 354).

If there is an admonition it is at once called a warning too. A whim is restated, without greater exactness, as an eccentricity. What is not 'commonplace, ordinary or normal' is further described as 'unusual', and 'not usual and normal', nor yet 'usual and commonplace' (GW 9, 410). But it is now no longer the narrator but Joseph Knecht himself whose words are reported. The supreme player of the game is as incapable of writing unrepetitive German as the man who undertakes to write his life. When he is determined to 'free himself from the fetters of his present condition' his purpose is to leave himself 'unencumbered'. When he is 'all attention' he is also 'absorbedly listening', and when he smiles, 'full of friendly sympathy', he looks with 'goodwill and satisfaction, in fact with a touch of amusement'. The praise he gives to a friend who has attracted so much fellow-feeling is in the same vein:

> 'I must admit', Knecht said smilingly, 'that you have described the episode remarkably well, splendidly. That is exactly how it was, and perhaps the lingering sense of insult and accusation in your voice was needed for you to bring it out as effectively as you did and to recall the scene to my mind with such perfect vividness. Also, although I'm afraid you still see the whole affair in somewhat the same light as you did then, and have not fully come to terms with it, you told your story with objective correctness . . .' (GW 9, 333)

Life as a Grand Master has left him, however, uncertain of the effect of his words, for he continues:

> Have you really failed to see that? But still you have described it very well, I must say. You've called back the whole sense of oppression and embarrassment over that weird evening. For a while I've felt as if I had to fight for composure again, and then been ashamed for the two of us. No, your story is exactly right. It's a pleasure to hear a story so well told.

And for good measure, a few lines, further on, 'Once again, Plinio, you have an excellent memory and you've told the story well' (GW 9, 333). Knecht's condescension towards Plinio echoes the mood produced by the narrator throughout — for the aloofness of supreme wisdom has been substituted a senile paternalism.

Yet as Knecht develops in his dissatisfaction with Castalia, the home of the game-players, his resolution to return to ordinary life outside not only seems like a symbolical resolution by Hesse to intervene in the affairs of the Weimar Republic, but also to be validated by the wisdom and knowledge he has achieved. The reference to Germany just before 1933 is unmistakable, despite the device of placing the novel in future times:

> Before long . . . the generals will again dominate Parliament, and if the people are confronted with the choice of sacrificing Castalia or exposing themselves to the danger of war and destruction, we know how they will choose. [*viz.* they will not be prepared to go on with the expense of maintaining Castalia when money is needed for armaments.] Undoubtedly a bellicose ideology will burgeon. The rash of propaganda will affect youth in particular. Then scholars and scholarship, Latin and mathematics, education and culture, will be considered worth their salt only to the extent that they can serve the ends of war. (GW 9, 392)

Because he fears these events and believes that the outside world needs teachers, 'men who can give the young the ability to judge and distinguish, who serve them as examples of the honouring of truth, obedience to the things of the spirit, respect for language', Knecht decides to leave Castalia, and though he seems less well equipped, so far as language is concerned, than he supposes, there is nothing self-evidently wrong in his decision. As the main part of the novel draws to a close, Knecht is in effect acting as Hesse would have done if he had abandoned his own withdrawn existence in Switzerland and taken some part in the efforts of German writers to speak in the cause of humanity.

All the greater the disappointment when Knecht comes so suddenly and mysteriously to an end. The prospect of his teaching career abruptly stops. After watching the boy Tito perform a mystic dance to the rising sun, he is invited or challenged by him to swim across the mountain lake to reach the other shore before the sun does,[11] and hoping to educate the boy in the values of truth and judgment, Knecht does not reject this test of strength: he takes off his clothes and dives in. His immediate death is as inconsequential as if he had been run over by a bus. Hesse claimed that the death was a sacrifice, 'valiantly and joyfully fulfilled', but, as Mark Boulby says, that is scarcely consonant with all the facts, and as a conclusion, it could hardly be more off-hand. It is as though Hesse had been unable to face the imagined realization of Knecht's intentions in anything like the circumstances which he, Hesse, would have had to face if he had taken a similar decision in his own day. And it is clear enough why he felt able to offer the novel for publication in Berlin in 1942. As a novel, from a strictly literary point of view, there was indeed little to be said in its favour. But politically it was harmless, a lame gesture towards an ideal in which Hesse had no confidence, about which, judging by the novel, he did not even seem to care.

To maintain that Hesse was typical of his generation would require a thorough sociological survey, and perhaps not be convincing even then, despite his popularity. To go further into his neutralism in politics would lead too far away from literature, and it was as a literary man, not as a politician, that he made his name. The significance of his writing for understanding the Weimar Republic and the period after it is of less importance than understanding its significance today. The quality of the praise given to Hesse by some of Britain's leading journalists, to say nothing of the awarders of Nobel Prizes for Literature, does not, it is true, put us in immediate danger of an authoritarian revolution, as inimical to those same journalists as that of 1933. What it does reveal, and it can do with being revealed, is the low level of thought and literary distinction required in order to establish a world-wide reputation. A democracy hoping to survive on no better awareness of reality than that — since reality and literature are intimately related — may expect to be disappointed.

Notes

1. K.-H. Deschner, *Kitsch, Konvention und Kunst*, Munich, 1957.
2. K. Rothmann, *Kleine Geschichte der deutschen Literatur*, Reclam, Stuttgart, 1978, p. 259.
3. *Demian*, in *Gesammelte Werke*, Frankfurt am Main, 1970, Vol. 5, pp. 52–3 (all *Demian* quotations transl. R.G.).
4. *Die Gedichte*, Zürich 1942, p. 245 (not in *GW*).
5. ed. cit., p. 248 (not in *GW*). The omission from the peace-time edition is notable.
6. *GW* 7, pp. 189–90 (all *Steppenwolf* quotations transl. R.G.).
7. *If this War Goes On, Reflections on War and Politics*, transl. Ralph Manheim, London, 1972, p. 65.
8. See Volker Michels, *Hermann Hesse. Politik des Gewissens*, 1977, Vol. 2, p. 614 and J. Mileck, *Hermann Hesse, Biography and Bibliography*, University of California Press, 1977, Vol. 1, p. 88.
9. See R. Freedman, *Hermann Hesse. Pilgrim of Crisis. A Biography*, London, 1979, pp. 360–2. The German translation, edited and revised by Volker Michels, to be published by Suhrkamp, should be consulted in due course.
10. *The Glass Bead Game*, transl. Richard and Clara Winston, Penguin, 1972, p. 15 (*GW* 9, 8).
11. For the symbolism here see Mark Boulby, *Hermann Hesse. His Mind and Art*, New York, 1967.

Irrationalism, Art and Violence:
Ernst Jünger and Gottfried Benn

Hugh Ridley

I

The Weimar Republic, as has often been observed, was a period of the progressive politicization of literature. After the traumas of war and revolution it no longer seemed possible for writers to isolate themselves from the currents of history. Everything they wrote took up an attitude to the institutions and foundations of the Republic, while these institutions, deprived of the sanction of tradition, seemed open to change and somehow dependent on support or modification from intellectuals.

Jünger and Benn both belong in the mainstream of Weimar culture. Jünger by his war-diaries and essays, Benn by his dazzling achievements in poetry and prose, assured themselves of a place in every anthology. Both must be seen as characteristic figures of the period. Despite their individuality and dislike of being classified (Jünger's favourite image was the lone soldier defending an already lost position, Benn's view of poetry a lonely 'conversation with oneself'), Jünger (b. 1895) was the perfect representative of the 'front generation', while Benn (b. 1886) epitomized the early Expressionist movement. Both writers made significant contributions to the 'conservative revolution', the 1920s upsurge of that anti-socialist radicalism which makes it so difficult to place many Weimar intellectuals on any normal right-to-left political spectrum. Yet it is interesting to notice how problematic political activity was for both writers. Jünger, as we shall see, embarked upon the 1920s with a war-record as distinguished as Goering or Rommel and the evident prospect of a field marshal's baton in Hitler's army. In 1939, however, he was 'on the marble-cliffs', 'above the mêlée', and the years of Weimar show clearly the struggle within him between practical and intellectual activity. Benn, who began the Weimar period utterly detached from the world, leading what he described as an 'irrelevant existence as a doctor in Berlin' after an 'irrelevant development' in the eventful years of the war — later he was to say that he was 'surrounded by a vacuum'[1] — celebrated the end of the Weimar Republic by an enthusiastic conversion to Hitler's revolution. The shadow of politics hangs over his work also and gives it, for all the polished perfection of its literary expression, a provisional quality which is typical of the whole Republic.

By nineteen Jünger was in the trenches. Like many of his generation he moved from the schoolroom to the Somme: unlike many, he survived, leading a charmed life in the worst battles the war saw. He fought in every campaign after the Somme, including Ludendorff's last offensive in March 1918, where, once more in the heat of the action, he collected his final wounds and was evacuated just before the final collapse. At the end of the war he had run up an impressive tally of wounds, had known a sense of mild curiosity as he compared the size of entry and exit wounds in his own chest, had killed in every frame of mind and with most weapons, and at the very end of the war, on top of almost every other military decoration, he was awarded the highest of all, one never before awarded to so young an infantryman: the 'Pour-le-Mérite'.

After the war, for a while Jünger did the correct thing, entering the tiny professional army allowed Germany by the Treaty of Versailles, and working on technical staff manuals. A dazzling career loomed before him, but, as the highly autobiographical short novel *Sturm* disclosed in 1923 (its genuineness can be guessed from the fact that for years Jünger did not include it in the various collections of his work) — the conflict between intellectual and practical work, the humiliating role given to the military at the time of the Kapp Putsch (which Jünger would obviously have preferred to join rather than put down) drove him from the army.

Jünger's war-books, the most famous of which was published in 1920, had made him a renowned soldier and also an ideological focal-point for younger members of the right wing. When he retired from the army in 1923 he found himself naturally at the centre of a militaristic movement of small, loosely collaborating ex-servicemen's organizations to which the name 'New Nationalism' was given. Its ideology included anti-democracy, anti-semitism, and the cult of dictatorship. Jünger remarked in one of the essays which he wrote to give ideological shape to the movement that its aim was to establish a 'national, social, military, and dictatorially organized state'.[2]

Among Jünger's associates from this time were many who would make their reputations later: Joseph Goebbels, Alfred Rosenberg, the Strasser brothers. As the National Socialist movement consolidated its position after Hitler's release from Landsberg in 1925 and through his organizational genius politically outmanoeuvred the New Nationalists, the Party made strenuous but fruitless efforts to recruit Jünger into its ranks. Jünger had once described the newspapers in which he conducted his political campaigns as 'busses which you get into without having any control over the quality of the other passengers and which you get off at the place you wanted to go to',[3] but he found that his bus had set him down at a place he did not want to go, and that it continued its journey to the National Socialist state regardless.

It may seem odd to link Gottfried Benn with this violent man of action. Benn did fight in the war of 1914, with more enthusiasm and vitality in its opening campaigns than during the famous years he spent in charge of a prostitutes' hospital in Brussels, but he had joined the army originally to learn medicine, and the hundreds of bodies he encountered (and which we encounter in his work) were the result not of military action but of the oldest enemy of all. Nevertheless the war marked a turning-point in Benn's life no less dramatic than for Jünger.

It has often been observed that Expressionism anticipated and gave literary expression to the chaotic experience of war. The 'Aufbruch' which featured in so much of their poetry found an equivalent in the mobilization of 1914, just as their general criticism of bourgeois society was conveniently strengthened by the Spenglerian sense of doom which the war brought to Europe. Heym's war-god did indeed rise up from long sleep and pour pitch and brimstone over a corrupt age. Jakob van Hoddis's vision of the end of the world ('Weltende') perfectly expressed the sense of crisis and collapse more fundamental than that which ordinary people could detect. That which the bourgeoisie sees as tragedy — their blown-off hats and their snuffly noses — stands in the shadow of greater catastrophes. With the coming of the War it seemed to many of the Expressionists that history had pronounced sentence on those who had not read the message of the shadows.

Jünger's war-experience was a response to a similar discontent with peace-time society. When he had found his way into the heart of the barbarity and comfortless horror of the war he had no doubt that the slaughter and degradation was nothing less than the final expression of the world of peace. In the Somme he saw the final pronouncement of a 'hopelessly lost age'.[4] The bloated economic satisfaction of the years of peace, the optimistic theory that advances in technology would wipe away all tears, the stifling ideology which saw in man merely a biological and social unit to be manipulated in the faceless cities — all this was redressed in war; the chaos and nihilism at the heart of that society which the Expressionists had rejected in peace-time had come into the open, their prophecy had become reality. It was for this reason that Jünger felt his experiences of war to be important. He had belonged to that section of the infantry which, having sat through the worst saturation shelling and thus experienced the high-point of the destructive materialism of the industrial nineteenth century, was responsible for launching counter-attacks and for reasserting movement and the freedom of the human will over against the dead-weight of matter. Their real victories were not those against the Allied troops, but those against the spirit of the pre-war world. They were accomplished not in retreat from reality, but in defiantly draining the worst dregs of material reality. The cup was filled by the age of peace.

In diagnosis Jünger and the Expressionists were agreed. In their response, however, they parted company. While the Expressionists were gratified to find some external support for their feeling that reality was breaking down, and while they might prophesy that war which was to come, they hated the War with all their heart. In response to its sickening inhumanity and slaughter, they tried to find social and political ways out of the War, as well as moral lessons which would make future war impossible. But Jünger affirmed war for its own sake, partly because of his own incredible suitability for it, and partly because of his hatred for those forces in society which had — in his view — brought an end to the War. He would never forget the experience of revolution in 1919. His affirmation of war never meant therefore a mere enjoyment of the slaughter; however insensitive he was to become to the deaths and bodies of those he did not know, he never ceased to cherish the memory of those whom he had known. Nevertheless his affirmation of war involved assent to total chaos and total destruction, founded on the mystical belief that only out of total destruction can a new spirit arise. Paradoxically, Jünger called that spirit which could be reborn amid the 'storms of steel' the 'spirit of life itself'. The residue of war for Jünger was a purer vision of the richness and purity of life.

T. E. Lawrence (with whom Jünger rightly has often been compared) summed up this spirit in a letter in 1930. He said of his experience in war: 'I had pushed my go-cart into the eternal stream and so it went faster than the ones which are pushed across stream or upstream'. In the desert, in the pure flame of the Arab wars, Lawrence had felt himself to be in touch with a force greater than any national upheaval, transcending all grief and loss, a force which, in the famous phrase in *The Seven Pillars of Wisdom*, Lawrence called 'the morning freshness of the world', that primitive and affirming spirit behind all life. In Jünger's words war showed 'a wild opening out of life, which revealed itself here at its most essential'.[5] It was this essentially aesthetic vision of life which was the legacy of the War. It stood side by side with rather more mundanely expressed nationalist opinions which the War had confirmed in Jünger (as in many of his generation). The Weimar Republic was singularly unfitted to be the inheritor of this storm.

A similar process of discovery can be found in the work of Benn, though the context is markedly different. It was in the dissecting-rooms and the mortuary that Benn came across the prosaic reality which needed transcendence, and in traditional medical science's mechanistic account of human behaviour and personality that he first felt a longing for escape, no less exotic than that which took Jünger into war. Similarly, though the escape was not into the activity of war so much as into a new dimension of inward experience, as Benn explored the subconscious and examined the collapse of the artificial edifice of the 'normal' personality, he discovered, like Jünger, a new and fruitful stratum of the life-force.

It was Freud of course who had first linked this discovery to the experience of war. In his celebrated essay 'Zeitgemäßes über Krieg und Tod' (Thoughts for the Times on War and Death) (1915) he had shown the connection between war itself and the stirrings of the unknown and hidden self. Just as civilization was forced by war to come to terms with the violent and hitherto repressed sides of itself, so in individuals the hidden and darker side of their nature lay in temporary hiding. Both society and the individual were seething with internal pressure, ready to explode.

Jünger, in his first analyses of the lessons of the War, fell back on language which (while different in origin from Freud's) obviously touched on common threads of experience. 'The human race', he wrote in 1922, 'is a secret and over-grown primeval forest. The tops of the trees are wafted by the winds of open seas and reach up ever more strongly away from the oppressive miasma of the soil towards the bright sun; while the tops of the trees are wrapped about with scent, colour and blossom, a tangle of strange growths luxuriate far below in the depths.'

The depths are man's subconscious, represented by his ancestry from apes and cavemen to more recent generations. History and civilization have refined man, but even as he slumbers on the 'rug of a polished, frictionless and smoothly integrated civilization' man keeps his past close to the skin.

> When the graph of life swings back towards the red line of the primitive, the mask falls, and primeval man breaks out, naked as ever, a caveman still in the utter uncontrollability of his rampant instincts . . . His blood, which once flowed cool and regular through his veins in the mechanical activity of his stony edifices, the cities, bubbles up . . .[6]

Freud had written of war, 'it strips us of the later accretions of civilization, and lays bare the primal man in each of us'. He had argued the essential health of this recognition, and that, in this one respect, 'we should adapt ourselves to war'.[7] Like Jünger and unlike the Expressionists, Freud argued that the eruption of war — felt by so many to have been a betrayal of valid principles of humanity, brotherhood, peace and so forth — was in fact merely the shattering of illusions and a return to reality. We may, again with some caution, suggest that Freud saw the fact (but not the activities) of war positively.

The shattering of illusion, the jolt with which an individual breaks through the thin ice of false assumptions and unfounded habit, is one of Benn's most common themes, and one to which his poetry and essays in the 1920s constantly return. In many of his early poems the shock is angrily delivered to the reader between the eyes. In 'Little Aster' (III, 7)[8] and other poems in *Morgue* (1912) the tone is a defiant challenge to accepted views of the world. Art, as Benn later remarked of fellow-Expressionists, is an axe swung against accepted reality (I, 15), and the impact of Benn's poetry was hardly more gentle. But in others of Benn's works, most famously perhaps in the Rönne stories which began to appear with *Gehirne* in 1915, the jolt hit Benn no less hard than his reader. While his poems might speak of the collapse of self as 'sweet and deeply longed for' (III, 52), it is evident that the problems presented by Benn's discovery that the self and the world were different to the pictures Benn had inherited of them ('deeper than the century believed' (I, 80) 'utterly different, inconceivably different from what science taught me' (I, 142)) was one of survival. 'How can one go on living?' (IV, 11) Benn asked in 1922, clearly unsure of the answer himself. Like Jünger he had used materialism to destroy the idealism of the nineteenth century and the new life he had dis-covered had yet to find a form of expression. It is no exaggeration to suggest that for the Weimar Republic too Benn's discoveries raised a question of survival.

For, of course, if civilization is sham and illusion, if reason holds no sway over the passions and instincts, if life so strongly depends on its roots in instinct and the blood, then the organization of the world by reason and its further control by the institutions of enlightened democracy is a vain charade against which reality has once rebelled in war and will again rebel. Not only is the self who contracts out of that 'smoothly integrated civilization' sure of his own credentials, but tradition and race have been lined up as the natural enemies of civilization. This had in any case been part of the legacy of cultural pessimism from the late nineteenth century (Thomas Mann had tried out these ideas in the nationalistic essays with which he greeted the outbreak of War in 1914); with the experiences of war, how-ever, the seed-bed had been created for the widest possible exploitation of possi-bilities latent within the tradition. Whatever Benn's contempt for the traditional bourgeois nationalism he encountered in the officers' mess, his most radical explorations of self and world were in harmony with the 'antidemocratic' ideology of the 1920s, on whose back Hitler was to ride to power.

It may well seem exaggerated to make this link so early in Benn's work. I should not wish to perpetuate the crude equation of Expressionism with fascism which, with the advantages of hindsight and with that extra perspective afforded by their situation in Moscow, Lukács and Kurella found it easy to make during their debates with Bloch and Brecht. It was by then easy to recognize the pseudo-revolutionary tone of much of Expressionism, the shallow and subjective nature of its rejection of bourgeois society, the irrationalism which underlay its social thinking. But to argue that these things led to Hitler, or to imply any community of interest between the Expressionists and the pseudo-radical conservatism of the National Socialists, would be a distortion of the intellectual integrity of Benn's early work.

Nevertheless, violence remains the common denominator of this work, a joy in destruction and an assault on the bourgeoisie which stands in a strange relation-ship to that passivity and anti-intellectual sinking back into the archaic which is one of the most commonly remarked features of Benn's work ('Oh, that we were our ancestors' ancestors, a lump of slime in some warm bog' (III, 25)). The world-picture of the nineteenth century — the breadth of concept is Benn's — needs to be smashed into 'rubble', and it is only violence and pain which can operate as a 'fist in the teeth of hedonistic democracies . . . sweeping over the paddy-fields of bourgeois *ratio* and utterly destroying them' (I, 17). 'Mankind, if it thinks in machines,' Benn remarked elsewhere with equal savagery, 'must be smashed and pulped' (II, 460). It is an assent to violence which, while not ruling out individual compassion or making a fetish of hardening the heart, puts Benn's work in the same category as Jünger's, whose links to extreme nationalism were so much less problematic.

A particular affinity of Benn and Jünger lay in their attack on the use of reason by bourgeois society, and its replacement not by the kind of pompous irrationalism which looked to the Middle Ages for its forebears, still less by a sentimental empathy with nature (both of these were favourite topoi of the conservative novel), but by a new, virile and instinctive reason. Benn repeatedly bemoaned the decline of reason from a virile weapon in man's struggle for survival, the only armour he possessed against a hostile nature, to its nadir in bourgeois society's preoccupation with hygiene and safety. The history of reason bears witness to a 'drive for security' (II, 104), as the great thinkers of the past have been netted by the lion-tamers of bourgeois society, with Kant's logic being trivialized into the basis of civil law (II, 41) and Darwin shepherded into the political lobby of the progressives (I, 69). The railway to the top of the Zugspitze, which allowed old ladies and children to reach the summit in comfort (II, 81), struck both Benn and Jünger as a comment on this distortion of reason. Jünger (who climbed the mountain just before the railway was opened to the public), was fascinated all the more strongly by the violence of reason as displayed in the War, for instance in the fact that the railways shipping munitions to the front had previously been seen as the vehicle for improving human communication and international concord, and he was convinced that, when the nations beat their ploughshares into swords, a necessary corrective had come into a distortion of human history, and that reason had rediscovered her true face.

Technology fascinated both writers, as it did their entire generation, and it was with similarly sadistic pleasure that both men commented on the ways in which technology let down just those hopes which the nineteenth centry had placed in it. Indeed, this demonstration was an integral part of their rejection of the progressive Weimar Republic. Benn, for instance, relished the story of the man who first introduced into America a variety of wheat hardy enough to withstand the most extreme of winters. His intention of helping the farmers of Kansas by his work was turned inside out when his innovation celebrated its success by glutting the market and ruining those very people whom it had been intended to help (I, 201–10). Technological improvement will change neither the basic social structure ('the poor always want to rise and the rich won't come down' (IV, 209)) nor the direction of history, which is circular rather than progressive.

Jünger's fascination with technology is a study in itself. From his experience of the trenches to his decision, perhaps sometime in 1934, to leave the organization of the world to 'the technicians and warriors',[9] Jünger recognized and studied technology as the historical force of the moment. That energetic vitality which he found in the activity of war and which became the ideological residuum of the experience of the battlefield, was identified in the work of the technicians, partly because of their struggle for 'planetary control' (Jünger's phrase for the spread of technology throughout the world), and partly too because of their closeness to the source of vital energy which Jünger, like the Futurists, saw in technology. He shared with many of the New Objectivity writers a relish for the technological as the millstone grinding down bourgeois attitudes and positions, but at the same time, however, he went far beyond the naive cult of technology (Brecht's image for this was of '700 intellectuals worshipping an oil-tank', invoking the tank to 'extinguish our selves, make us collective')[10] in that he recognized immediate social and political positions as latent within the spread of technology. Indeed his war-experience had taught him that nationalism had a natural affinity with the mastery of technology. As we shall see in a later chapter, similar claims were made for an affinity between socialism and technology. It can be shown that Jünger's long study of technology, *Der Arbeiter* (1932), corresponded in almost every respect to the National Socialist state which came into being some months later, and was even seen as a blue-print for that state.[11]

The changes in technology were having, as everyone noticed, an immense effect upon the intellectual. We shall see how Benjamin made these changes the starting-point for his redefinition of the intellectual, seeing — as Jünger saw — both destructive and constructive effects of technology on intellectual life. For Jünger the emergence of violence into intellectual life was only possible through the preliminary destructive work of technology, breaking down the social role of the free intellectual and discrediting traditional art-forms. He welcomed these changes and allied his nationalism to the historical movement represented by technology. In a notorious phrase he gladly seized the chance to be involved in 'the high treason of the spirit against the spirit'. With the victory of the Workers, the 'museal' concept of art as an object of value, for collection, contemplation and preservation would be replaced by a dynamic and pragmatic evaluation of the usefulness of art of the Workers. His various studies of photography emphasize his interest in the impact of technology upon art, and the parallels between his diagnosis and that of Benjamin are striking.[12]

Benn too noted, although with extreme distaste, the shifting pattern of intellectual life. He saw the emergence of the technologically sophisticated, socially integrated, committed writer with dread. He regarded Tretjakov — who, as shall be demonstrated below, was the model for Benjamin's redefinition of the role of the intellectual — as a pathetic and absurd figure, and lost no opportunity to sneer at the more conventional figures of literary engagement in politics, those writers who 'sit next to ministers at banquets, a carnation in their button-hole, five wine-glasses set out for their use, and sign petitions about the problems of the age' (IV, 208). Yet it is clear that Benn felt the historical impossibility of traditional intellectual stances. Despite the traditional manner in which he defended the activity of art against 'Americanism' (a synonym for many of the ideas of New Objectivity) with its slogans 'Tempo, Jazz, Cinema, Overseas, Technical Activity' (IV, 194), his own poetry involved a continuous assault not only on the language of poetry but also on its extra-historical situation. Benn obviously held to the 'double life' of poetry as an act of despair rather than of hope. His work shows the tensions implicit in the defence of culture during Weimar, and an anxiety to find a redefinition of intellectual activity which would be in keeping with the present.

In the exposure of their work both to technology and to violence Benn and Jünger may be seen as characteristic figures of their age. Perhaps, however, the most representative pattern traced by their lives and thought in Weimar was that constellation of aesthetic and political language, in which the aesthetic is torn between a preservation of its purity and the possible realization of itself in the real world. The debate was, of course, anything but new. It had been Thomas Mann who had attacked the Expressionists, during the chaotic months of the Bavarian revolution, for their naive belief in putting ideas into social practice. They had been a symptom of the growing discontent of younger intellectuals with their isolated position in pre-war society, and while writers such as Thomas Mann were determined to find 'personal and ethical' answers to this isolation, Heinrich Mann and the activists were convinced that 'political' dimensions to their work would end their isolation.[13] The debate is well known, and it left its mark across nearly all the writers of Weimar, as the development of Jünger and Benn demonstrates.

II

In Jünger the problem may be briefly stated. Having experienced, at an elevated and intense level, the spirit behind the War, and having identified it both with 'life' and nationalism, Jünger found himself preaching a political concept based on an aesthetic experience. His nationalist movement was intended to mobilize those resources of the human spirit which war had revealed, as he set out deliberately to put into political practice the lessons of those years. Writing again in 1925 of the 'inner experience' of the War, Jünger said: 'If this strength is present, without making use of the external agencies, then it has renounced all shaping of the external world and the happiness which lies in living effectiveness'.[14] Yet once Jünger had embarked on the road of political practice, he constantly faced the challenge of realizations of his ideas in which he had to distinguish between his vision and its substantiation in practice. Repeatedly he stressed the political impact of his ideas in preference to their actual substance, but no less often the choice between a particular realization and the original vision was settled in favour of the latter. In virtually every case the realization was being offered by the National Socialists.

The blood — to take but one example — is incessantly flowing in the pages of Jünger's books and essays. The blood of opponents, but also the blood of the narrator and his compatriots, flowing on the ground and pulsing through their veins. It symbolized — like the sap of Jünger's tree — the irrational, the dynamic, the archaic. Very evidently to others it also symbolized the Aryan race, and it was not long before Jünger, in the midst of his political campaigns, noticed that the language of blood formed a major part of the National Socialist programme. In April 1926, therefore, the first differentiation took place. Jünger rejected any attempt 'to ascertain the value of the blood intellectually, that is to say by means of modern science'. In obvious reference to the work of the various 'researchers' in the National Socialist movement (perhaps also to the sketches of Aryan buttock shapes undertaken by Hitler) Jünger continued 'We don't want to hear any more about chemical reactions, blood-injections, skull shapes and Aryan profiles. In the blood movement is more admirable than any goal.'[15] In this spirit Jünger prided himself on a political programme which operated 'with fluctuating concepts, which keep the unedifying crowd of the dogmatic at bay'.[16] On the one hand exhorting his readers 'let us throw ourselves into this age'[17] and exploring the dynamics of a non-dogmatic ideology, Jünger was therefore at the same time anxious to preserve his distance from the practical manifestations of that ideology, as much because of a distaste for reality itself as out of dislike of any particular manifestation of his ideology.

Aestheticism and violent politics were closer neighbours than is healthy either in writers or aspiring politicians. Small wonder that Walter Benjamin should describe Jünger's position as 'an uninhibited translation of the principles of *l'art pour l'art* to war itself'.[18] He accurately saw the fateful consequences of this confusion of ways of thinking. But there was in Jünger's thought a final dimension of violence which, no less than the confusion of aestheticism and politics, characterized his work during this period. I shall approach this, conveniently, through the same topic: race. So far I have noted merely how Jünger both advocated the blood as a political positive and delineated his idea from the more practical theories of his fellow radicals of the Right. There were, however, negative elements in the theory too, a view of 'enemies of the blood'. Here, since Jünger was anxious to think positively, his ideas were on the surface less outspoken. He dealt with the 'problems' of the Jews, the Freemasons and the Roman Catholic Church only because it was part of the accepted canon of nationalism to have a view about these sinister forces threatening German nationalism. But this dismissiveness about the 'enemies of the blood' led Jünger to pass over to Alfred Rosenberg and the National Socialists the responsibility for handling the anti-semitism of the nationalist movement, thus allowing Jünger to get on with the 'positive' elements in his programme. 'When we have managed to replace the present state with a purely nationalist state, then all the anti-national powers will have a nasty shock,' Jünger remarked, in passing promising also that Jews, Freemasons and Catholics would 'feel an iron fist at their throat'.[19] The violence is not merely anchored ideologically in Jünger's view of primitive and violent man: it is casual too, dismissive from the intellectual heights of 'pure' nationalism.

For Benn the relationship between aesthetic and political thinking was no less problematic. He often spoke of art and politics as separate realms, claiming for instance, in the midst of a polemic with Johannes R. Becher, that works of art were totally separate from history and had no influence on and no echo from them. They were 'an isolated phenomenon, individually unfruitful and mono-maniac' — indeed, their remoteness from history 'protects their quality' (I, 47). 'In the midst of the general European nihilism' (Benn's summary of the state of Europe in the early 1930s) there was only one transcendent activity: 'the transcendence of the pleasure of artistic creation' (I, 416). The very notion of transcendence showed the gulf which existed between the state of society and the activity of the artist. Benn once wrote that 'the artist signifies the gulf from the junk-heap of civilization' (I, 76), and while, in a lighter vein, he suggested that this meant only freedom for him to worry about poetry while the rest of Berlin worried about Hertha (the local football club), it is evident that he saw the gap between society and art to be permanent and unbridgeable. One of his best-known poems contrasts the sense created by poetry with the chaos of the world outside, and may stand as a testimony to the separation of art and life in Benn's Weimar work:

Ein Wort, ein Satz —: aus Chiffren steigen
erkanntes Leben, jäher Sinn,
die Sonne steht, die Sphären schweigen
und alles ballt sich zu ihm hin.

Ein Wort — ein Glanz, ein Flug, ein Feuer,
ein Flammenwurf, ein Sternenstrich —
und wieder Dunkel, ungeheuer,
im leeren Raum um Welt und Ich. (III, 208)[20]

(A word, a sentence — from codes rise up life known and sudden sense.
The sun stands still, the spheres are hushed — and everything is focused
on that word.
A word — a ray of light, a flight, a fire, a jet of flames, a shoot
of stars. Then, once again, the immensity of darkness, in the empty
space round world and self.)

The poet's word is light, but it does not change the darkness of history. As Benn remarked less poetically in 1929: 'There are no mediations between receptive and productive mankind' (IV, 195).

By 1932 and the collection *After Nihilism*, however, Benn set out to find ways in which the constructive elements in art might be transplanted into other areas of life. How, in other words, the aesthetic might help society to find answers to its problems. How the overcoming of nihilism might be artistically solved in a wider compass than merely within the individual work of art. Art (because of its contact with the irrational) had freed itself from the general weariness of an over-refined and over-rational society and had managed to be constructive according to the laws of artistic form. Could this run over into societal and political activity?

Before 1933 Benn's attempt to see such a merger of the two spheres of activity were relatively modest. A discussion of Goethe's scientific thinking offered a model for artistic activity outside the immediate sphere of art (especially relevant to the present, Benn believed, since Goethe's controversy with Newton had involved an attack on the over-dominance of reason), but since Goethe was an artist anyway the example did little to remove the gap between society and art on any larger scale. By the time Hitler had come to power, however, Benn's despair at the moribund state of society under Weimar led him to a total equation of art and politics, whose consequences in Benn's enthusiastic support for Hitler are well known. During a period of some 18 months after Hitler's assumption of power, Benn equated the formal organization of a work of art with the political organization of the totalitarian state. (This was, in part, the political allegory which Thomas Mann's *Doktor Faustus* was to explore.) The eccentric biological theories of the irrational which Benn had been tentatively putting forward for fifteen years because of the place they ascribed to the artistic activity as a return to the source of life suddenly found their equivalent in the biological tenets of National Socialist race-thinking. As if by magic, the state became an art-work, the hand of the politician (even by then more than drenched in the blood of opponents) took on an artistic touch, and under the dual categories of form and power art celebrated its triumphal entry into the reconstructed temple of art. Violence was approved, for — as Benn wrote in an attempt to link fascism and Expressionism early in 1934 — the Expressionists also 'smashed reality' in order to free the way for their personal vision of the world-order. Eugenics (far from being the 'scientific' distortion of the original elan behind race-theories which Jünger had condemned) 'is subsumed in the question of form' (I, 475), and the state and art which Benn had pronounced eternally separate had entered on marriage after the briefest of courtships. In a speech due to have been delivered over the grave of Stefan George (he had been foresighted enough not merely to die outside the new Germany but to request that no orations be held over his grave by its spokesmen), Benn reached the trite consummation of that union. Discussing George's poem 'komm in den totgesagten park' (an anthology piece of enormous beauty in which not even the most unrestrained undergraduate interpretative zeal could discover anything remotely political), Benn proudly commented that the formal perfection of the poem breathed 'that spirit which marched in the columns of the brown battalions' (I, 627). To compare literature to the spirit of its age is far from unreasonable — but the comparison of George's sonnet with the sweaty violence of the SA argues not only a political naivety of the first water but a positive mania to complete the broken arcs of art and society. No less than Jünger's exuberant beautification of war, Benn's efforts all ran in the direction of that 'aestheticizing of politics' which Walter Benjamin recognized as the main ideological weapon of fascism, and to which (as demonstrated in a subsequent chapter) he opposed the 'politicizing of art'.[21]

The confusion of art and politics was as deeply rooted in Jünger and Benn as it was in their age. The function exercised by these — intellectually outstanding — members of the conservative revolution was not only to provide what Heinrich Mann, in his vitriolic attack on the court-poets of nationalism in 1914, called 'intellectual props to barbarity'. To the extent to which they did this their recantation followed on so quickly as to undermine the original support. What makes them symptomatic of the weaknesses of Weimar's intellectual life was not the views they held — although these were and still seem at times extreme and unpleasant — but their utter confusion as to the function of their writing in society and, correspondingly, their uncertainty about the status of those views. Breathing the fire of politics they filled the page with the colder water of aesthetic delight; cocooned in the vacuum of a monomanial obsession with poetry and inner dream, they saw their visions as a fulcrum to change the world. Jünger, looking back on the 'Mauretanier' days of the 1920s in the fascinating early chapters of *On the Marble Cliffs*, blamed the age itself for the uncertainties and extremities of his thinking. 'There are ages of decline', he wrote, 'in which the inner form is lost which life is to follow'.[22] Karl Kraus, however, reviewing those remnants of Weimar culture which had trickled over into Hitler's Germany, had a different explanation. It was not the age which had lost its way, but the intellectuals who had lost the language with which to illuminate that way. Kraus said of Benn's welcome for Hitler's state that it derived not from the vision of a rebirth of man (which had been Benn's claim), but from 'the decline of language, that true being which has power to unmask the language which people speak to-day'. He was echoing, in sorrow and anger, his comments in 1914 that those who welcomed the War knew nothing of it and — such was the poverty of their imaginative capacities —could not envisage the reality to which their empty rhetoric referred. 'If they could imagine it', Kraus remarked severely, '*it would not happen*'.[23] Benjamin obviously had Kraus's methods in mind as he lampooned the pompous and unreal attitudinizing of Jünger's assent to war and echoed Kraus as he referred to language as 'a touchstone for each and every position taken'.[24] His sense of intellectuals' need for a new starting-point was rooted in his recognition of how utterly past positions had been found wanting.

NOTES

1. Letter to Gertrud Zenses of 24 February 1929 in *Ausgewählte Briefe* (Wiesbaden, 1957), p. 32. See also his autobiographical sketch in Kurt Pinthus' anthology *Menschheitsdämmerung*.
2. 'Zum Jahre', *Die Standarte*, 3 January 1926.
3. 'Schlußwort zu einem Aufsatz', *Widerstand,* 1 January 1930.
4. Cf. *Der Kampf als inneres Erlebnis*, in *Werke* 5, 1 (Stuttgart, 1961 ff), pp. 14, 82 etc.
5. *Der Kampf als inneres Erlebnis*, loc. cit., p. 108. T. E. Lawrence quoted by H. Arendt, *Origins of Totalitarianism* (George Allen & Unwin, rev. ed. 1966), p. 220.
6. *Der Kampf als inneres Erlebnis*, loc. cit., pp. 17–18.
7. S. Freud, 'Thoughts for the Times on War and Death' in Standard Edition, Vol. 14 (Hogarth Press, 1962), pp. 280 f. 299.
8. For convenience, all references are to Dieter Wellershoff's complete edition of Benn's work, published by Limes, Wiesbaden, 1959–61. The Roman numeral refers to the volume number.
9. G. Benn, 'Können Dichter die Welt ändern?' (IV, 214).
10. B. Brecht, *Gesammelte Gedichte* (Frankfurt, 1976), p. 316.
11. See for instance the comments of Hermann Rauschning (former Gauleiter of Danzig) on the centrality to the NS State of Jünger's work *Die Revolution des Nihilismus*, Zurich & New York, 1938, pp. 100, 156, etc. Also W.-D. Müller, *Ernst Jünger: ein Leben im Umbruch der Zeit* (Berlin, 1934), pp. 64–5.
12. Karl Prümm gives an excellent account of these links in *Die Literatur des Soldatischen Nationalismus* (Kronberg, 1974), p. 277 ff.
13. T. Mann, *Betrachtungen eines Unpolitischen* (Berlin, 1919) p. 296. The contrast of ethical and political forms one of the constant themes of the work.
14. 'Der Kampf als inneres Erlebnis', *Die Standarte*, 11 October 1925.
15. 'Das Blut', *Standarte*, 29 April 1926.
16. 'Schlußwort zu einem Aufsatz', *Widerstand,* 1 January 1930.
17. 'Großstadt und Land', *Deutsches Volkstum*, August 1926.
18. W. Benjamin, 'Theories of German Fascism', translated by Jerolf Wikoff in *New German Critique*, No. 17 (Special Benjamin issue, Spring 1979) p. 122.
19. 'Die antinationalen Mächte', *Arminius*, 30 January 1927.
20. Although the final version of this poem lies outside the Weimar period, a draft from the 1920s shows the place of these ideas in Benn's thought at that time.
21. The last words of Benjamins 'Author as Producer' (1934).
22. *Auf den Marmorklippen*, in *Werke* 9, 1, p. 207.
23. Cf. K. Kraus, *Die dritte Walpurgisnacht* (written May–September 1933) (Munich, 1955) p. 121; and 'In dieser großen Zeit' in *Die Fackel,* 5 December 1914, variously reprinted.
24. 'Theories of German Fascism', p. 125.

The Novel as History:
Hermann Broch's Trilogy—*Die Schlafwandler*

David Horrocks

I

In September 1929, when the original versions of his three novels were near to completion, Hermann Broch had still not fixed upon a title for the trilogy as a whole. Of those he had considered, the one he liked best was, as he explained in a letter to Frank Thiess, too abstract to be commercially viable. It was simply 'Historical Novel'. At first glance this bare designation does not seem entirely inappropriate. A clear historical emphasis is indicated by the dates that figure prominently in the titles of the work's three parts: *1888 Pasenow oder die Romantik, 1903 Esch oder die Anarchie* and *1918 Huguenau oder die Sachlichkeit.*[1] Indeed, the 30-year span covered by the novels, corresponding as it does exactly to the reign of Emperor Wilhelm II, leads the reader to expect a novelistic treatment of the Wilhelmenian period as a whole. Such expectations are not, however, fulfilled. National politics and public events are conspicuous by their absence.

The first novel contains one brief critical reference to Bismarck's fondness for innovative policies ('neuerungssüchtige Politik'), as seen from the conservative perspective of the elder von Pasenow, but the most obvious events of national importance in the Germany of 1888, the year of the three Emperors, are never even mentioned by any of the characters. The second novel, apart from some reference to the growth of the Social Democrats and to trades union activities in connection with a dock strike in Mannheim, is almost wholly concerned with the private sphere of the central character, Esch. The 'anarchy' of the title has no direct political significance, nor does the choice of the year 1903, which seems to have been dictated solely by the desire to have a symmetrical 15-year division. The Great War and revolution are, as one would expect, important themes in the third novel, but the former is directly portrayed only in the opening chapter, with its description of Huguenau's desertion from the trenches, and the latter appears only in the form of a minor uprising led by the workers of a paper mill in a small town in the Mosel valley near Trier.

In the final version of *Huguenau* the war is given greater prominence by the introduction of a number of parallel narratives in the manner of Dos Passos, two of which, the stories of Lieutenant Jaretzki and the Territorial Reserve Ludwig Gödicke, are set in a military hospital. The chapters concerning Jaretzki, which consist largely of dialogue, afford Broch ample opportunity for bitterly satirical comment on the effects of the War and are strongly reminiscent, both in tone and content, of scenes from *Die letzten Tage der Menschheit* (The Last Days of Mankind) by Karl Kraus, whose work Broch greatly admired. These two stories constitute, however, only two strands in the complex fabric of the third novel, the major portion of which deals with the private world of the central character, Huguenau.

38

It will be clear from this brief survey that *Die Schlafwandler* (The Sleepwalkers) is not a historical novel in the normally accepted sense of the term. To understand why Broch considered calling it such it is necessary to examine the somewhat idiosyncratic conception of history he arrived at after a long period of study, stretching back some 15 years before the novel's composition. Broch's preoccupation with historical problems dates from the start of the First World War. His first serious literary work, the satirical *Cantos 1913*,[2] written partly in verse and partly in prose, anticipates in its comments on historical progress the theory of disintegration of values later incorporated in *Die Schlafwandler.* It also contains a critique of Wilhelm II in which the concept of 'romanticism', so important in the trilogy, already plays a part. An unpublished notebook of the same year contains eight sides of excerpts from and notes on a standard work of historical methodology, Ernst Bernheim's *Lehrbuch der historischen Methode* (Manual of Historical Method). Numerous essays and sketches on historical themes then follow during the war years.[3] They testify to a vast amount of reading, not only of historians like Ranke and Mommsen but also of philosophical investigations of history by such as Dilthey, Rickert, Simmel and Windelband.

It would be wrong to interpret all this intellectual enquiry as the mere pursuit of an academic interest. For Broch knowledge was always inseparably bound up with ethical considerations, and it seems certain that what prompted his historical investigations and gave them an urgency far exceeding that of normal study was the reality of the War itself. 'The countenance of death is the great awakener,' he was later to write. The statement comes from an essay published in August 1933 in *Die Neue Rundschau*, at a time when death's countenance was again visible on the horizon.[4] Broch follows it with the interesting speculation that, for the philosopher Nietzsche, a key experience which more than any other influenced his thought was the brief spell he spent as a medical orderly in the Franco-Prussian War. What had led Nietzsche to question all established values, Broch goes on to argue, had a far more widespread effect at the time of the First World War when death assumed infinitely greater proportions: 'not until then was the collapse of all values evident; fear descended upon mankind at the loss of all life's values; whether new ones could ever be constructed was the anxious question that had to be faced'. (GW 6, 316) Although Broch writes here in terms of a general human experience, the significance of the moment for his own personal development is barely disguised. The reference to Nietzsche is revealing in two respects. First, Broch's own experience of war was similar to that of the philosopher. Having been declared unfit for military service in 1915, he spent the remaining war years in Teesdorf near Vienna, where his father's textile mills were situated, running a military hospital. Secondly, Broch's own philosophy in general, and his philosophy of history in particular, are centered around a concept which was of key significance in Nietzsche's thought: that of value.

It is above all the emphasis he puts on the prime importance of values that accounts for the apparent down-grading of empirical facts in Broch's approach to history. The mere chronicling of events, he believes, contributes little to understanding. To make those events intelligible the historian must seek out the values that lie behind them. His task is 'discovering historical man and his experience by a process of induction from given empirical reality' or 'establishing a hypothetical value-subject that corresponds to the given value-object'. (KW 10/2, 25)

In his early essays Broch acknowledges the closeness of his ideas to those of Herder, who stressed the importance of empathy, and those of Dilthey, especially his notion of 'reliving' the past. He goes beyond both these thinkers, however, by denying the existence of a direct correlation between values and reality. That is to say, he is acutely aware of the discrepancy between what men believe they are doing and what they actually do. In exploring this discrepancy Broch emphasizes three factors, all of which play an important rôle in *Die Schlafwandler*. The first is the way in which men seek to make sense of their actions by imposing a logical framework on them, spurious though this logic may be. The second is a phenomenon that a modern historian usefully terms 'time-lag',[5] the way in which value-systems remain in being and continue to influence men's actions long after they have been outstripped by events or advances in knowledge. This is a key element in Broch's notion of 'romanticism': seeking refuge from reality in outmoded systems of value or belief. The third is the extent to which the actions of a person are determined by supra-individual values such as those of a class, nation or religious confession. These are what Broch terms 'fictive value-centres' as opposed to 'effective value-centres' which are concrete individuals.

I have stressed the importance of the First World War for the genesis of Broch's historical ideas because in a real sense the beginning of his vast novel *Die Schlafwandler* lies in its end. The chapters of the historico-philosophical treatise entitled *Zerfall der Werte* (Disintegration of Values) were only included in the third novel of the trilogy at the very last stage of its composition in June and July 1931, but the ideas expressed in them had been formulated long before Broch conceived the plot of the work. Indeed the opening passage of the treatise as it stands in the novel is word for word the same as the first paragraph of an essay written circa 1917 but unpublished in Broch's lifetime. It reads:

> Is this distorted life still reality? Is this hypertrophic reality still alive? What began with a grandiose gesture of willing self-sacrifice is ending with a shrugging of the shoulders — they know not why they die. Bereft of all sense of reality, they are falling into the void; yet they are surrounded and killed by a reality that is theirs, since they understand its causality.[6]

The questions posed here as to how men can experience as unreal and nightmarish the reality of a war that they themselves created and originally welcomed are followed in the later version of the novel by an even more fundamental question: 'Are we mad because we have not gone mad?'. The point of this paradoxical formulation, which strikingly resembles the now well known 'catch 22' of the American novelist Joseph Heller, is, as Broch goes on to explain, the fact that individuals continue to behave normally and have no difficulty in finding logical justifications for their actions whilst at one and the same time they experience the totality of events as illogical. By rights, he is saying, people ought to have gone mad. Is the very fact that they have not done so itself a sign of madness? Towards the end of the passage Broch answers his own question in the affirmative when he diagnoses a kind of communal schizophrenia: 'a splitting asunder of the totality of life and experience that goes much deeper than any division as between isolated individuals, a split that reaches down into the individual himself and into his sense of a unified reality.' (GW 2, 403) One of Broch's major aims in stepping back in history and creating the fictional worlds of

Pasenow and Esch was to trace the origins of this mass sense of dissociation from reality.

II

The initial phase in what Broch sees as a process of progressive disorientation is portrayed in the novel *Pasenow oder die Romantik*. Outwardly it is the account of a crisis in the personal life of Joachim von Pasenow, a 30-year-old First Lieutenant in the army and younger son of a Junker family. Initiated in spring 1888 by his affair with a Bohemian bar 'hostess' called Ruzena, the crisis is resolved in the autumn by his conventional marriage to Elizabeth von Baddensen, the daughter of a baron from a neighbouring estate in West Prussia. This personal psychological drama is, however, seen by Broch as symptomatic of a deeper, historically significant crisis of values.

Joachim's involvement with Ruzena threatens his hitherto secure hold on reality. Conscious of the disruptive effect of the relationship on his ordered, punctual existence, he pictures it variously in terms of cracks forming in a central pillar of his existence or his ship having sprung a leak. Both images are important within the tightly woven symbolic fabric of the trilogy as a whole. The first forms part of a pattern of motifs to do with building which, throughout the work, symbolize the disintegration of values and man's attempts to build new systems.[7] The ship image, as an indicator of an individual's control — or lack of control of his destiny, occurs later in relation to both Esch and Huguenau.[8] In the context of 1888 both images might also be seen as highly ironic. Outwardly, after all, Germany is set to build further on the firm foundations of the 'Gründerzeit' and the new emperor will shortly be steering the ship of state on its 'new course'.

Joachim's disorientation is further presented in terms of a blurring of vision and a sense of being caught in an invisible net or dragged down into a morass. These are the reactions of a representative of the landed gentry to the confusing reality of the metropolis Berlin, which is the natural sphere of Ruzena. She, the dark-haired lover, is associated with the darkness of the big city in which Joachim fears he might disappear without trace, whereas the blond Elizabeth is at home in the clear light of her father's country estate or, when she visits Berlin in the spring, in the 'small rural paradise' of the family's suburban home in the Westend. This overly schematic contrast between town and country pervades the whole novel. To an extent it is the confrontation of a still largely feudal way of life — the elder von Pasenow still entertains notions of a '*jus primae noctis*' in relation to the Polish maids on his estate — with the modern world of industry and commerce. Joachim is troubled by the sight of workers at the gates of Borsig's machine factory, which he passes on his daily walk to the barracks, for they appear to him to be just as exotic as the Bohemian girl, Ruzena. He is even more disturbed by the area of the Alexanderplatz and the stock-exchange, where the hustle and bustle produce in him a sensation of vertigo. His antipathy towards the business world stems largely from his acquaintance with Eduard von Bertrand, a former colleague who has abandoned the army for a successful career in cotton importing. With his offices in Bremen, Hamburg and Liverpool, his trips to America and India and his command of the esoteric language of commerce, Bertrand strikes Joachim as a foot-loose adventurer, a traitor who has betrayed the ideals of the army by opting for a life spent in unscrupulous pursuit of profit.

Here is a clear example of two men who, in terms of Broch's historical theory, belong to different 'Partialwertsysteme' (partial value-systems). Joachim, whilst he retains links with a feudal way of life based on the land, is primarily a soldier, whose whole ethos is conditioned by his occupation. The younger son of the family, he has been sent away at the age of ten, in accordance with tradition, to the cadet school in Culm. The subsequent 20 years spent wearing the King's uniform have shaped his whole outlook on life. The clothes have made the man. Joachim associates his uniform with all that is clear, ordered and disciplined. It has become almost a second skin, a protective casing that insulates him from all the instability, questionable morality and indeed anarchy he sees in civilian life. His first encounter with Ruzena takes place, significantly, on one of the rare occasions when he has, albeit reluctantly, donned civilian clothes. And appropriately it is Eduard von Bertrand, the turncoat, the businessman who has exchanged his Prussian uniform for a suit of English cloth, who supplies Broch's commentary on the historical significance of Joachim's attachment to uniform. The military ethos is, he says, a kind of substitute theology, compensating man for the loss of an all-encompassing value-system centred in religious faith. It is also 'romantic' because 'it is always romanticism when things secular are raised to the level of absolutes'. Broch is thus not content merely to stress the importance of military values in Wilhelmenian Germany by dwelling on the motif of uniform, as writers like Heinrich Mann and Zuckmayer had done before him; he locates it also in the wider context of a process of secularization, stretching back to the Middle Ages. Bertrand's remarks on the rôle of uniform anticipate the theory of the decline of values which will be expounded at length in the third novel of the trilogy.

Bertrand acts as Broch's spokesman with regard also to that other element of the concept 'romanticism' which we have defined as seeking refuge from reality in outmoded value-systems. His remarks on this subject are prompted by the death of Joachim's brother Helmut in a duel with a Polish landowner. The fact that in the age of railways two men can still shoot at each other with pistols strikes Bertrand as a remarkable example of the way in which irrational conventions continue to operate despite historical progress. When Joachim tries to defend his brother's behaviour in terms of 'Ehrgefühl' (sense of honour), Bertrand dismisses all such feelings as atavistic: 'I think that the feeling people have about life always limps along roughly a half or even a full century behind life as it really is.' (GW 2, 54) The metaphor of limping is one Broch often uses to convey the process of time-lag in history. As early as *Cantos 1913* he talks of progress 'falling, as it were, over its own feet', and the same notion finds concrete expression in the often lengthy descriptions of the gaits of characters in *Die Schlafwandler*, examples of which are the analysis of Joachim's father's walk at the very beginning of the work and the repeated references to the crutches on which the trades union secretary Geyring hobbles along in the second novel, *Esch*. Bertrand attributes Helmut's death in the duel to 'Trägheit des Gefühls' (emotional inertia), a related image that equally stresses the way in which the weight of traditional values impedes progress.

The death of his brother Helmut is an experience of central importance for Joachim von Pasenow. His confrontation with 'the countenance of death' when he returns to the family estate for the funeral could have the effect, Broch suggests, of awakening him to the realization that his own values are essentially dead ones. Momentarily this is in fact what happens. As he contemplates his brother's coffin, Joachim has the strange notion that he himself is lying in it and that it is the coffin of a child. But this symbolic glimpse of the truth is suppressed as he returns to 'reality' by assuring himself that, behind the black funeral drapes, the familiar furnishings of the room he remembers from childhood are still intact, especially the framed Iron Cross won by one of his ancestors in 1813. Though the word itself is not mentioned, the fleeting perception of truth Joachim has here, as he steps outside his limited value-system, is an early instance in the trilogy of the experience Broch calls 'sleep-walking'. It is not possible here to discuss the title symbol in all its complexity, but it is worth stressing that the image is not used with negative connotations. On the contrary: it invariably occurs in conjunction with a sense of freedom from the established values that normally determine an individual's actions, affording an insight into the true nature of his situation and therefore also holding out the possibility of change — a change which is suggested by the dual sense of 'wandeln' in German.[9]

Joachim's reaction to the momentary knowledge vouchsafed to him as he looks at his brother's coffin is one of fear. Like a child he reaches out with his hand to confirm that the solid objects which make up his secure world are still in place. In doing so he fulfills Broch's third criterion of 'romanticism': fear of knowledge.[10] After the death of Helmut the first novel is substantially an account of Joachim's refusal to recognize his own better knowledge or that communicated to him by Eduard von Bertrand. Although the sight of cavalry exercising in the military riding school reminds him one morning of clowns, prompting the heretical notion that 'the Fatherland is being defended by a circus', he continues to seek security in military values. Although the faith of his army colleagues, as he witnesses them at worship in the garrison church, strikes him as empty and hypocritical, he himself increasingly takes refuge in the Lutheran beliefs of his childhood. And although the fate of his father, who becomes more and more deranged after Helmut's death, provides ample evidence of the bankruptcy of the Junker's feudal way of life, Joachim ultimately opts for it by rejecting Ruzena and entering into a conventional marriage with Elizabeth.

The spurious logic by which he attempts to rationalize what is essentially a flight from reality is nicely conveyed by an incident towards the end of the novel, when he visits a lawyer to arrange a financial settlement for Ruzena, the girl he is rejecting. Originally he has in mind an annuity, because he knows how un- reliable she is with money. But when the lawyer proposes a lump-sum payment, arguing that this will allow Joachim to sever all connections with the girl at a stroke, thus rendering the whole affair 'non-existent', he seizes on the opportunity to simply annul the reality which has been causing him so much confusion. He is also confirmed in his resolve to extricate himself from his emotional entangle- ment by another piece of advice from the lawyer: 'I suppose convention is still always the best guide'.[11]

Having thus patched up his leaking ship, Joachim eventually lands, as Bertrand ironically points out, 'in the harbour of marriage'. But the terms in which his wedding night are described — more like a funeral than a honeymoon — suggest that he has opted for a living death. It is at this point that Broch abruptly breaks off the narrative with a laconic five-line final chapter, indicating that Joachim has served his purpose as a model figure within the historical scheme of the novel and that his subsequent story is of little significance.

III

August Esch, the central character of the second novel, makes a striking contrast with Joachim von Pasenow. As a native of Luxembourg, living and working in the Rhineland cities of Cologne and Mannheim, he is comparatively rootless. As a humble bookkeeper for a wholesale wine-merchant he lacks the sense of security that comes from belonging to an established ruling caste. Family tradition and religious faith, both of which Joachim is able to fall back on in a crisis, are also denied him. Esch is an orphan and a self-styled free-thinker. For all these negative reasons he provides Broch with a model example to illustrate his theory of the collapse of values.

The only system of values Esch seems to know is that of his job, which allows him to impose a semblance of order on reality, even if it is only the order of columns of figures that neatly balance out. At the very start of the novel, however, he is sacked because of an alleged error in the books, and his dismissal leads to a feeling of disorientation more acute than that experienced by Pasenow. Although with the help of the trades union official Martin Geyring he quickly finds a new post as a clerk in a Mannheim shipping company, he continues to brood on the injustice of his dismissal, which he sees as evidence of a fundamental flaw in creation. Appropriately and amusingly Broch has him express his metaphysical anguish in the language of his occupation. The lack of justice in the world is attributed to an enormous error in the books; the lack of order is seen as a situation where, in contrast to the clear debit and credit columns of his ledgers, nobody knows left from right.

Esch's perplexity increases as he discovers that his own personal case is not an isolated example of injustice. In a cabaret in Mannheim he watches with horror a knife-throwing act, identifies instinctively with the 'victim', a Hungarian girl called Ilona, and determines to 'save' her. His trades unionist friend, Geyring is then jailed for allegedly inciting dockers to strike when in fact he has been trying to dissuade them from taking industrial action. Esch's anger at this injustice is directed at the president of the shipping company he now works for, whom he suspects of having sent *agents provocateurs* to the union meeting addressed by Geyring. His subsequent discovery that the president — none other than Pasenow's former colleague Bertrand — is a notorious homosexual reinforces Esch's conviction that he and not Geyring deserves to be in prison.

Further support for Esch's view that the world has gone awry is provided by basic incongruities that he discovers in the behaviour of people he comes into contact with. 'Mother' Hentjen, the landlady of a pub he frequents in Cologne, has a puritanical abhorrence of men and their sexual appetites, yet she tolerates flirtation with her waitresses because it is good for business. Fritz Lohberg, an acquaintance in Mannheim, is a vegetarian, a temperance fanatic and an enemy of smoking, which he sees as a threat to the health of the German nation, yet he runs a tobacconist's. Herr Gernerth, a respectable family man, earns his living as a theatrical impresario, organizing female wrestling bouts in which the costumes provided for the women are deliberately designed to burst at the seams. These are all examples of what Broch means by anarchy. It is an anarchy of values rather than an anarchical situation in the political sense, and it anticipates, as the rather forced examples of the widow Hentjen, Lohberg and Gernerth show, that moral schizophrenia which he diagnoses as a general condition at the time of the First World War.

The plot of the second novel, too complex to recount in detail here, is essentially the story of Esch's forlorn efforts to restore justice and create some sense of order in this 'anarchic' world. Ultimately they end in stoic resignation when he takes refuge in a marriage with 'mother' Hentjen and returns to the secure haven of his old occupation as a book-keeper in his home country, Luxembourg. There is a clear parallel here with the development of Joachim in the first novel, and Broch goes to similar lengths to chart the confused logic by which Esch justifies his actions and attempts to make sense of the world. One example of many is the illusory notion that by persuading the knife-thrower Teltscher to abandon his act in favour of the more profitable business of women's wrestling, he is somehow 'redeeming' his assistant Ilona. He even sacrifices his job in Mannheim and joins the venture himself: it does not occur to him that he is in effect promoting the exploitation of several women in the vain hope of saving one. This is a classic instance of what Broch in the first chapter of the Disintegration of Values terms 'underpant logicality', and indeed the tangled thought processes by which Esch arrives at his decision to abandon his job are recounted at a moment when he is literally taking down his underpants before going to bed.

The reference to underwear is more than a wry joke. For Pasenow, underclothing was the very embodiment of anarchy, against which his uniform acted as a protective casing. Whereas he sought to sublimate his sexual instincts for the sake of preserving order in his life, Esch frequently indulges his own as a means of working off his frustration and anger at the lack of order in the world. This is most apparent in his relations with the widow Hentjen. The descriptions of their love-making suggest that she personifies an intractable reality that Esch is desperately trying to mould into some sort of meaningful order. The repeated references to her 'matter-of-factness,' 'rigidity' and 'muteness'[12] anticipate the picture of the modern world, as Broch sees it, in the final phase of the process of disintegrating values. Esch's hopes that a 'new life' will be born of their union remain unfulfilled, because she proves infertile.

Despite the unmistakably satirical tone of much of the novel, Broch's portrayal of Esch is by no means wholly negative. His desperate search for values in an anarchical world may seem quixotic, — the comparison with Cervantes' hero is made explicit in a passage in *Huguenau* — but the very fact that he rebels against the status quo, even if he has no very clear idea of what to put in its place, has the author's sympathy. Constantly described as 'a man of impetuous attitudes' Esch at least is not guilty of that 'emotional inertia' which characterized Pasenow. Indeed, Broch sees him as an archetypal rebel, comparing him not only to Luther, but suggesting also in a number of passages a parallel with Kleist's Michael Kohlhaas.[13]

The more positive side of Esch is stressed in a dream-like encounter with Eduard von Bertrand, in the third section of the novel. In his obstinate and confused pursuit of justice he has come to associate the industrialist not only with Geyring's wrongful imprisonment but with all the wrongs in the world, and he sets off for von Bertrand's country retreat in Badenweiler with the firm intention of killing him. The journey, however, turns into a 'sleepwalk' in which, freed briefly from the narrow, determined world of his normal life, Esch is allowed an insight into that logic at work in the process of history which Broch is to explain in the treatise of the third novel. Bertrand, acting as Broch's mouthpiece, points out to him that there can be no hope of a rebirth of values as a result of individual crusades like his own. The process of disintegration must run its course until a zero-point is reached. This he envisages in unmistakably apocalyptic terms, conjuring up a picture of inevitable destruction that anticipates the slaughter of the First World War and sets the stage for the central character of the third novel, Huguenau:

> Many will have to die, many will have to be sacrificed so that space can be made for the knowing, loving saviour. And only his sacrificial death can redeem the world and establish a new state of innocence. But beforehand the Antichrist must come, the madman who is without dreams. The world must first become devoid of air, emptied out as under a vacuum receptacle, .. the void. (GW 2, 324)

Esch's decision to marry the widow Hentjen, which follows closely on the encounter with Bertrand, may be a renunciation of rebellion and a resigned acceptance of reality, but Bertrand's vision remains with him and his eyes, unlike those of Pasenow, are at least directed to the future.

IV

It is as if the prediction of Bertrand has become a reality when, at the outset of the third novel, Wilhelm Huguenau deserts from the trenches. For that spring morning in 1918 'the world lay as if under a vacuum receptacle'. The bare facts of Huguenau's story, which forms the central strand in the complex third part of Die Schlafwandler, are quickly told. On deserting from the army, Huguenau, a businessman from Colmar in Alsace, makes his way to a small town in the Mosel valley near Trier. Passing himself off as the agent of patriotic big-business interests, he enlists the support of the local military commander, the now 60-year-old Major von Pasenow, for his scheme to take over control of the town's newspaper, the political line of which is, he claims, subversive. The paper's proprietor is August Esch. The fraudulent scheme succeeds, and Huguenau establishes himself briefly as a respected figure in the community. In November, however, amidst the confusion of a workers' uprising, he murders Esch and rapes his wife, the former widow Hentjen. Then, pretending to have rescued the dazed and injured Pasenow from the mob, he escorts him to a hospital in Cologne. From there, equipped with the necessary papers, he makes his way back to Colmar to resume his former civilian life as if nothing had happened.

Incredible as it may seem, this strange interlude in Huguenau's life is not accompanied by any of that sense of disorientation that Broch emphasizes so much in the cases of Pasenow and Esch. The whole episode is seen rather as a vacation — appropriately so, since it takes place in vacuo, that 'vacuum of values' which Broch sees as an inevitable transitional phase after the collapse of the old and before the birth of new values. Described by Broch as 'the appropriate child of his age', Huguenau is, for the duration of his vacation at least, devoid of all values. The designation 'child' has a literal significance too, since his actions have a childlike freedom and spontaneity. He feels little need to rationalize them, as do Pasenow and Esch, and he is uninhibited by any moral scruples. Even his dupery of Esch is not calculated, but carried out instinctively as in a trance. To this extent he too is a sleepwalker, since he acts autonomously throughout, undetermined by the narrow business ethic by which he has previously lived and to which he eventually returns. His murder of Esch is a case in point. It is not motivated by financial gain — he has already securely lodged the capital, raised from unsuspecting local dignitaries to enable him to gain control of the newspaper, in a Cologne bank account. It is rather an 'acte gratuit', similar to the murder in Gide's Les Caves du Vatican.[14] Reprehensible from a traditional moral point of view, the killing is nevertheless 'ethical' in Broch's terms by virtue of its autonomy.

Broch's ambivalent attitude towards Huguenau is an inevitable consequence of the dialectical philosophy of history underlying the trilogy, since the 'value-free' man must represent at one and the same time the nadir in a long process of disintegration and the starting-point of the regeneration of values. It is the negative side of the figure that is indicated by the concept 'Sachlichkeit'. This 'matter of factness' or 'objectivity' — there is no single equivalent in English that adequately expresses all the word's connotations — represents for Broch an extreme form of that positivism which, according to his theory of history, has increasingly dominated the modern world since the break-up of the 'Platonic' medieval order. It is the end-product of a five-hundred year process, which began in the Renaissance when man ceased to view reality through the mediation of God and turned his attention directly to the world of objects, a process Broch defines as: 'turning one's attention to the immediate object . . . away from the language of God to the language of things'. Above all it is manifest in modern science's 'obsession with facts'.

Broch's choice of the term 'Sachlichkeit' was no doubt also influenced by the contemporary movement in the arts known as 'Neue [new] Sachlichkeit'. Certainly those chapters of his historical treatise where he discusses modern architecture as symptomatic of the spirit of the age suggest that this is the case. As early as 1911 he had written an essay on the Austrian architect Adolf Loos who, with his disdain for elaborate ornament and insistence on austere functionalism, is regarded as one of the forerunners of the movement.[15] In Die Schlafwandler his early critique of Loos in developed into a general theory, according to which the absence of ornament in modern architecture is a visible indication of the absence of values in a world where pure functionality has become the sole criterion of human activity.

Huguenau's thought processes are described as 'devoid of ornament' just like modern architecture. They are conveyed in appropriately terse, staccato sentences that contrast markedly with the long-winded, tortuous passages of 'free indirect speech' used by Broch to express the confused logic of Pasenow and Esch. They are strictly functional too, always concerned with the matter immediately in hand — 'la chose', as Huguenau, a native of Alsace, revealingly likes to call it. As the child of the age of 'Sachlichkeit' he is also very much at home with inanimate objects, experiencing none of that sense of alienation from the world of concrete things that characterizes the heroes of the first two novels. Whereas Pasenow feels threatened by the machinery of Borsig's factory in Berlin,

Huguenau positively delights in contemplating the printing press on which the local paper is produced. Not that he understands its workings: he treats it rather as a child does a new toy, or a primitive a fetish. In this last respect he exemplifies Broch's cyclical theory of history, which envisages a return to primitivism after the process of rationalization that accompanies the disintegration of values has run its course.

Apart from a child called Marguerite, with whom he feels a great affinity, Huguenau is the only figure in the third novel who is wholly in his element in the confused world of 1918. All the other characters feel disorientated and are conscious in varying degrees of the collapse of values which is Broch's theme. In a letter to his publisher's wife, he explains his decision to include a number of parallel narratives in the novel:

> The book consists of a series of stories, all of which are variations on the same theme; that is to say man's re-exposure to isolation, a re-exposure determined by the disintegration of values — and it also brings to light the new productive forces that are engendered by this isolation once it has actually become manifest. (GW 8, 57)

The sense of isolation stressed here is most directly linked to the First World War itself in the narrative that deals with the doctors, patients and nurses of the local military hospital. One of the doctors in particular, Flurschütz, acts as a spokesman for Broch's views when, in a reference to Gogol, he talks of the wounded soldiers as dead souls, and goes on to confess that he has given up reading because language itself has become mute. Ideally, he says, men should invent some new form of communication to overcome their isolation. This unlikely possibility appears to be realized in another strand of the narrative, that which concerns Ludwig Gödicke. Severely wounded and almost buried alive in the trenches, Gödicke, a stonemason in civilian life, is involved, metaphorically speaking, in the laborious process of piecing together again the shattered fragments of his being. Beyond a few inarticulate expressions he never recovers the power of speech, but this does not prevent him from establishing one of the few meaningful relationships in the whole novel, his silent friendship with a watchmaker called Samwald. Another story, less directly linked to the War, charts the progressive dissociation from reality of the lonely middle-class woman, Hanna Wendling, whose lawyer husband is away from home in the army. In her isolation she becomes increasingly alienated from the furnishings and decor of her fashionable home — a clear illustration of the link between ornamentation and values in Broch's theory.

Isolation and estrangement also characterize Broch's portrayal of Pasenow and Esch in the third novel. The former, as commandant of the little Mosel town, is cut off from his family and roots in Prussia. In addition, he feels out of place in a war fought with what are, by his traditional military standards, 'unchivalrous weapons'. Frustrated by the restrictions imposed on his newspaper by military censorship, Esch comes to see the War more and more in terms of the apocalyptic vision conjured up by Bertrand in Badenweiler. Convinced that man's only salvation lies in a revival of religion, he organizes prayer meetings, in which he is eventually joined by Pasenow. These activities, satirized though they are in all their naïveté, are nevertheless evidence of those 'productive forces' which

Broch sees as emerging from man's isolation, for they illustrate his theory that true religions originate from sects and disintegrate to form new sects. On a less spiritual level too, the brief friendship between Pasenow and Esch, two characters who are politically and socially poles apart, is one of the most positive features of the novel.

Another such relationship is the subject of the *Geschichte des Heilsarmeemäd-chens in Berlin* (Story of the Salvation Army Girl in Berlin), a strange story, written for the most part in ballad-like verses. Narrated by Bertrand Müller Dr. Phil., who is also the fictional author of the treatise *Zerfall der Werte* (Disinte-gration of Values), it tells of a brief and wholly platonic relationship between Marie, a Salvation Army girl and Nuchem, an orthodox Jew. Broch brings together these two representatives of radically different religions in a 'godless' Berlin which he describes in terms of aridity and petrifaction reminiscent of Eliot's *Waste Land*. Each of them illustrates an aspect of the role of religion in his philosophy of history. Although his faith is incomparably older, the Jew, in his adherence to an abstract Law devoid of all ornamentation, is seen as the epitome of modern man. The Salvation Army, on the other hand, is interestingly com-pared to the Jesuit movement of the Counter-Reformation, not only in its military organization, but also in its attempts to re-centralize all values by taking religion out on to the streets and exploiting 'ornamental' aids such as tambourines. Broch's alter ego, Bertrand Müller, sympathizes with Marie, especially with her practical efforts to relieve suffering in the city, but he judges the religious aims of her move-ment to be 'pathetic and inadequate waste of effort'. For himself, he prefers to go on living in the tenement block he shares with Nuchem and other Jewish refugees from Eastern Europe, because he thinks their essentially provisional way of life is highly appropriate in an age when everything has become pro-visional. In doing so he deliberately chooses to experience to the full the estrange-ment and isolation Broch regards as typical of an age of transition between the collapse of old values and the creation of new ones, a phase he calls 'no longer and not yet'.

V

Interspersed among the parallel stories and the central narrative concerning Huguenau are the chapters of Broch's treatise *Zerfall der Werte*. Structurally, this disruption of the linear narrative mirrors the collapse of values which is the central theme, and the concrete examples of the stories link up with ideas of the treatise to produce an elaborate contrapuntal effect. By making the theory just one strand in the narrative, alongside others, and by attributing it to Bertrand Müller, a pessimistically-inclined intellectual, suffering from malnutrition in the Berlin of the final year of the War, Broch gives the impression that it should be viewed relatively. On the other hand, in a letter to his translator Willa Muir, he claimed that it was not only the intellectual key to the whole work, but also 'the outline of a *new* philosophy of history'.[16] He certainly attached great importance to the ideas of the treatise because he repeated them time and again in his essays of the thirties, and elements of the same theory, such as the concept of a 'vacuum of values' figured prominently in one of his last works, the study *Hofmannsthal und seine Zeit* (Hofmannsthal and his Time).

Relativized or not, it has to be said that much of Broch's philosophy of history is of questionable validity. This is particularly true of his idealized vision of the Middle Ages which, like that of Novalis in *Christenheit oder Europa,* is more a theodicy than a historical account. No amount of special pleading along the lines that it is not to be taken literally but only as a 'model' or 'logical construct' can disguise the fact that it conflicts with the findings of conventional historiography. The same applies to the cavalier fashion in which he lumps together, both temporally and geographically, Renaissance and Reformation.[17] Nor is his emotive description of the former as 'that criminal and rebellious age' likely to make much sense to more orthodox historians. Such judgements make clear that his theory is anything but neutral. In fact it bears all the hallmarks of that cultural pessimism, born of a reluctance to accept the pluralism of values in the modern world, which characterized the thinking of many intellectuals at the time of the First World War and during the years of the Weimar Republic.[18]

The negative portrayal of the modern metropolis in *Pasenow* is evidence of this pessimism. It may be presented from the perspective of a conservative Junker, but his attitudes are close to those of the author, as can be judged from Broch's later essay *Geschichtsgesetz und Willensfreiheit* (Historical Laws and Free Will), where modern man's rootless, disorientated existence in big cities is set against an idealized view of peasant life. Pasenow's association of the decline of values with the rise of commerce also reflects Broch's own attitudes. Again and again he identifies the businessman, and often specifically the Jewish business-man — examples from *Die Schlafwandler* are the impresario Gernerth and the theatrical agent Oppenheimer — with the evils of the modern world. To an extent this may be a reaction to his own father, the Jewish textile manufacturer in whose business Broch somewhat reluctantly worked until the age of forty, but it is also characteristic of a widespread 'internal' anti-semitism of the time, a phenomenon Broch later remarked upon himself.[19]

By virtue of its cyclical nature, Broch's philosophy of history is not, however, wholly pessimistic. Out of the 'vacuum of values' it envisages the eventual emergence of a new unified and integrated system on the medieval model. In this respect it may be regarded as an example of that 'hunger for wholeness' which Peter Gay, in his study *Weimar Culture*, identifies as a dominant feature of the age. Certainly Broch gives ample expression to such longings in the trilogy, whether through the revivalism of Esch; Jaretzki's desire for 'a new kind of intoxication or some such so that we can all belong together again'; or the ominous reference in the closing pages of the work to 'longing for a leader figure'. All these yearnings are, to be fair, viewed sceptically. Broch himself makes no attempt to show what form the new 'wholeness' will take. He merely invites the reader, in the light of the logic of his historical theory, to accept that its eventual coming is inevitable.

I am not competent to judge that logic, still less the involved epistemological arguments on which it depends, but in its determinism Broch's philosophy of history seems to me to be vulnerable to most of the criticisms levelled at such systems in Isaiah Berlin's well known essay *Historical Inevitability.* One passage from it could almost have been directed specifically at Broch. Referring to 'the contemporary collapse of values' as just one example of what he calls 'non-empirical figments', Professor Berlin goes on: 'There has grown up in our modern time a pseudo-sociological mythology which, in the guise of scientific concepts, has developed into a new animism — certainly a more primitive and naïve religion than the traditional European faiths which it seeks to replace.' Ironically, it is precisely its close resemblance to primitive animism that Broch singles out as a virtue of the epistemological concept which is the cornerstone of his whole theory.[20]

The shortcomings of Broch's philosophy of history are one thing: The extent to which it affects *Die Schlafwandler* as a novel is another. Apart from the intellectual difficulty of the treatise itself, especially the chapters on logic and epistemology, there is a clear tendency in *Huguenau* for the characters to become mere puppets, manipulated by the author to illustrate this or that point from the theory. This is less apparent in the more conventional narratives of *Pasenow* and *Esch*, although they too are marred at points by rigidly schematic characterization and structure. Perhaps this is inevitable in a work that attempts to impose a logical framework on historical events in order to make sense of their apparent absurdity. Whether Broch's logic is in the end any less spurious than that of his creations Pasenow and Esch is a moot point. The verdict of Broch's translators on this, reported by Willa Muir in her autobiography, seems to me to show sound common sense:

> We refused to be bludgeoned by Broch's logic, we did not admit the supremacy of abstract philosophizing, we set up a stout resistance to his arguments. We felt that Broch, in his attempt to be rigorously logical, had merely rationalised his deeper fears.

NOTES

The majority of references are to the standard ten-volume edition of Broch's works published by the Rhein-Verlag, Zürich 1952–61, for which the abbreviation GW (Gesammelte Werke) is used. Works not included in this edition are referred to in the new Suhrkamp Kommentierte Werkausgabe, as yet incomplete, using the abbreviation KW. The fullest bibliography is that by Klaus W. Jonas, contained in the *Broch-Brody Briefwechsel*, Frankfurt am Main, 1971. More recent items on *Die Schlafwandler* are listed in the new Suhrkamp edition of the novel, KW Vol. I.

1. Pasenow or Romanticism, Esch or Anarchy, Huguenau or Objectivity. The narrow identification of the heroes with the abstract nouns of the titles in Edwin and Willa Muir's translation is misleading, especially their version *Esch or the Anarchist*.
2. First published by Manfred Durzak in *Neue Deutsche Hefte* 110/XII (1966).
3. The most important are published for the first time under the heading Wert- und Geschichtstheorie in KW Vol. 10/2, 11–94.
4. *Das Böse im Wertsystem der Kunst* (Evil in the Value-system of Art), in GW Vol. 6.
5. Gordon Leff in *History and Social Theory*, London 1969.
6. For the early essay see KW 10/2, 11. For the passage in the novel, GW 2, 400.
7. For a good analysis of this see H. Reinhardt, *Erweiterter Naturalismus*, Cologne/Vienna 1972, p. 178ff.
8. Cf. especially GW 2, 386 and 395.
9. In my view the best discussions of the title symbol are those by Dorrit Cohn, *The Sleepwalkers*, The Hague/Paris 1966, Chapter IV and Hartmut Steinecke, *Hermann Broch und der polyhistorische Roman*, Bonn 1968, pp. 103–55.
10. Cf. GW 2, 475. 'wer die Erkenntnis fürchtet, ein Romantiker also . . .' (someone who fears knowledge, that is to say a romantic . . .)

11. 'Die Konvention ist wohl immer noch der beste Leitfaden.' GW 2, 139. 'Leitfaden' suggests 'clue' or 'thread' that will lead out of the labyrinth.

12. 'Stummheit' (muteness), which is a leitmotif of the whole trilogy, indicates not only literal lack of communication but also modern man's disrespect for the word in general. For a discussion of this see the brief talk on the novel Broch gave in the Volkshochschule in Vienna in 1931. KW 1, 728–33.

13. Amongst other things the comparison is suggested by Esch's passionate sense of justice, 'die rechtschaffene Buchhaltung seiner Seele', the fact that the particular injustice he has suffered is soon subordinated to 'größere und höhere Ziele', and that he is prepared in his fervent desire to restore order to the world, 'notwendig Köln an allen vier Enden anzuzünden'.

14. A comparison made by Reinhardt, op. cit., p. 147.

15. *Ornamente*, KW 10/1, 32–3.

16. GW 10, 319. The italics are Broch's own.

17. A point made by Robert A. Kann in 'Hermann Broch und die Geschichtsphilosophie', *Historica*, Vienna 1965.

18. Similarities between Broch's ideas and those of Spengler are noted by Hermann Krapoth, *Dichtung und Philosophie*, Bonn 1971, 108.

19. In a letter of 1938 to Sidney Schiff. GW 10, 373–8.

20. Cf. GW 2, 597.

Alfred Döblin's Berlin Alexanderplatz and Literary Modernism

A. F. Bance

Alfred Döblin's *Berlin Alexanderplatz* (1929) is one of the few German works both frequently and unequivocally cited in general discussions of Modernism. It is the first, and only, important German novel to concern itself with the life of a metropolis, and, in an age of mass culture, to do so seems a guarantee at least of modernity, if not of Modernism. The city is, after all, the alembic in which the Modernist consciousness was precipitated, from Baudelaire to Joyce and T. S. Eliot. In Döblin's novel, the hero and his milieu are given almost equal weight: indeed, the consciousness of the individual and the collective life of the city often coalesce. It was only on the insistence of his publisher that Döblin adopted the subtitle 'Die Geschichte vom Franz Biberkopf' (The story of Franz Biberkopf).

Berlin Alexanderplatz was a radical departure from the author's previous works, and remained unique among them, not only for its popular success. Döblin had read, and indeed reviewed, Joyce's *Ulysses*, and technically was much influenced by it, as a recent study has conclusively shown.[1] The stylistic and formal innovations of Döblin's prose unquestionably place him among the avant-garde of novelists in Germany between the wars, a select group including Hermann Broch and Hans Henny Jahnn, the only major German writers to follow in the footsteps of James Joyce. Here of course it is not simply a question of writers employing a few new-fangled literary devices, such as inner monologue (which was not new to German literature, in any case, since Arthur Schnitzler's *Leutnant Gustl*, published in 1901) but of a revolution in the writer's expectations of the reader, a refusal to provide the usual narrative guide-words or 'markers' being only one symptom of this change. In *Ulysses*, Joyce breaks down not only traditional narrative techniques but also distinctions of genre, of dramatic, epic or lyric. He demands that his reader should forgo the comfort of traditional linear development and stylistic uniformity, and he forces him to 'perform' the text in his reading of it, to reconstruct the novel's plan or structure for himself, while at the same time making constant leaps of the imagination to encompass brilliant play with syntax, inventive neologisms, and onomatopoeic effects.

Döblin's style of narration varies from episode to episode, mixing inner monologue, free indirect style ('erlebte Rede') and third- and first-person narrative. Particularly striking, and an innovation in the German novel, is the use of inner monologue in conjunction with third-person narrative within a sentence. There is a good deal of dialect and colloquial conversation; the narrator employs in his own right the racy style of Berlin slang, as well as other lively effects, such as onomatopoeia, and rhyming couplets heading a number of the sections or 'books', reminiscent of a *Moritat* or *Bänkelsänger* (street-ballad or broadsheet) style, and helping to maintain a strong, archaic didactic line throughout the novel. Mythical material is introduced, such as the story of Orestes; biblical passages, such as the chapter on Job and the story of Abraham and Isaac, as well as frequent quotations from Jeremiah and Ecclesiastes.

While the will to stylistic experiment does not necessarily make a Modernist, any more than the absence of experiment precludes Modernism, Modernism and innovation are often found together; and Modernist writers do frequently explore the possibilities of formal experiment as a natural outlet for their particular kind of vision. But with the introduction of the term 'vision', we can no longer defer the pressing problem of definition. Modernism is a concept which clearly calls for definition if it is to mean anything more than merely 'the modern' or even 'the contemporary'. One difficulty is that whereas *by* definition the modern is what is present, Modernism is now a term of historical placement like Romanticism or Realism, a period term that can be used to refer to a literary event in the past, although (and this is the complication) the period we call 'Modernism' may not yet be over.

Modernism is a crisis of culture which befell some of the creative minds of Europe in the late nineteenth century. To define the crisis is to define the movement, and nobody has dealt more delicately with the problem of definition than Lionel Trilling in his essay 'On the Teaching of Modern Literature', where he puts forward his reasons for choosing certain texts for the Modern Literature course at Columbia College, and points out the inherent difficulty of dealing academically with matters which concern us so personally, as we 'try to make a shape out of the very things of which we are ourselves made' (David Jones). For as Trilling says, the essence of modern literature is to pose uncomfortable and personal questions about our marriages, our professional lives, and our relationship with family and friends. With quiet irony Trilling presents the examination-question version of matters so insidious and threatening that we usually deal with them either unconsciously or within the privacy of our own thoughts. The force and terror of modern works, the rage of Lawrence and the subversiveness of Gide, become in the academic version 'notable instances of the *alienation of modern man as exemplified by the artist*' (Trilling's italics).[2]

To attempt to come any closer to a characterization of Modernism only leads to the accumulation of more or less embarrassing, and yet unavoidable, phrases akin to 'alienation', such as 'the mocking suspension of accredited values', 'the flight into subjectivity', 'the divorce between inner worlds and public worlds', 'the mode of perceiving itself as the object of perception', 'the abandonment of "man the measure"', 'the rejection of scientific certainty'. (All these expressions have been culled from writings on Modernism). The balance has to be corrected, as far as it can be, by a similar list concerning the evasive or redemptive measures taken by art on behalf of society to manage this crisis of Modernism, at the same time that it draws attention to it: for example 'the reinvention of faith as poetic imagination', 'the special intensity of concern with the spiritual life', 'surrendering oneself to experience without regard to self-interest or conventional morality', 'the frequent exhilaration of the Modernists', 'recourse to myth as a way of ordering the futility and anarchy which is contemporary history'. The two poles of Modernism are, on the one hand, what Thomas Mann called in *Der Tod in Venedig* (Death in Venice) 'sympathy with the abyss', and on the other hand, an almost religious view of the power of art to redeem a world of subjective chaos. Modernism profoundly explores unreason, but may or may not celebrate irrationality: the writer takes on the task of imposing order on chaos, yet in Modernist literature (it is claimed) aesthetic order is abandoned or radically modified as Modernism 'downgrades the value of aesthetic unity in behalf of a jagged and fragmented expressiveness'.³ Hermann Broch is not untypical of German commentators on Joyce's *Ulysses*, and he finds it the consummate work of art, stating for the last time a disillusion with art and with culture, a 'swan-song' that is a highly composed product of the highest rationality, full of disgust for the rationality and composure of civilization.⁴

The concept of 'art to end all art' is the contradiction at the heart of many discussions of Modernism. In the novel, some of the effects of this 'terminal' function of Modernist art are seen in such features as the abandonment of 'knowability' of character, the problematic relationship between individual and collective, and the expansion of the metaphorical possibilities of language and structure, at the expense of the discursive or descriptive (metonymic) function of the traditional novel. Hermann Broch goes so far as to say that would-be naturalistic reportage, in the manner of the nineteenth-century novel, is in fact highly romantic (op. cit., 'Das Weltbild des Romans', p. 223–24). The Modernist must go one step further in his naturalism and include the act of perception itself as the *object* of perception. The writer gives the personal vision a substance that the everyday, seen world has always had, and irrevocably undermines the reader's confidence in his own grasp of reality by exposing him to a different reality that is not seen until it is communicated, like Kafka's existential terror. It is in the nature of things that although the writer can lead us into this new territory, he is not available as a guide or mentor within it, for he does not have the philosophic composure that would allow him to stand above his material.

I turn back now to *Berlin Alexanderplatz*, to consider to what extent the term Modernist applies to the novel. As his ground structure, Döblin takes a conventionally chronological progression in one man's life. The story-line might be called somewhat over-emphatic for a Modernist. When Franz Biberkopf emerges from Tegel prison in Berlin, after serving four years for manslaughter, he finds it hard to adjust to the disordered world outside. He is determined to stay decent, however, and initially he succeeds, getting by with jobs such as door-to-door salesman and street vendor on the Alexanderplatz. But in the first of three increasingly serious setbacks he is to suffer, a colleague robs him of the favours of a compliant widow. Soured by this betrayal, he takes to drink and subsequently falls in with a dangerous petty criminal, Reinhold, a member of the Pums gang, specializing in warehouse burglaries. This character, Reinhold, tires of his mistresses after a month or so, but has difficulty getting rid of them, and at first Franz obliges him by taking them off his hands. Eventually, however, Franz decides that order must be restored, and attempts to regularize Reinhold's love-life by preventing him from discarding the current girl-friend. Reinhold's deep resentment is given expression one night when the Pums gang take the unsuspecting Franz along on a 'job' to act as look-out. When he realizes what is going on, Franz refuses to participate, and is bundled into the get-away car. Another car gives chase, and Reinhold seizes the opportunity to push Franz out of their own vehicle. He is run over and loses an arm. This disaster convinces Franz that life is too hard for the honest. He throws in his lot with the gang, finds a girlfriend, the prostitute Mieze, and is so proud of her that (in a parody of a scene from Hebbel's nineteenth-century tragedy

Gyges und sein Ring) he undertakes to show her off in his room to the hidden Reinhold. Subsequently, Reinhold completes his revenge on Franz by murdering Mieze after a failed attempt to seduce her. Arrested, he declares Franz to be the murderer. Franz has gone into hiding, but, gradually realizing that through his stupidity he *is* ultimately responsible for Mieze's death, he brings about his own arrest by staging a shooting incident in a night-club. He suffers a nervous breakdown in the prison wing of a mental hospital, and almost dies. When he recovers he emerges from prison for a second time, but as a changed man. The nature of the change in him is not clear, but we are led to believe that he has undergone some kind of spiritual regeneration.

The narrator is in control throughout the book, one might almost say brutally so in his imposition of a moral meaning upon the chaos of the metropolis. How are we to construe such a strong narrative line, such un-Modernistic willingness to act as the reader's guide and mentor? For the editor of the selected works of Döblin, Walter Muschg, the didacticism of the narrator serves religious ends, for this is Döblin's 'first Christian work', foreshadowing, by implication, the author's later conversion to Catholicism.[5] Other critics have put forward equally committed interpretations, notably socialist ones, but the idea that Döblin has written a straightforwardly didactic novel contrasts markedly with the views expressed in a letter to the *Eckartjournal* in 1928 (the year he was working on *Berlin Alexanderplatz*) where Döblin denies to literature any priestly or hortatory function. 'I am of the opinion that only he who knows can take upon himself "the cure of souls", for that means to direct, create objectives, propel, lead'.[6] He touches indirectly on this subject again elsewhere, in a tribute to Freud on his seventieth birthday: 'Note the simple, clear style . . . it is not really a style; he says, without artifice and without phrases, what he means; that is the way someone talks who knows something'.[7] In contrast to his view of Freud, Döblin does not see himself as enjoying an intellectual, emotional or philosophic composure. It is perfectly accurate to say of him, what has been said of the Modernists in general, that he presents dilemmas and offers his struggle with them as the substance of his testimony. The strong story line is as 'artificial' as the strong narratorial persona. The first is offset by the licence Döblin takes with his narrative thread, the abrupt changes of theme and style, and the abandonment of conventional syntax. The strong narratorial presence is counterbalanced, not to say neutralized, by the crucial vagueness and openness of the ending, so that interpreters have felt free to take from it a whole range of meanings, from the political to the religious. It is when the narrator is at his most self-assertive that he can least be taken at face value, for I would suggest that his apparent strength is a strategy to enable Döblin to circumvent the dilemma of the Modernist writer's lack of magisterial power over his material.

Take, for example, the brief opening summary of the story, rendered very much in the style of the age, the racy, 'muscular' style of the boxing commentator (boxing was a prominent sport in the inter-war years, popular especially with the more demotically-inclined Weimar writers, like Brecht and Horváth): 'He is being viciously poked and punched. He can hardly get to his feet again, he's almost out for the count. Finally he is torpedoed with terrific, extreme brutality'. This language, the style of the boxing commentary, parallels the animal strength of the hero. There is a further parallel between the tough, muscular narrator seeking to impose his will and interpretation upon the events of the book and the chaos of the metropolis, and the tough, strong, somewhat boneheaded protagonist determined to impose his own idea of order upon a world in which he represents only an infinitesimal and insignificant particle.

Döblin's attitude to the life of the city is characteristically Modernist in its ambivalence: simultaneously futuristic and nihilistic, relishing the advance of technology (*poésie brute*) and recoiling from its effects, Döblin's obsession with the 'whore of Babylon' is finally transcended in the story of Franz Biberkopf's fate. Döblin's evocation of the city includes passages of montage, 'excrescences' like the details of tram-routes, excerpts from the Berlin telephone directory and from prison regulations, weather reports, advertisements, a list of local government departments, and statistics of births and deaths. There are long descriptions of the city abattoir. There are potted biographies of randomly-selected Berlin characters, whose dual function appears to be to demonstrate, on the one hand, the narrator's omniscience and his privilege of arbitrarily using his power over the material; and on the other hand, the little that can be known about persons, even if one is in full command of all the external facts about their lives. These life-stories read like case-histories. They are built around the illnesses endured by the subjects, and the causes of their deaths. Döblin was a panel-doctor in the working-class district of Berlin East around the Alexanderplatz (as well as conducting a prosperous practice in the affluent west end of the city) and these short biographies convey something of a doctor's synoptic view of human life, his dubiously privileged insights into the often short and unfulfilled lives of ordinary people, and his ultimate impotence to know them or to help them. This crushing portrait of Berlin life reduces the hero to his proper size by the end of the book, as it does the narrator, who for all his show of control and conviction must fail as an interpreter in the face of Franz's overwhelming spiritual crisis.

I want to suggest that Döblin's narrator and his hero, and perhaps to some extent Döblin himself, are confronted with those truths which form the consciousness of Modernism itself. Conventional notions are under attack, including the notion of individual identity itself, or the concept of man as a predominantly rational, coherent being in a structured universe. The narrator's moral stand is transparently theatrical, for the hero's consciousness is clearly conditioned by external forces to such an extent that he must be exonerated from absolute responsibility for his behaviour.

The anachronistic certainty of the narrator — epitomized by the archaic doggerel of his street-ballad style — enhances, through an ironic contrast, the uncertainty of the times. The entertainment provided by the narrator's brashness is part of the colourful aesthetic show in which Döblin reflects the brittle world of inter-war Berlin. Franz's disorientation is the disorientation of Germany itself in the Weimar period, masked by the bright modernity of an age of mass culture. The modishness of the thriving entertainment industry of Berlin in the 'Golden Twenties' is caught in the title of a 1928 foxtrot called 'Es liegt in der Luft eine Sachlichkeit' (modernity is in the air), echoed in *Berlin Alexanderplatz* in a passage of word-play which prefigures Günter Grass, and lays bare the hysteria and ominous self-delusion of such determined modernity: 'Es liegt in der Luft was Idiotisches, es liegt in der Luft was Hypnotisches, es liegt in der Luft, es liegt in der Luft, und es geht nicht mehr raus aus der Luft' (There's something idiotic in the air, there's something hypnotic in the air, it's in the air, it's in the air, and it will never leave the air: p. 209). What is 'in the air' is the obverse of a coin whose reverse is existence in a cold impersonal society requiring the individual to endorse the latest interpretation of the status quo.

I have suggested already that Döblin shares the preoccupations of typically Modernist works. But there is some evidence that the book succumbed to such a confrontation with the conflicts of Modernism almost against the author's will. When Professor Julius Petersen, a well-known Germanist at Berlin University, conducted a seminar on the novel and sent the resulting study to Döblin, the author was pleased with it, and in a letter of November 1931 conceded the critical point that the ending was 'apparently tacked on'. He could offer no defence except that the book was only the first of two volumes that he planned to write: 'The second was to have portrayed (will portray?) the man of action, even if not the same person; the ending is a bridging exercise, so to speak — but the other bank is not there'.[8] Döblin went on to explain a conflict in his novel between a passive and receptive element with tragic overtones, and a more optimistic element — 'the ego in nature' versus 'the ego above nature'. He had had every intention of leading Franz Biberkopf on to the second phase, that of political activism; but he failed. Against his will, simply by the logic of the plot and the plan of the novel, it ended thus. It was beyond redemption, it escaped from his control. 'The dualism cannot be resolved', he concluded, referring Petersen, significantly, to *Manas*, the book that preceded *Berlin Alexanderplatz*, a verse epic influenced by the *Baghavadgita*, in which an Indian Prince journeys to the Kingdom of the Dead. The Hindu world-view which is the philosophical setting of *Manas* is the antithesis of the commitment to political activism that Döblin had originally hoped to bring about in Franz Biberkopf. If, as seems to me to be the case, Döblin was contemplating an escape from the Modernist crisis through the advocacy of meaningful political action, then *Manas* did not point in the right direction. The surrender of the ego, the transformation of the self through boundless suffering, and the doctrine of the identity of all beings, 'the murderers and the murdered, the executioner and his victim', as Döblin expressed it in a later summary of *Manas*[9] — and therefore, one might add, the exploiter and the exploited, the capitalist and the worker — can surely only lead to an inwardness and a quietism completely inimical to political solidarity and action.

For all the modernity, the concrete realism and reportage of the novel, the ending of *Berlin Alexanderplatz* has the appearance of a response to the particularly German tradition of *Innerlichkeit*, inwardness. Although the breakdown of the relationship of 'Innen' and 'Außen', inner and outer worlds, is an aspect of Modernism in other literatures, it is of special and long-standing significance in the German tradition. Inwardness here means a preference for the exploration of inner states, a higher degree of interest in the reality of the individual sensibility than in the worldly circumstances that alone condition that sensibility. For whatever reason, the extreme limits of this subjectivity have quite frequently been reached in German literature, so that it is possible to speak of a tradition of renunciation of the experience of the outer world for the experience of the imagination alone, a renunciation that results from a painful sensitivity towards the isolation of the individual and the gulf between objective and subjective worlds. (Goethe's *Werther* or Büchner's *Lenz* are prime examples.)

In so far as international Modernism was drawn to the pole of subjectivity, it was not strange to the Germans when it came, and yet, as might be expected in view of the different German tradition, the German reaction to Modernism diverged from responses elsewhere. The Anglo-Saxons were more likely, for example, to see techniques such as stream-of-consciousness *as* techniques, a way of extending realism to a new realm, the inner lives of characters. But for many German writers the kind of subjectivity which accompanied the rise of the Modernist novel threatened a return to a dangerous *Innerlichkeit*, and a decline from the attempt at a fruitful synthesis of the dualism of the self and the world. It is not surprising therefore that in *Berlin Alexanderplatz* Döblin was attempting to fulfil a venerable ambition of synthesis, the resolution of this dualism. But neither is it surprising that the attempted evasion of dualism in *Berlin Alexanderplatz* gives rise to a 'tacked on' ending incongruous with the Modernism of the book's overall tendency.

The dilemma reflected in *Berlin Alexanderplatz* is that, in the German view, subjectivity and the formal developments of the twentieth-century novel are taken together as recording quite accurately the fragmentation of existence and the sensation of lack of control over the objective world: therefore it is difficult to maintain the traditional role of the German novel as the vehicle for a Weltanschauung, and of the narrator as interpreter of the given world, which is his function in the particularly German *Bildungsroman* (novel of education) tradition, for example.

It follows that no German writer tracing the footsteps of Joyce could afford simply to take over the techniques of *Ulysses* and consider their employment to be a solution to the so-called 'crisis of the novel'. Döblin was quite right to reject the suggestion that he was merely a Joyce imitator. *Ulysses*, he said, had to be seen only as 'a good wind in my sails'.[10] The elements of inner monologue, montage, parody of the scientific style, and so on, were for Döblin a means to an end very different from that of *Ulysses*. 'I know' said Döblin in 1932 'that Joyce has nothing to do with substantial areas of my work: it can only be a matter of peripheral similarities'.[11] The point is that Döblin is not willingly subscribing to the use of Modernist techniques either as part of the creation of a new realist genre, or as an end in itself, as autotelic art. What emerges from Döblin's struggle with Modernism is an attempted reversion to the traditional German solution to the problem of subjectivity — a tradition of transcendentalism, idealism, of belief in a 'superreality' underlying mere appearance.

It is in this same tradition of transcendence that Döblin eventually finds the resolution of another familiar German problem that exercised him in the twenties: how to reconcile knowledge and action, *Erkennen* and *Handeln*, 'Wissen und Verändern' ('knowing and changing' — this latter phrase being the title of a political tract of 1931, subtitled 'Open letters to a young person'). In *Wissen und Verändern* Döblin typically maintains an abstract, liberal view of socialism, untarnished by notions of materialism or class-conflict. But the question of how to proceed from the platonic realms of theoretical insight to practical action without compromising that insight is an old German problem that particularly plagued Weimar writers, faced with a clear need for action but conceiving it as inevitably the rape of theory, 'the inevitable tragic decline of the intellect from its own standards'.[12] Weimar intellectuals were less than fertile in generating practical solutions to the question of what is right action in the sphere of reality. In *Wissen und Verändern*

Döblin squares the circle of the 'thought versus action' dilemma by equating the two: thought *is* action! It is a similar sleight of hand by which Döblin attempts to derive a political and moral advantage from Biberkopf's fate in *Berlin Alexanderplatz*: the theme of 'transformation' is characteristic of his novels, and, of course, of his Expressionist beginnings. Döblin's dilemma appears to be that, while on the one hand he finds it hard to come to terms with the new 'poetic', non-prescriptive role of the novel and its autonomy, which is to say its Modernism as an art form, on the other hand his world is too modern and his awareness of the contemporary crisis too acute to allow a very close examination of this somewhat outdated prescription for spiritual regeneration, Biberkopf's metamorphosis.

To return to the specifics of Döblin's work: how does this particular kind of protagonist fit into his most Modernist novel? His choice of the limited proletarian hero may have been influenced by the view of the novel's function which he expressed in his *Ulysses* review of 1928: 'The heroic, and in general the significance of the isolated person, the individual, have been very much reduced, overshadowed by the factors of the state, the parties, economic complexes. Much of this applied earlier, too, but today a man really is no bigger than the wave that carries him'.[13] The condition of modern man could hardly be less ambiguously presented than through the medium of a decisively non-intellectual, un-heroic product of the metropolis. Again, the use of the proletarian and underground milieu may have something to do with Döblin's desire to show off his superior knowledge of the lower levels of Berlin society (around 1930, Döblin became involved in literary and political controversies connected with his suspicion of the left-wing intellectuals' 'cult of the proletariat' coupled with their basic ignorance of working-class life). To employ a 'low' character as an exemplary representative of modern man is in itself a deliberate provocation to bourgeois readers, stressing the natural democracy of Modernism, the idea of the crisis of traditional (class-based) culture, and the exposure — akin to that of psychology — of subliminal and ulterior motives in us all. This aspect of *Berlin Alexanderplatz* has led some to identify the novel with the *Neue Sachlichkeit* ('neo-objective') movement in Weimar Germany, which attacked authority in general and outdated notions of literary decorum in particular. But it is typical of Modernism to be fascinated by the lower depths, the asocial elements on the margins of society and the shadowy milieu they inhabit.

Biberkopf's alienation from the life of the city is expressed in the confusion and disorder he feels after leaving prison; and in a phrase reminiscent of Kafka's *The Trial*: 'the punishment is beginning'. The true punishment lies in his freedom, not in his imprisonment, which represented security and order. This punishment that is freedom is expressed in metaphors taken from the most commonplace areas of city life. The attempt to escape the Law (the law of existence) is shown to be futile and terrifying in its consequences, in the scientific-symbolic description of the smoke in the beer-hall which obeys the physical laws of its nature and seeks escape, but in doing so finds itself dissipating in the cold night air outside the lighted hall (p. 66). Such an image, occurring as it does in the midst of a scene of social satire worthy of Georg Grosz, tears a sudden rent in the fabric of the everyday world of inter-war Berlin and gives a glimpse of the terrible, because boundless, perspective of a universe in which human beings are components of a collective obeying the physical laws inherent in *its* nature, one of which enjoins a constant, fruitless attempt to escape from the grip of these laws. 'How do I get out of this prison?': Biberkopf's words (p. 28) are taken up, and their metaphysical implications made explicit, in the *Epilog* that Döblin wrote at the end of his life: 'What do I actually know? I know that in this era we human beings . . . are sorely tried. Our skin rasps against the walls that surround us until it bleeds. We strike them and hear our hands slapping and the way we scream . . .'[14]

This perspective renders pathetic all attempts to impose a man-made order on the world; but from the discrepancy between man's puny attempts to establish order, and his ignorance of the laws of the macrocosm to which he is subject, arises a good deal of the humour of the book. The 'smoke' episode itself has a wry outcome: 'The smoke hardly knows what's happening to it; it clutches its forehead, which is no longer there, it wants to think but it can't. The wind, the cold, the night have got it, and never more was seen' (p. 66). There is humour too in the recital of the rules of the transport company, and in the copybook example of the man who breaks them (p. 41). Much of the texture of the book is composed of the language of various kinds of official announcements and prescribed forms, each of them announcing the essentially transient (because man-made) nature of the apparently permanent (because colossal) metropolis.

The delusion of strength is a theme running through the novel. Among the varied forms it takes is the description of the bull sent to the slaughter-house and cut down in all its strength and vigour. The point made here is again that of the subservience of the individual — however powerful — to the macrocosm. The strength of the animal is in the last analysis not its own: 'from the sun came your blood, the sun was hidden in your body, now it is emerging again' (p. 123). All life beneath the sun comes from the sun. Despite the individual's illusion of strength, he has merely been lent a part of the strength of the whole. In the novel, the delusion of physical self-reliance appears a pathetic and highly temporary self-aggrandizement, as does the presumption of spiritual or intellectual self-reliance. Other intellectual frameworks, such as physics, are rejected too (the application of Newton's laws of motion to describe a brutal killing creates a sense of outrage against the amorality of the scientific perspective). Psychology suffers the same fate: in the mental asylum at Buch, the psychologists' attempts to devise clever diagnoses of Franz's spiritual crisis are satirized as irrelevant.

The hubris of these intellectual systems is really no different from Biberkopf's pride in the strength of his muscles, as a metaphor for the sin of the great city which rips nature apart and busily builds, demolishes and rebuilds itself. The leitmotif of the steamhammer on the Alexanderplatz punctuates the novel. We are constantly told of the demolition of buildings and plans for new ones: the city never rests. But human beings are still rooted in nature, and, for all its power, the city does not nourish them. The cold black waters of the lake in Freienwalde, the scene of Mieze's murder, symbolize both the unplumbed depths of a mind such as that of the psychopathic murderer Reinhold, in whose brutality the underlying *Angst* of the city has surfaced; and of the force of nature as perceived from the city: that is, an unknown quantity lying out in the great void beyond the city lights, disregarded yet representative of an immeasurable power that will ultimately engulf Berlin as it has engulfed other cities, other civilizations before.

What man cannot forsake is the delusion of strength derived from the projection of his own thought-system (as laid down in the 'given' of his language-inheritance) on to the surrounding world, and his elevation of that system into an immutable truth. We are forcibly reminded of Nietzsche, influential upon Döblin as upon all the German Modernists: 'In as much as man has through long ages believed in the concepts and names of things as in eternal truths, he has acquired that pride by which he raised himself above the animals: he truly believed that in language he had knowledge of the world.'[15] The narrator seems to endorse this remark in one of his frequent, free-standing interpolations in the text: 'and have all one breath, and a man has no pre-eminence above a beast . . .' (p. 127: *Ecclesiastes* 3:19). The interpolation occurs in the midst of Döblin's version of the Book of Job, which could almost be a parable to support a sermon upon Nietzsche's text. In Döblin's version, what Job cannot accept is, firstly, the fact that he is threatened with the loss of his very thoughts, his consciousness; and secondly, the weakness to which he has been reduced. (Once again, the motif of pride in strength is in the foreground.) We are reminded of Kafka's reasoning protagonists, who can see no way to grace *except* through their powers of reasoning, and yet whose clever ratiocination stands between them and whatever kind of salvation is available to them. What Hermann Broch calls 'the myth of philosophy itself', which is to say 'the myth of Jacob who fought against the angel in order to be blessed by him',[16] is also the appropriate myth for Kafka, and for Döblin. Job is a Modernist figure, suffering through his *Erkenntnis*, his formidable insight and consciousness, yet unable to relinquish the 'superiority' they give him. As God says to Job: 'Although you suffer thus, and suffer because of your thoughts, yet you do not wish to lose them?' (p. 125).

The greater man's efforts to demonstrate his strength, the more obvious his weakness becomes, and Biberkopf is the paradigm for the process. No setting could be more appropriate for such a statement than the capital of Weimar Germany in the phase of its illusory prosperity and stability (roughly 1924 to 1929), bolstered by American money, a house of cards which was to collapse overnight when American credits were lost subsequent to the Wall Street crash. As Biberkopf represses (to his peril) the feelings of insecurity that he experiences upon leaving Tegel, the sensation that the roofs of the houses are slipping and falling down upon him, so has Berlin suppressed the terrible experience of insecurity brought about by the Great War, finding oblivion in an explosion of commercial and cultural activity and heedless promiscuity. Döblin ensures that the First World War is never far from the reader's mind in the pages of *Berlin Alexanderplatz*. Characters make recent history an excuse for moral decline in the post-war era (with some justification, since the war obviously represented a monstrous collapse of civilized standards) so that reference to the war is brought in as a convenient justification for any immoral act (p. 331). Instead of teaching men about the insubstantial and unreliable nature of their man-made reality, war has taught them another lesson; one of callousness, towards themselves as much as to others. Franz's military experience (it is implied on page 262) helps him to endure his amputation, and thus inhibits him from learning the lesson which he ought to have learned from the episode that caused it. The missing arm becomes a psychological support which allows Franz to pretend to be a war-hero, and a fraudulent Iron Cross completes the effect. He now has an outer sign and justification for the disorientation that he suffered as a result of the war, becoming Hero and Victim at the same time (a familiar and dangerous combination whose outcome is all too clear to us in the train of events that led directly from the First World War to the Second).

The modern city (to summarize the tendency of these remarks), and post-war Berlin in particular, of which Franz is the representative, has suppressed precisely the kind of knowledge that informs Modernism: the belief in perception as plural, life as multiple, reality as insubstantial. These insights are offered to Franz at the beginning of the novel by some Jews who try in vain to help him: they are offered again by the Old Testament-like 'Angels of Death' (whose speech-cadences are distinctly Eastern European-Jewish) at whose hands he finally accepts them. Döblin takes a delight in subjecting the most recalcitrant material (the thick-skulled protagonist) to a process of transformation by firing in the furnace of self-knowledge. The role of mythical and biblical references — whose applicability to themselves is frequently denied by the novel's characters — is to undermine the smugness of modern city man. This Döblin does by the cumulative intensity of experience, which eventually breaks down the hold upon the protagonist of the metropolis and its aggressive rejection of three or four thousand years of human experience, of which the Jews are appropriate representatives. The change in Franz can only be presented metaphorically; as a struggle with the Angels of Death, as the buffeting of a great storm which Franz survives, as a withdrawal into the innermost recesses of the mind, where we cannot follow, and in other metaphors often taken from quite commonplace contexts.

Such a metaphor, and I would suggest, a crucial one, is a botanical image containing a pun which is very apposite to Döblin's purpose: 'How does a plant protect itself against cold? . . . The most important defence is conversion of the starch (*Stärke*) contained in the cells into sugar' (p. 324). *Stärke* translates as both 'starch' and 'strength'. In the conversation that Franz has with Death in the hospital at Buch, Death announces that strength leads to the delusion of conservation and resistance to change: 'Bewahren, bewahren, so ist das furchtsame Verlangen der Menschen . . . Du hast dich in Stärke hineingekrampft . . . Ich bin das Leben und die wahre Kraft, du willst dich endlich nicht mehr bewahren' ('To preserve, to preserve that is the timorous desire of men . . . You convulsed yourself into strength . . . I am the life and the true power, now at last, at last you no longer wish to preserve yourself') (p. 388).

Death expresses himself in the same doggerel rhyming couplets as the narrator ('Du willst dich erfahren, du willst dich erproben, das Leben kann sich ohne mich nicht lohnen'), and their shared advantage of omniscience makes them comparable figures, if not broadly co-terminous. As Death cannot be held to account, no more can the narrator. The starch-sugar metaphor is characteristic of his Delphic style, and offers a better epilogue for the novel than the 'ending with fanfares' that Döblin could not resist tacking on to celebrate Franz Biberkopf's return to the world as a kind of Expressionist New Man. The conversion of starch into sugar is discussed from the point of view of the usefulness of the process to mankind: 'The usefulness of many commodity crops is, however, not greatly increased by the formation of sugar: the best evidence of this is the undesirable sweetness of frozen potatoes. But there are cases where it is only the sugar content brought about in a plant or fruit by frost action that makes it utilizable, as with wild fruit, for example' (p. 324). The usefulness of the transformation depends upon a changing standpoint, that of consumer reaction. But if for a moment we apply the metaphor to Franz's own metamorphosis, as we are transparently invited to do, it is clear that there *is* no ultimate consumer of metaphysical verities except man, the subject, himself — unless it be God. The 'usefulness' of the change Franz undergoes cannot objectively be established. The ending of *Berlin Alexanderplatz* must be an open one. For all Döblin's efforts to avoid the Modernist's dilemma of subjectivity, Franz has done no more than arrive at the Modernist position of 'the man of faith without a faith'. But this is a position in which he is at least immune to the credos inspiring the fanaticized masses who march past his window with flags and bands and singing. 'I'm not going to rush into swearing loyalty to anything in this world', he resolves (p. 410). The knowledge Franz has gained through his suffering in Buch is, Döblin would like to say, an irreducible, transcendental truth, whose function is to protect him from all the man-made half-truths he is offered. The same function is performed, however, by the Modernist's sceptical awareness of the human capacity for self-delusion, and I would suggest that, almost in spite of himself, it is as a Modernist that Alfred Döblin emerges from *Berlin Alexanderplatz*.

NOTES

1. See Breon Mitchell, *James Joyce and the German Novel 1922–1933*, Athens, Ohio, 1976, especially Chapter 7, 'Joyce and Alfred Döblin: Creative Catalysis', pp. 131–50.
2. Lionel Trilling, 'On the Teaching of Modern Literature', *Beyond Culture*, first published 1955, London, 1966, p. 12.
3. See Irving Howe, 'The Idea of the Modern', *Literary Modernism*, Greenwich, Connecticut, 1967, p. 29.
4. See Hermann Broch, 'James Joyce und die Gegenwart', *Gesammelte Werke, Essays*, Bd. I, ed. Hannah Arendt, Zurich, 1955, p. 188.
5. See p. 423 ('Nachwort') of the dtv edition of *Berlin Alexanderplatz*, Olten, 1961. Page references to the text of the novel relate to this edition throughout.
6. *Briefe, Ausgewählte Werke in Einzelbänden*, hrsg. von Walter Muschg, Olten 1970, p. 146.
7. Quoted in Walter Schönau, *Sigmund Freuds Prosa: Literarische Elemente seines Stils*, 1968, p. 258; cit. Peter Gay, *Freud, Jews and Other Germans*, New York 1978, p. 50 n. 41. The title of Döblin's tribute was 'Zum siebzigsten Geburtstag Sigmund Freuds', appearing in *Almanach für das Jahr 1927*, 1927, p. 33.
8. *Briefe*, p. 165.
9. *Aufsätze zur Literatur, Ausgewählte Werke in Einzelbänden*, (ed.) Walter Muschg, Olten, 1963, p. 389.
10. See 'Mein Buch Berlin Alexanderplatz', reproduced in *Berlin Alexanderplatz*, Olten, 1961, p. 413.
11. Breon Mitchell, op. cit., p. 149–50, notes 28 and 29.
12. Hanno König, *Heinrich Mann*, Tübingen, 1972, p. 187.
13. *Aufsätze zur Literatur*, p. 288.
14. Ibid., pp. 397–8.
15. Friedrich Nietzsche, *Werke*, (ed.) Schlechta, Munich, 1954, I, p. 453.
16. Hermann Broch, 'The Style of the Mythical Age', *Gesammelte Werke, Essays*, Bd. I. p. 253.

Lion Feuchtwanger's Erfolg:
The Problems of a Weimar Realist

M. E. Humble

It is a commonplace that nineteenth-century German realism was a tender plant which failed to bloom for lack of the fertilization which only a vigorous metropolitan culture could have provided, and that German prose realists suffered from their provincial situation and the political backwardness of the social group to which they belonged.

German writers of the twentieth century have been acutely conscious of these criticisms and some have made a deliberate effort to place their work in a European tradition. One writer, Lion Feuchtwanger, produced a series of novels which can claim in their range, vividness and humanity to bear some comparison with Balzac's *Comédie Humaine*, while bringing to the conspectus of society which they present specifically Modernist techniques of narrative. Feuchtwanger bears at present the stigma of the forgotten author of best-sellers, and is remembered, if at all, as a historical novelist. Furthermore, the fact that the only reprint of his works at present available comes from the GDR has led critics to place him among the Socialist Realists, or at least as one of their precursors.

The son of a prosperous Jewish entrepreneur, Feuchtwanger grew up in Munich, where he studied German, philosophy and anthropology at the university and gained a doctorate for a dissertation on Heinrich Heine's fragmentary drama *Der Rabbi von Bacharach* (The Rabbi from Bacharach). He travelled extensively in Southern France, Italy and North Africa, where he was caught by the outbreak of the First World War. Poor eyesight prevented his active participation, but he was close to events in Bavaria throughout the turbulent and chaotic post-war period and he was acquainted with some of the men (such as Ernst Toller, Erich Mühsam and Gustav Landauer) who played a part in successive left-wing governments there.

Feuchtwanger's first literary efforts were confined to sketches and dramas and showed no indication of his later epic gifts. However, his interest in history (not for its own sake, but for the light it shed on the present) bore fruit in such works as *Warren Hastings. Gouverneur von Indien* (Warren Hastings, Governor of India) (1916), in which the characters were presented according to a scheme which was to become typical: the opposition of unscrupulous activists, of whom the title figure may be considered representative, and passive contemplatives, such as some of the Indian roles in the play. Feuchtwanger's interest in the former type may be traced to a passing enthusiasm for Nietzsche shared in varying degrees by many writers of his generation and class; there are signs of this interest in the early sketches *Die Einsamen* (The Lonely Ones) (1903), the play *Der Fetisch* (The Fetish) (1907), the novel *Der tönerne Gott* (The Clay God) (1910) and the play *Julia Farnese* (1915). Feuchtwanger's interest in Oriental literature and philosophy, which he had studied and adapted for *Vasantasena* (1915), initiated a mode which included the publication of Alfred Döblin's *Die drei Sprünge des Wang-lun* (The Three Leaps of Wang-lun) (1915), based on a revolutionary uprising in eighteenth-century China, as well as works with an oriental setting by Hesse (*Siddhartha* and *Morgenlandfahrt*) (Journey to the East), and the chinoiseries of Klabund (Alfred Henschke), one of the most popular writers of the twenties.

The conflict of active and passive principles in his early works reflects the general cultural situation in Germany at a time when the aggressiveness of the Wilhelmine era was giving way to a quest for alternative approaches to reality.

In the drama *Jud Süß* (Jew Süss, 1916) Feuchtwanger traces a similar polarity of active and passive principles in the meteoric career of Josef Süß Oppenheimer, financier to the court of Württemberg in the early eighteenth century. Süß, who had risen to power and wealth by means of a series of crimes and intrigues, is disgraced and sentenced to death for his misdeeds. However, he refuses to save himself from the scaffold by converting to Christianity, although his religious faith had been no more than nominal. He thus renounces the amoral activism by which he had directed his life, and follows a course which Feuchtwanger considered typical of twentieth-century man: 'a path taken by our shared evolution . . . from Europe to Asia, from Nietzsche to Buddha, from the Old to the New Testament'.[1]

Both *Jud Süß* and *Warren Hastings* were reworked during the twenties. The second version of the latter, *Kalkutta 4. Mai*, resulted from collaboration with Bertolt Brecht — a partnership which also produced *Leben Eduards des Zweiten von England*, an adaptation of Marlowe's *Edward II*. Brecht influenced Feuchtwanger in the direction of 'Sachlichkeit' (objectivity) and towards the epic treatment of drama.

The popular success of the *novel* entitled *Jud Süß* was unequalled in his career. It was completed in manuscript in 1922, but initially rejected by several publishers, who considered that the historical novel had had its day. Only after a book-club had commissioned a shorter work with a more immediate appeal, *Die häßliche Herzogin Margarete Maultasch* (The ugly Duchess Margarete Maultasch, 1923), was *Jud Süß* accepted, and its sales took both author and publisher by surprise. The novel was filmed twice, the first time in Britain in 1934, with Conrad Veidt in the title role; and again a little later at Goebbels' instigation, in a version produced by Veit Harlan, which combines technical virtuosity with crude tendentiousness and abandons any notion of faithfulness to the original. In all likelihood Feuchtwanger's reputation has been damaged by the false association so easily made between the film and the novel.

The 500-page novel gave clearer definition to the East-West dichotomy, which had been a key element of the original drama's structure, by means of references to topography and a primitive kind of anthropology. Such philosophical-historical speculations may be dismissed by some as a typical example of the ideological ballast which has vitiated the achievement of even those German novelists who appealed to a very large readership. However, they deserve serious consideration, not only because they reflect prevalent preoccupations of Weimar intellectuals, but also because they provided a framework, however attenuated in form, for Feuchtwanger's attempts, in *Erfolg*, to describe the post-war period he had experienced at first hand.

The narrative of *Erfolg* consists of several closely woven strands. At the centre of the action stands the case of Dr. Martin Krüger, art historian and Deputy Director of the State art galleries in Munich, who is sentenced to three years imprisonment, on a trumped-up charge, because his sympathy for the artistic avant-garde has displeased the reactionary authorities, as represented by the Minister of Justice, Klenk, and the Minister of Education, Flaucher. His friend and later wife, the graphologist Johanna Krain, attempts to secure a retrial and a release for Krüger; supporting her in her efforts are Krüger's Jewish defending counsel Geyer, the motor designer and constructor Kaspar Pröckl, and the Swiss writer Jacques Tüverlin. Krüger dies of a heart complaint after two years in his cell, a few days before he is due to be amnestied.

The novel is set during the catastrophic inflation of 1922–3. As it gathers momentum and the precarious unity of Germany is threatened by reaction and irridentism, a movement calling itself 'die Wahrhaft Deutschen' (the true Germans), under the leadership of Rupert Kutzner, gains the support of heavy industry and of large numbers from within the dissatisfied petty bourgeoisie. At first the traditionally conservative ruling class in Bavaria is suspicious of Kutzner's demagogic tactics, and although rivalries within this clique lead some of its members to make overtures to Kutzner, this suspicion remains strong, so that when the time comes for a Putsch, Kutzner discovers, contrary to his expecta-tions, that he cannot count on the support of Flaucher, now Prime Minister of Bavaria. Feuchtwanger follows very closely the events leading up to and following the Munich Putsch of 1923, in which Hitler attempted to gain the support of Dr. Gustav Ritter von Kahr, who at that time held the office of State Commissioner during a state of emergency.

The third strand of the narrative centres on the relationship between Johanna Krain and the writer Jacques Tüverlin. Johanna is divided between her duty to her jailed husband and her growing attachment to Tüverlin, who, under the pressure of events, develops from an uncommitted dilettante to an advocate of reform determined to publicize the scandalous victimization of the innocent in Bavaria and the full background to the Krüger affair. He is prompted in this course, first, by his disillusionment with the entertainment industry, which he had hoped to steer towards a serious treatment of social issues, but which falls instead under the domination of commercially minded impresarios, and secondly, by his discus-sions with Kaspar Pröckl, for whom Brecht provides the model of a committed revolutionary who doubts whether any intellectual pleading, in the form of art or science, can bring about any change in the social sub-structure.

Many of the novel's characters are based on identifiable historical figures which make *Erfolg*, to a large extent, a *roman á clef*. Of these Kaspar Pröckl and Franz Flaucher have already been mentioned; others include Kutzner (Hitler), Crown Prince Rupprecht (Kronprinz Maximilian), General Vesemann (Luden-dorff), Krüger (August Liebmann Mayer and Bruno Frank), Anna Elisabeth Haider (Marieluise Fleißer and Paula Modersohn-Becker), Balthasar Hierl (Karl Valentin), Konrad Stolzing (Ernst von Possart), Dr. Lorenz Matthäi (Ludwig Thoma) and Josef Pfisterer (Ludwig Ganghofer).[2] Some of these characters can be traced to very insignificant originals; others are recognizable portraits of promi-nent members of Feuchtwanger's closely-knit literary circle.

The model for Balthasar Hierl, Karl Valentin, was an entertainer from whom the young Brecht learned a good deal about the epic treatment of comic charac-ters; a Munich folk-hero who received such adulation from his public that he remained immune from Nazi counter-measures, despite his scurrilous attacks on the regime. Feuchtwanger reinforces his criticism of the 'Wahrhaft Deutschen' in an account of one of Hierl's sketches, 'Der Handschuh. Nicht von Schiller' (The Glove. Not by Schiller). Hierl informs his friend Resi that he has found lying on the street two tickets to a meeting of the Eddabund, an aristocratic club where Kutzner makes his best speeches and reveals his secret plans. He describes the recent sighting he has had of the leader in his grey car, elegantly dressed and holding a pair of gloves. An argument ensues on the question of whether Kutzner will appear that evening with or without gloves, and the dispute is beginning to reveal both differences in Weltanschauung and character-flaws when the protagonists realize that the meeting has already begun. Their quarrel distracts their taxi-driver and causes a crash, and they eventually arrive at the hall only in time to witness the final acclamation of the leader. As the spectators leave they ask whether he was wearing gloves; the answers differ and the evening ends in a street fight in which all present resolve their differences by turning on an innocent bystander.

As part of Feuchtwanger's satire of incipient Nazism the incident is of minor significance; as part of his general appraisal of popular mentality, however, it has an important place in the novel. Other events are integrated into the trend of the novel's critique by means of a number of recurrent images and leitmotifs, which give the documentary aspect of the novel an extra dimension. Animal behaviour, like that of the lemmings which Krüger finds described in a book he read in prison, provides an analogy to the movements, attitudes and habits of human beings, for which the Marxist theories of Pröckl give an inadequate explanation. The lemmings resemble to some extent and by implication the Bavarians, whose tribal consciousness is shown to be so strong. Another example of a human-animal analogy points up this general resemblance: Klenk and the complex of images connected with Bavaria that he represents is identified with the Steinbock (ibex), a creature which prefers the remoteness of mountain heights to the crowded plains, stubborn isolation to co-operation with others towards a clear goal.

> These ibexes were strange, old-fashioned beasts who refused to bow down, were destined to extinction or to a bare existence in zoos. They were haughty and lived like hermits. They clambered up steep rock-faces, mysteriously sure-footed, insensitive to the severest cold. . . . They could only be tamed as long as they were young: when fully grown they acquired a gloomy, malicious humour, and grew so obstinate that nobody could manage them. (p. 491)[3]

Other motifs draw on traditional culture or on works of art and literature with which Feuchtwanger would expect his readers to be familiar. One of Tüverlin's writing projects, *Weltgericht* (Doomsday), draws an analogy between the contemporary social and political situation and the millennium, in a manner reminiscent of Karl Kraus, who, like Feuchtwanger, had conveyed a mood of apocalypse in *Die letzten Tage der Menschheit* (The Last Days of Mankind) by means of a loosely connected series of scenes and dialogues based on direct observation.

Central to an understanding of the novel are the debates on the function of art. Franz Landholzer's picture 'Josef und seine Brüder oder: Gerechtigkeit' (Joseph and his brethren or: Justice) is introduced on the first page of the novel and is merely one of several works by various hands which provide the initial impetus for the action. It is through his involvement with Anna Elisabeth Haider, the painter of a nude self-portrait which shocks the Munich gallery public, that Martin Krüger is tried and convicted. These pictures, together with a powerful 'Kruzifixus' by Andreas Greiderer, are made to throw light not only on the character of the artist, but also on that of the observer and owner.

Specific works of art occupy a key position in the discussions of art's function. The seventeenth-century artist Alonso Cano represents an insipid and decorative type of art to which Krüger is temporarily attracted and against which Kaspar Pröckl in particular reacts in the name of an art which induces social concern. The trivialization of serious art is the theme of Tüverlin's association with the show-business tycoon Pfaundler, who transforms Tüverlin's satirical review *Kasperl im Klassenkampf* (Kasperl in the class war) into a leg-show with the title *Höher geht's nimmer* (You can't get any higher). Similarly the apostle-play in Oberfernbach (modelled on the Passion play at Oberammergau) is stripped of what spiritual content it once had and changed into a catchpenny spectacle under the influence of the American dollar, as represented by Daniel Washington Potter. The dilution of an *engagé* approach to art is seen throughout in relation to the title and principal abstract motif of the novel — success — defined for the most part in material terms; the failure of the committed is juxtaposed with the hollow triumph of the dilettante. The wealthy connoisseur Heßreiter is a typically superficial art fancier, who purchases the Haider self-portrait and displays this intensely private and anguished work to his friends, only to be forced to auction it to another industrialist, Andreas Reindl, when his business, manufacturing garden gnomes, is caught up in the economic whirlwind of the inflation.

More often than not, an example of art which acts as a palliative of an intolerable situation, such as the work of the Heimatdichter Josef Pfisterer, is opposed to one which shocks the complaisant majority, as represented by the paintings of the artists Krüger supports before his imprisonment. All the artists and writers in the novel are confronted with the alternatives of pursuing efforts to create art which might serve enlightenment, or of bending to commercial pressures and reactionary opinion and seeing their ideas debased. Most are either forced into the latter course, or renounce art altogether, finding no future for it in a society which has lost its way. Tüverlin, who embodies many of Feuchtwanger's own attitudes, can be said to rescue part of the original inspiration for his review, despite the alterations demanded by Pfaundler, by allowing a serious point to emerge, in some of the items, from beneath a sensational surface.

The bullfight scene in the review, in which showgirls play matadors and Balthasar Hierl is the bull, is a powerful image of backward Bavaria's (or Germany's) difficulties in adjusting to the twentieth century in general and the post-war situation of defeat in particular. Tüverlin's attitude to the phenomenon he describes is complex and ambivalent: 'Tüverlin had made the bull a harassed dull-witted creature doomed to destruction, a creature full of strength, not unlikeable, lacking only in cunning, a quality without which in that age it was hard to live.' (p. 399) The ambivalence is a sign of the love-hate relationship towards his adopted country which he later openly declares: 'Tüverlin loved the people among whom he lived. With all the intensity of the true writer, who despite the coldness of his insight cannot live without hating or loving his subject, this highly developed man loved the uncouth, slow-witted Bavarians with their crude art.' (p. 571)

However, it is the Spaniard, Francisco Goya, who takes on the mantle of an artist who comes to terms with his own times, faithfully reflecting its failings without succumbing to its temptations. In his approach to his subject matter he resembles not Tüverlin, but the hapless Krüger, who during his harsh imprisonment rejects his former ideal, the dandy aesthete Cano, and turns to the more astringent products of his compatriot: 'He drank in the story of the violent painter with his greed for life, who knew so well the terrors of the Church, of war, and of the judicial system'. (p. 344) Although the narrator does not point the comparison, one can see in the particular Goya motifs singled out for mention aspects of the general situation in Bavaria and of Krüger's own personal plight: 'the giant rising from mist and consuming a living man' can be identified with Krüger's view of authority from the perspective of his prison cell, while 'peasants belabouring one another with clubs during a land demarcation dispute' can be compared with the Bavarians' stubborn pride in their homeland and their suspicion of strangers.

This last characteristic, already illuminated by the image of the bullfight, receives further elaboration in the figure of Kasperl, portrayed in Tüverlin's review by Hierl. Here a positive slant is given to what elsewhere bears the brunt of his criticism, and the balance of love and hate tips in favour of the former:

> Tüverlin had not made Kasperl merely a virulent caricature, but had allotted him a sympathetic role and a lot of triumphs. Kasperl was knocked about a good deal, but more often it was he who gave the knocks. He knocked everyone on the head, until the big-wigs and the smart Alecks lay dead all around. But Kasperl still remained, stupid, predictable, triumphant, ingenuously enquiring: 'What's your cut, mate?' (p. 397)

Hierl is said to have an instinctive awareness that Kasperl (who occupies a place in German folklore corresponding to that of Mr. Punch in Britain) embodies 'specifically Bavarian characteristics'. He presents Kasperl as the great survivor, who by the example of his resilience gives hope to the 'little man' that there is a way through the labyrinth of war, inflation, insurrection and intrigue to some sort of stability.

Kasperl's reappearance towards the end of the novel has the ambivalence already apparent in the presentation of this and other images of the Bavarian character. Here Tüverlin's observation of a Kasperltheater during the Auer Maidult (a Munich fair) takes on a special significance as he ponders all the individual tragedies (Krüger, Amalia Sandhuber) with which he has been directly and indirectly associated. After the ritual call to his audience: 'Seid ihr noch alle da?' (are you all still there?) Kasperl deals with his enemies one by one: a loud-mouthed officer, a tax official, a policeman, a doctor who can work miracles, even Jack Dempsey and finally the devil himself. Although he receives heavy blows, he defeats them all and returns to his refrain: 'Are you all still there?' for the beginning of his next show. To the children (and to the reader, with his memory of Kasperl's earlier appearances) the question is a testimony to the little man's unflappability. However, to Tüverlin, at this moment, it points to the negative aspect of his dual view of Bavaria, resulting from its refusal to move with the times, its failure to extricate itself from the tangled post-war political and economic situation. In order to account for Tüverlin's feeling of hopelessness, Feuchtwanger introduces Nietzsche's notion of eternal recurrence — an idea which had been adopted by conservative circles in their challenge to Liberal views of progress: 'It is a tough peasant persistence: the eternal recurrence of the same. The city simply will not admit that anything has happened in the last decade.' (p. 755)

However, when Tüverlin later discusses with Johanna the possibility of a film on the Krüger case, his mood is shown to have changed. Now the loyalty of the Bavarians to their national customs no longer has the deadening connotations of stagnation, and the momentary return of the bullfight image points to the positive aspects of Bavarian stolidity: 'The brass band was playing, "So long as the green Isar flows through the town you'll find Munich full of good cheer", and then it played the "March of the Toreadors", and then, "A health to good company".' (p. 771) Tüverlin proceeds to establish a connection between enlightened faith in gradual progress through the power of reason and the figure of Kasperl. Once again he is associated with the Nietzsche tag of eternal recurrence; now, however, it is given a positive meaning: 'My book is all about Kasperl in the Class War. . . . You can also say, the eternal recurrence of the same thing. Everybody knocks Kasperl on the head, but he always gets up again in the end.' (p. 761)

Tüverlin's personal crisis, both in his relation to Johanna and to his work, is resolved, while the success of the film of the Krüger case and of Tüverlin's book (sub-titled *Das Jahrmarkt der Gerechtigkeit*) (The Funfair of Justice) closes the novel on a positive note. However, that note is only credibly sustained by means of pointed references to earlier discussions of art, in which the theme of Tüverlin's relation to his work is carried forward and developed. These references are the culmination of a complex debate about art, which involves not only Tüverlin, but also Pröckl and Krüger.

The first significant discussion of art takes place between Krüger and Pröckl in the prison where Krüger is held. To Pröckl Krüger's interest in Goya is merely a sign that he is lapsing into his old ways, misusing his enforced leisure and failing to develop a revolutionary consciousness. Krüger replies by accusing Pröckl of himself retreating from reality by espousing a revolutionary dogma; indeed, he sees his friend as one who lacks the normal human feelings which are the motor behind even the abnormalities of Goya's art:

> The reason why you've fallen for communism . . . is simply that from your birth you've been endowed with remarkably little of the social instinct. . . . You're a poor devil, you can't sympathise with other people; that's the reason why you try to acquire artificial means of doing it. . . . Furthermore, you're a puritan. You lack the most essential human attributes: a capacity for sensual enjoyment and a sympathetic heart. (p. 345)

Pröckl's own account of his discovery of Marxism harmonizes with Krüger's characterization. He had come to accept it, not for humanitarian reasons, but because it provided a firm ground on which he could stand after a period of drifting and disorientation:

> But at the moment when he applied the principles of scientific Marxism to them they arranged themselves spontaneously; causes and effects appeared; the wheels fitted into one another. It was as if he had tried till then to drive a

car with whip and reins, and had not been able to move it from the spot; but now he knew its mechanics. (p. 384)

The imagery is appropriate to Pröckl's profession of engineer. What, however, can be the place of art in the Weltanschauung of such a man? It is a question he attempts to answer in a later chapter, as he struggles at the typewriter with an article entitled *Über die Funktion der Kunst im marxistischen Staat* (On the function of art in the Marxist state). Conscious of having reached a personal crisis, he resolves to visit Franz Landholzer, the painter of 'Joseph and his Brethren or: Justice', one of the pictures which had shocked the public at the beginning of the novel. Plagued by doubts as to the value of his own art — the ballads in which 'image and knowledge were fused', but allowed no room for debate on serious issues — Pröckl hopes to draw from Landholzer some stimulus to develop an art which has the power to confront these issues and force its witnesses to do likewise.

Pröckl discovers that Landholzer is confined in a mental hospital after a frustrated career as a cartographer, during which his brilliant inventions have been ignored and then pirated by others. In his insanity he has painted not only the Josef picture but also a caricature of his official superiors described as 'a sort of Last Judgment', echoing the attempts by Tüverlin and Krüger's defending counsel, Geyer, to expose the Bavarian legal system. Landholzer's ravings contain such a weird mixture of truth and nonsense that his visitor is momentarily confused. However, Pröckl's clarity of mind returns when he examines Landholzer's pictures. The first, 'Das jüngste Gericht' (The Last Judgment), presents a surreal conglomeration of figures in legal garb surrounded by instruments of torture. A wooden sculpture bristling with weapons, entitled 'Militarismus' (Militarism), has four faces, two of which are recognizable as those of Hindenburg and Ludendorff. 'Abendmahl' (The Last Supper) is a painting presenting the four beasts of the Apocalypse and two images of Judas, while a wooden relief of an animal shown with bent forelegs, as if kneeling, is described as 'Das bescheidene Tier' (The modest animal), or 'Der Amboß seines Schicksals' (The anvil of his fate).

The relation of such works to the fantasies of betrayal and victimization of a paranoiac is clear enough; more important is their relation to Pröckl's creative dilemma. After showing Pröckl a self-portrait, Landholzer insists on a shave; and as his heavy beard is cut away a face comes to view which Pröckl recognizes as identical to his own. It is surely significant that Landholzer is confronted, not with any character who may be said to correspond in one way or another with Feuchtwanger (such as Geyer, Krüger and Tüverlin), but with Pröckl, who is partly based on Brecht. Pröckl proceeds to destroy Landholzer's work, abandon his own art and emigrate to the Soviet Union, where a position as engineer in a car assembly plant has been offered to him.

When Pröckl marks his decision to emigrate to the USSR by writing to himself a postcard in the form of military orders outlining his next moves, the narrator recalls an earlier argument with Tüverlin on the place of art in the Communist state. On that occasion Tüverlin had written to himself in terms which clearly rejected class-consciousness and permitted individual self-expression. The narrator points out that Pröckl is unmindful of that episode as he commits his marching orders to paper. Pröckl's commitment to a materialist theory of art is maintained:

It wasn't true that the quality of any work rebounded on its author: at best the glory was due to the age in which it came into being. Whether a work came to completion or not did not depend on the gifts or the labours of the individual; it depended simply on the age, on economic and social conditions. (p. 684)

Furthermore, he defines Landholzer's art as the dead end of an individualist aesthetic and even attempts to interpret Krüger's work on Goya as a revolutionary act according to his own theory.

Tüverlin's type of self-expression, in contrast to Pröckl's, implies a lack of commitment to a firmly held point of view which corresponds to Feuchtwanger's own stance throughout most of the novel. Furthermore, he has different interests: in the first of his conversations with Pröckl they had spoken not only of art under Communism, but also 'of the increasing migration of peoples, of the mingling of European civilization and Asiatic culture, of the sources of error in an attitude of mind based solely on sociological theories' (p. 242). The clash of European and Asiatic cultures, and their symbiosis, thanks to improved communications, are in Tüverlin's view twentieth-century phenomena far worthier of attention than the class war. The strength of Feuchtwanger's own concern with the East-West dichotomy has already been noted.

Erfolg does not conform to the common categories of the novel. As one would expect from its sub-title, 'Drei Jahre Geschichte einer Provinz' (Three Years in the History of a Province), it contains elements of the chronicle, and the narrative is interrupted from time to time by documentary chapters and sections within a chapter.[4] Feuchtwanger's habit of inserting information known to any twentieth-century reader, as if he were reporting the ethos and way of life of a people belonging to a much earlier period of history who have left few remains of their existence, has a distancing effect, whatever the standpoint in time or place of the reader. Even the most everyday occurrence has to be seen against the background of a particular culture which it is part of the novelist's task to analyse. 'The fashions of those times were cumbrous and ridiculous. The men buttoned stiff linen collars round their necks, ugly, superfluous and constricting affairs, and laboriously tied round them useless neck-bands, called "ties".' (p. 441) In so far as the narrator fails to achieve total objectivity, it is in favour of an enlightened stance from which many of the phenomena he is describing are seen as primitive survivals of a bygone age, even though the novel was published only six years after the last of the events it describes.

Otherwise the narrator remains in the background, and Feuchtwanger makes considerable use of modern techniques of narrative in order to reveal his characters' thoughts. Besides the subjunctive to indicate reported speech there are many passages which reproduce consciousness directly, such as Justice Minister Klenk's thoughts, during a drive through the Bavarian countryside: 'A picture either appeals to you or not: there is no point in making as much fuss about it as Krüger. . . . What does that *enfant terrible* of Bavarian politics mean by trying to poke a finger into its machinery? Why is he always up in arms? Can't the fool hold his tongue?' (p. 73) To let his characters speak and think for themselves without pointed commentary on the part of the narrator was an effective means of communicating what was outrageous, just as the direct reproduction of certain bare facts is sufficient to rouse in the reader a sense of injustice. The technique is comparable with that of Karl Kraus' *Die Fackel*, in which reports from other publications are juxtaposed in such a way that a point of view emerges without direct intervention.

The pleas of both Tüverlin and Feuchtwanger for objectivity must be seen in the context of Feuchtwanger's views on the historical novel. Feuchtwanger was criticized not only for adopting the standpoint of someone living in the year 2000, but also for introducing a number of anachronisms into a novel set in the years 1920–3. The historically aware reader will note that radio broadcasts began in Bavaria only in 1924, that Eisenstein's film *Battleship Potemkin* (the model for *Panzerkreuzer Orlow*, which Klenk sees during a visit to Berlin) was first shown there in 1926, and that the North Pole expedition described in Book V, Chapter 1 took place in 1928. An answer to such criticism is surely implied by the account of Tüverlin's approach to his work on *Weltgericht* (Doomsday). Having provided an explanation for his use of documentary material ('In order to distil a drop of higher reality he needed endless quantities of raw, unsifted actuality' (p. 493)) he goes on to exonerate himself from an apparently cavalier attitude to historical fact.

Pointing to a range of mountains in the Bavarian Alps he questions Johanna: 'Can you see the Braune Wand? . . . Can you see the nine peaks in front of it?' When she replies that they are invisible from their vantage point he continues:

> 'Yet if you go 25 miles further' he said, 'you can photograph them. But then you can't photograph the Braune Wand, for it will be hidden. Well, I don't want to photograph this or that detail of the second or third years, but to paint a picture of the whole decade. I alter details which are true today according to the record because at a distance of fifty, or perhaps even of twenty years, they will have become untrue. There's a difference between the reality of official documents and historical truth. . . .' (p. 494)

Tüverlin's apologia can be placed alongside certain remarks of Feuchtwanger in his essays, in one of which he claims that one of his chief aims in writing — not to restrict the narrative to an account of a few individuals but to provide a panorama of a whole society — could only be fulfilled if the writer maintained distance and detachment:

> As a modern German writer I have no interest in a hero or heroine. I choose for this novel groups of characters and not single individuals. Eight of the persons forming one group stand, if you like, a little higher than the others, after them come thirty figures who are almost equal to them in importance, and after these a further hundred who are unimportant, but who give to the work that fullness of life which I am after.[5]

Distance is necessary to reveal the economic forces which underlie the course of events; indeed, it is one of the paradoxes of *Erfolg* that while the debate on art undertaken in its pages reaches a conclusion which challenges a narrow view of Marxist aesthetic doctrines, the novel itself comes near to fulfilling one familiar Marxist criterion: that it should show the extent to which men are under the sway of economic forces of which they have no direct knowledge. However, Feuchtwanger insists that he is not describing the fate of a particular class, or indeed concentrating his attention on any one social group; rather, as his sub-title, 'Three

Years in the History of a Province', indicates, his primary concern is with a region, or, as he puts it: 'The land of Bavaria is the real hero of my novel'. Nor did he believe that economic and material factors were *exclusively* behind what he recognizes as 'historische Notwendigkeit' (historical necessity) — the common law according to which a number of individual fates take their course: 'I am neither a fatalist nor a Marxist, who believes that only economic and material laws govern the world. Nor am I an individualist, who believes that every man can be master of his future.'[6]

Distance is, moreover, essential to an adequate treatment of the theme of justice. In refusing to identify himself openly with any ideology, prevalent or incipient, Feuchtwanger ensures for himself a view of the party battle — which some would claim was the undoing of the Weimar system — based on a humane reliance upon natural law. He is thus able to unmask the injustice practised in the name of the law during the years of the Weimar Republic, sharing as he does with Kurt Tucholsky and others outrage at the manner in which the law is corrupted by the very persons whose office it is to uphold it and maintain its position above the various political ideologies fighting for dominance. Justice itself can become a commodity sold to the highest bidder. When Tüverlin adds the subtitle 'Funfair of Justice' to his exposure of the deficiencies of the Bavarian legal system, the phrase calls up the following associations in Johanna's mind: 'She saw gigantic piles of worm-eaten lumber among which people wandered anxiously seeking for something useable; and over every booth was a sign-board with the word "Justice", and the sellers stood there solemnly in black legal gowns.' (p. 774) In the face of such a situation some sort of commitment is required. In the end it receives most eloquent expression in a passage Tüverlin finds in Book III of Marx's *Das Kapital* after reading Pröckl's last message from the Soviet Union: 'We must portray the petrified state of German society, and force it to dance by playing its own tune to it. We must teach the nation to feel horror at its own condition in order to give it courage.' (p. 773)

In so far as Tüverlin can be identified as his mouthpiece, Feuchtwanger thus achieves a position which on the one hand accepts that art is both possible and permissible even in a turbulent time, and on the other eschews a purely dilettante and commercial approach. It is a position which is precariously maintained: first, against the view that the energies devoted to art are better applied directly to the improvement of society in the form of political, even revolutionary action, and secondly against the view that art creates a special realm in which the reader or spectator can find solace and relief from day-to-day problems. Like many writers of his generation Feuchtwanger was later prompted by the events of the thirties to believe that fascism could only be destroyed if he and others stood alongside those political groups which had declared their implacable opposition to it, even if this meant a loss of artistic freedom.

Since the setting of *Erfolg* is confined for the most part to Bavaria, it may be claimed that it does not break free of the bugbear of provincialism which is attached to so many German novels, and its status as a work illuminating the general Weimar situation may be put in doubt if one bears in mind that its action begins in 1921 and ceases in 1924. However, the choice of Bavaria as a setting may be considered wise in view of the overriding aim of the trilogy of which *Erfolg* forms the first part, 'to bring to life for posterity this evil time of waiting and transition, the darkest experienced by Germany since the Thirty Years War', as so many of the dangers to which the Republic was exposed had their origin in Bavaria during these years and there took an especially virulent form.

It may also be claimed that Feuchtwanger's presentation of the Nazi phenomenon in its early stages is naïve and trivial. Indeed, it would be simple to point to the discrepancies between Kutzner and his model, to demonstrate that the former appears as a buffoon and man of straw, merely the creature of more influential individuals who prefer to remain in the background, and to place him beside Chaplin's treatment of Hitler in *The Great Dictator*. In defence of Feuchtwanger it may be said that at the time of writing (1927–30) he was in no position to foresee the catastrophe, secondly, that at the time of the Putsch, Hitler, however great his ambitions, was still confined to Bavaria, still building up his movement and still dependent on others more powerful than himself, and thirdly, that the individual Kutzner (or Hitler) is less important to Feuchtwanger than the particular forces which he represents, in accordance with his theory of the historical novel. 'A good legend, a good historical novel, is in most cases more credible, more real, more momentous, more effective and more lively than an accurate and precise representation of the historical facts'.[7] These lines help towards an understanding not only of *Erfolg*, but of the numerous historical dramas and novels produced by German writers in exile after the Nazi takeover of power. Some of these portray Hitler in disguised or stylized form, in order to make the reader more aware of general truth behind particular detail, and the meaning of the events described or adumbrated for his own time, whether that is 1930, 1981 or 2000. True, some writers found retreat into history a necessary means of coming to terms with a situation in which they felt detached from the society which might have provided material for their art, or of putting forward certain views without directly challenging identifiable public figures. That cannot however be said of Feuchtwanger at the time when he was writing *Erfolg* and the other parts of the Wartesaal trilogy (*Die Geschwister Oppermann* (The Oppermanns, 1933) and *Exil* (Exile, 1940)), although these show signs of a withdrawal into the private sphere which is an index of the difficulties their author must have faced during exile. *Erfolg* remains therefore remarkable for the sharpness of its prescience and the rigour of its analysis of the social forces from which Nazism drew its strength.

NOTES

1. 'Über *Jud Süß*', in: *Centum opuscula*, ed. Wolfgang Berndt (Rudolstadt, 1956), p. 390.
2. For information on the models for the characters in *Erfolg* see Synnöve Clason, *Die Welt erklären. Geschichte und Fiktion in Lion Feuchtwangers Roman 'Erfolg'* Acta Universitatis Stockholmiensis (Stockholmer Germanistische Forschungen) 19 (Stockholm 1975), pp. 49–64, 112–21, and Ulrich Weisstein, 'Clio the Muse: An Analysis of Lion Feuchtwanger's Erfolg' in: *Lion Feuchtwanger. The Man, his Ideas, his Work. A Collection of Critical Essays*, ed. John M. Spalek (Los Angeles, 1972), pp. 157–86.
3. Lion Feuchtwanger, *Erfolg*. Gesammelte Werke in Einzelausgaben Band 10 (Berlin and Weimar 1973). All page references are to this edition.
4. E.g. Book I, Chapter 4, II. 14, III. 10, IV. 1 and 4, IV. 9 and V. 1, also pp. 60, 340 and 506.
5. 'Mein Roman *Erfolg*', in: *Centum opuscula*, pp. 397–9.
6. Ibid., pp. 397–9.
7. Ibid., p. 513.

Kleiner Mann — was nun? and Love on the Dole: Two Novels of the Depression

A. V. Subiotto

In his autobiography, *There Was a Time* (1967), Walter Greenwood tells of the rejection slip he received from the first publisher to whom he sent the manuscript of his novel, *Love on the Dole*, in 1932:

Dear Sir
We have read your novel with great interest. Unfortunately our Spring List is to include a book on a similar theme translated from the German, Mr. Hans Fallada's 'Little Man, What Now'...[1]

This suggests that, despite vast differences in their social backgrounds, a disparity of political enthusiasm, dissimilar methods of writing and literary traditions, and contrasting historical and economic situations that formed the context of their writing, these two novelists shared a burning thematic interest that transcended the diversity of their depictions. It was pure chance that *Kleiner Mann — was nun?* (Little Man What Now?) appeared first, in 1932, and a year later *Love on the Dole* found a publisher; both touched a chord in the public and became immediate and lasting best-sellers, *Kleiner Mann — was nun?* being translated into twenty languages and filmed in both Germany and the USA, while *Love on the Dole* enjoyed comparable success. Even now, half a century later, these novels still read well, spark the imagination and stand as accurate and moving documents of a turbulent time of crisis in European society. Indeed, it is the central theme of depression and unemployment, shared by the major industrial countries around 1930, that clearly provides a basis for comparison of the two novels, while the unique approaches of their authors as well as their critical reception yield many contrasts that in their turn illuminate the specific situations in Germany and Britain.

Walter Greenwood was born in Salford in 1903 where, while still at school, he peddled newspapers, delivered milk and worked in a pawnbroker's shop, before and after school hours. He left school at thirteen to become first a clerk, and later a groom in a cotton millionaire's private stable. During the depression, between illnesses and periods out of work and on the dole, he worked mending packing-cases, as a sign-writer, a warehouseman and salesman. Greenwood's autobiography is a sober, moving account of his life up to the acceptance of *Love on the Dole* in 1932, and it shares numerous details and incidents with this fictional chronicle of life in the grim industrial surroundings of Salford. Greenwood's father was a barber and his mother, who imposed a strict moral upbringing on her family, had strong literary interests, with aspirations to culture, education and rising in the world. Greenwood himself had a drive to self-education, and there are frequent indications in his style and attitudes that betray this autodidactic streak. Thus, despite the handicaps of his social environment, Greenwood was given a certain support and incentive when he began writing. The strength of his work lay in its veracity and its rootedness in the dispiriting milieu around him, but this was also an obstacle to success, as many an editor would indicate that he thought a story good in itself, but 'its subject matter was not the sort of thing to interest his readers who paid their money for romance, entertainment and excitement'.[2] There was certainly little likelihood that Greenwood, writing from such personal experience, would furnish escapist literature of this sort. In *There Was a Time* he wrote:

> Indeed I had two occupations, writing a novel and taking as little time off from this as was necessary to keep my weekly collections for Jackson's Emporium [selling goods on credit] just above the ten pounds a week mark, the ten per cent commission being my face-saver at home. As for future prospects for all left out in the cold . . . The three million registered as being on the dole did not include the debarred who were being supported by parents or married children. Trade union membership had shrunk to the level of 1913 and men and women who had dreamed dreams of Jerusalem in England's green and pleasant land saw, in the spectral ranks of the unemployed, the tarnished face of Empire.[3]

The gentle Fabian vision of a socialist future full of peace and plenty haunts the pages of *Love on the Dole* where it is blotted out by the raw harshness of families and communities struggling for food, clothing, shelter. A year before his death in 1967 Greenwood described the now bulldozed streets where he had played as a child: 'They were built when the British Empire was at the pinnacle of its wealth and power, and they had sheltered defrauded generations for whom life had been an endless struggle both insulting and depraved.'[4] He was well aware that a hundred years of exploitation and attrition had eroded and degraded the dignity of the working man. His cry of outrage, like a Jarrow march, helped stir the national conscience, owing its power to the detailed and vivid evocation of milieu; the claustrophobic network of working-class streets in Hanky Park is recreated by Greenwood with economy and succinct realism.

Hans Fallada, too, found fame with the identical theme in *Kleiner Mann — was nun?* In the *Berliner Börsenkurier* the critic Herbert Ihering described how the book took Berlin by storm, and the reason for this was voiced by the *Literarische Welt* in its issue of July 1932: 'One man has expressed what all are suffering: . . . Fallada has given us the epic novel of a divided society, an abused people, who seem to have nothing in common except want and the hate this generates of man against man.'[5] As in *Love on the Dole* it was the astounding verisimilitude of *Kleiner Mann — was nun?*, sustained throughout into the minutest detail, that was identified as its most appealing quality by many leading literary figures.[6]

Though Fallada's immediate inspiration was, like Greenwood's, his personal experience of unemployment and its devastating effects as it spread through industrial and social life, his very different origins and upbringing ensured a distinctive treatment of his material; the similarities and contrasts between the two are equally illuminating. Fallada (his real name was Rudolf Itzen) was born in 1903, in Greifswald, where his father was a local judge. The family moved to Berlin for several years and later Leipzig, as Fallada's father rose in his career. As a young man Fallada underwent training and worked as a book-keeper on various agricultural estates, at the same time writing two unsuccessful novels. He twice served prison sentences for embezzlement, as a result of which he found himself in the late Twenties in straitened circumstances, eking out a living in advertising and as a local reporter. He married Anna Issel ('Suse') in 1929 and a fortuitous second meeting with the publisher Ernst Rowohlt led to a modest position in his review department. In his autobiographical *Heute bei uns zu Haus* (The Way we Live Now) (1943) Fallada looks back on the grim aftermath of the Wall Street Crash in 1929. Despite the success in 1931 of *Bauern, Bonzen und Bomben* (Peasants, Politicians and Power), a novel based on first-hand observation as a reporter of the disturbances among the farming communities of Neumünster, he too was caught up in the financial troubles that beset Rowohlt. A receiver was appointed to salvage the finances of Rowohlt and Fallada lost his post when he refused to take a sharp cut in salary. He then spent his time pushing his son's pram around the Berlin suburb of Neuenhagen, where he was soon known as 'der arme Arbeitslose mit dem Kind' (the poor out-of-work man with the child) and writing *Kleiner Mann — was nun?*, that was ironically to be the financial salvation of Rowohlt in the following year: 'What was more natural in such a situation than to write a book with the title: 'Little Man What Now?' I wrote it in the afternoons and evenings of the most depressed period of my life.'[7] Fallada joined the ranks of the unemployed in Germany when the crisis was almost at its peak, for more than six million were without work, while in Britain the figure was less than half. But the statistics only indicate the extent of hardship and misery, not the intensity with which it struck individuals, families and communities. Greenwood's depiction in both *There was a Time* and *Love on the Dole* is acute and unrelieved by any ray of hope, whereas Fallada, at least in retrospect, invests this time with a suffused personal happiness.

The contrast between the two writers is a matter of class. Greenwood was rooted in the working-class, the urban proletariat in industrial Manchester, which, because it lived precariously from week to week between birth and death on what meagre reward it could command as the price of its factory labour, had no resources — economic, moral or spiritual — to fall back on, once the blight of economic recession struck. Even when in work the wages were so mean that none could rise above the abrasive, interminable struggle for mere survival, as Larry Meath, Greenwood's politically conscious and articulate 'mouthpiece' in *Love on the Dole* tries to impress on Sally Hardcastle, whom he would like to wed:

> And how many times had he repeated: Forty-five bob a week: ten shillings rent, twenty-five shillings food, five shillings coal, gas and insurance; five bob left for clothes, recreation, little luxuries such as smokes and holidays. You gave a week of your life, every week, so that you might have a hovel for shelter, an insufficiency of food and five bob left over for to clothe yourself and the missis in shoddy. 'Aye, and what of the other things?' he asked himself. Books, music, brief holidays . . . His brain refused further contemplation. (*LoD* p. 150)

Fallada, on the other hand, belonged to the middle class, with its pretensions that were also its weaknesses, the major one — certainly uppermost since the astronomical inflation period of 1921–3 — being a consciousness of higher status than the working-class when its actual power was at a nadir, measured in terms of savings (which had disappeared), solidarity (negligible in terms of trade union

organization) and security of employment (extremely vulnerable to the acceler-
ated rationalization of business and commerce). This 'false consciousness', constantly nourished by the fear that the step downwards into the proletariat is the
ultimate degradation, echoes through *Kleiner Mann — was nun?* and is perhaps
characteristic of its author as well. In contrast, the hero of *Love on the Dole*, Harry
Hardcastle, who at the start of the novel has just left school and whose parents
want him to take a job as a clerk in the pawnshop, resists this pressure which will
cut him off from his mates and their tight-knit social habits. He sees himself
'doomed to clerking', a 'scrivener', and detests 'the uniform of offices, Eton collar,
stud bow and those abominable knickerbockers'. (*LoD* p. 19) Harry's single
ambition is to be taken on at Marlowe's, the massive engineering plant employing
most of the men in the neighbourhood. Greenwood allows the young lad — and
perhaps himself — an idealized perception of the 'romantic work' of 'these gods of
the machine and forge' (*LoD* p. 20), but Harry's euphoria at now being a 'man' is
rudely dissipated when he too is laid off after completing his apprenticeship to
make way for cheaper, younger labour. The process of attrition grinds on through
the novel as Harry, in common with his fellow-workers, sinks powerlessly lower
and lower through the dole and the Means Test close to the bread-line. His love-
affair with a local girl, Helen, leads to a shot-gun marriage and ejection from his
father's home, and it is only through 'connections' that he finally lands a job with
the bus company. His good-looking sister Sally, dejected and hopeless after the
death of her fiancé, Larry Meath, has yielded to the advances of the wealthy bookmaker, Sam Grundy, who uses his influence in the right places. The relentlessly
accurate observation and the unrelieved greyness of Greenwood's narration has
led economic historians to describe the novel as 'more vivid and penetrating than
a score of studies'.[8]

A scene at the Situations Vacant counter of the Labour Exchange sets the scene
for the main theme of *Love on the Dole*:

> Engineers in overalls, joiners and painters and clerks in seedy suits;
> stevedores, navvies and labourers in corduroys. They came singly and in
> couples, stood in front of the taciturn clerk, offered their unemploy-
> ment cards, received answer by way of a shake of the head, turned on their
> heels and went out again without speaking. (*LoD* p. 156)

Harry is at first buoyantly convinced he will easily find alternative work, but after
a fruitless search he has 'a feeling in his heart as though he had committed some
awful crime in which he was sure to be found out', and 'a tinge of shame coloured
his cheeks; he licked his lips and slunk along by the walls'. (*LoD* p. 159f) The inward
demoralization recurs and intensifies from page to page:

> You fell into the habit of slouching, of putting your hands into your pockets
> and keeping them there; of glancing at people, furtively, ashamed of your
> secret, until you fancied that everyone eyed you with suspicion . . . You
> prayed for the winter evenings and the kindly darkness. Darkness, poverty's
> cloak. (*LoD* p. 169)

A mate of Harry's, Billy Higgs, young and three years out of work, was 'a thread-
bare, shuffling, stoop-shouldered furtive old man, that, not long ago, had known
laughter' (*LoD* p. 154); and in Harry too the disintegration of moral fibre, the loss

of a man's self-respect, takes physical form: 'There was a dull vacuity in his eyes nowadays; he became listless, hard of hearing . . . A living corpse; a unit of the spectral army of three million lost men' (*LoD* p. 170). The inability to change anything only exacerbated their sense of helplessness and bottled-up fury: Harry's 'urgent, desperate yearning for work made him squirm' (*LoD* p. 230), while his father, prone to violent outbursts which expressed his raging resentment at never having sufficient money for his family, is finally beaten into the ground by the ignominy of the Means Test:

> The canker of impotence gnawed his vitals. He felt weak; as powerless as a blind kitten in a bucket of water.
>
> His wife, frightened by his silence, looked at him through her tears to see him sitting there, head bent, sparse grey hair catching the fire's glimmer, an arm resting on the table, the other on his knee, his hand dangling limply. (*LoD* p. 248)

Almost the last scene in *Love on the Dole* depicts Harry striding home smiling and ebullient with his first week's wages from the bus company in his pocket, when he catches sight of an unemployed mate in the classic image of the Thirties:

> He was standing there as motionless as a statue, cap neb pulled over his eyes, gaze fixed on pavement, hands in pockets, shoulders hunched, the bitter wind blowing his thin trousers tightly against his legs. Waster paper and dust blew about him in spirals, the papers making harsh sounds as they slid on the pavement. He was an anonymous unit of an army of three millions for whom there was no tomorrow. (*LoD* p. 255)

The desperate plight of the unemployed was aggravated by stern measures implemented by the Government in 1931 and which play a central role in *Love on the Dole*. Owing to Britain's economic and financial troubles in the summer, there were heavy international withdrawals of deposits and as a consequence of this flight from the pound Ramsay MacDonald's Labour Government fell in August. Immediately he formed a National Government from a coalition of parties to save the situation, but a prerequisite for urgently needed international loans was a reduction in unemployment benefit — to which Labour agreed in an attempt to quieten the Conservative opposition. Notwithstanding this 'betrayal' of Labour, Britain was still forced off the gold standard in September to save the pound, and at the General Election called in October Labour were routed. Labour had been made to appear a frightful Bolshevist ogre destroying the country and so lost two million votes compared with 1929. The landslide return of conservative National Government supporters confirmed the harsh measures enacted in the September budget: salary cuts of 15 per cent affected the public sector, unemployment payments were reduced by 10 per cent, contributions were increased, the benefit period was limited to twenty-six weeks per year, and a needs test was instituted for 'transitional' payments. Thus, on top of a cut in the dole came the infamous Means Test, which took account of any earnings by members of a household, as well as of savings and pensions. The head of a family could be 'knocked off the dole' if sons or daughters were in work; the disintegrating effect on the fabric of the family can be observed in *Love on the Dole*.

Nevertheless, the sense of community and solidarity — if only because of mutual adversity — is dominant in the novel. The action takes place almost entirely within the compass of the streets of Hanky Park, tightly packed with identical houses and human beings sharing the same fate. There is no need for the author to articulate the 'them' and 'us' antagonism: it is inherent in the descriptions he gives, from the 'great exodus' from Marlowe's at noon on Saturdays to the press of women waiting to flood into the pawnbroker's. In the dole queue and on the spontaneous demonstration that erupts against the Means Test the victims seek the companionship of their kind, and even the innocuous picture of light-hearted mill girls clattering home in clogs to array themselves in gaudy finery for Saturday night is a tacit testimony of the dreary, narrow uniformity of the years that await them. Wider horizons are closed to these folk except in dreams and fantasy. The restricted confines of their lives are maintained and reinforced by the street-corner bookmaker, the Clothing Club money-lender and the pawnbroker: 'A trinity, the outward visible sign of an inward spiritual discontent; safety valves through which the excess of impending change could escape, vitiate and dissipate itself'. (*LoD* p. 24) Another such trinity, this time of communal edifices, providing a focus and an opium for dangerous energies again includes the pawnshop which 'stood at one point of a triangle; the other two points were occupied, respectively by a church and a palatial beerhouse, each large, commodious and convenient'. (*LoD* p. 27) There is nevertheless a noticeable absence in *Love on the Dole* of higher social classes. The policemen are only working men in uniform, tools of the establishment; and even the immediate exploiters — the bookie, money-lender and pawnbroker — live in symbiosis with this community, their mutual interdependence lending an intense, claustrophobic air to the novel. Yet this close-knit, oppressive atmosphere which expresses the doomed lives of the downtrodden has a positive aspect in the powerful supportive quality of the community. Aggressions and antagonisms are vented by individuals on their own kind not through innate hostility but because they are powerless to get to grips with the real cause of their frustrations, the nebulous rulers of the country's destiny.

In contrast to the sense of fellowship in distress that pervades *Love on the Dole*, Fallada's novel focuses on one person, the shop assistant Johannes Pinneberg, as he struggles to survive and maintain his family in an engulfing tide of rationalization and redundancy. Where Greenwood gives us a network of interweaving lives Fallada depicts an individual in a precarious and exposed relationship with his surroundings, isolated from any sense of community, restricted to his wife and child for companionship and warmth. Pinneberg has no past: we see the totally impersonal footing he is on with his mother, the only relative he has, who invites him to Berlin for her own purposes. The tone is set in the very first chapter when Pinneberg and his girl-friend, Lämmchen (Bunny), learn from the doctor that she is pregnant; Pinneberg is aghast when the doctor tells him an abortion is out of the question, and on taking her home he impulsively proposes marriage. Despite this initial 'duress' in Pinneberg's relationship with his wife, Lämmchen represents, as many critics have observed, a stay and support for Pinneberg that is characteristic of Fallada's portrayal of marriage generally. She encourages him and embraces him protectively against her pregnant motherly body: 'Bunny only wanted to hold her husband in her arms for a while. Outside lay the wild wide world, full of tumult and hostility, . . . All of you, he thought, in your cramped little rooms, of this no man can rob you . . .' (*LM* 201–5, *KM* 112–14) Unfortunately, Pinneberg's perception of marital bliss is negative: a private island, a refuge from the hazards of a hostile environment. There is something forced in his picture of where they will move to, after his dismissal by the grain merchant Kleinholz in Ducherow: '. . . something cheaper; but at any rate, four walls, a roof overhead, and warmth. And, of course, a wife. It was fine to lie in bed at night and feel someone breathing at one's side'. (*LM* 123, *KM* 70) This is followed by three more sentences evoking the philistine pleasures of marriage and a cosy senti-mentality.

The sanctuary of the home, one's own four walls, is a motif that runs through the novel and counterbalances the parallel theme of Pinneberg exposed to the rough buffetings of economic realities in the world of work. Of the four 'homes' the couple have, the opulent room in the flat of Pinneberg's mother is the least friendly because it is theirs on sufferance and open to intrusion. The earlier, lugubrious flat in Ducherow, the almost inaccessible rooftop rooms at Putt-breese's and the dilapidated shack outside Berlin all offer a sense of security, however illusory, against a threatening world. Lämmchen feels this cosiness particularly about Puttbreese's: 'We can be alone here — no one can poke their nose into our affairs. It's lovely.' (*LM* 229, *KM* 127); and intensely as she awaits the birth of her son:

> It was pleasantly warm in the room; gusts of damp December wind that swept now and again against the windows only made it all the more cosy . . . It was lovely to sit at home, alone in the darkness, waiting for her husband, and from time to time feeling the child stir within her. She was getting so large and broad, she seemed to keep on overflowing . . . (*LM* 233–5, *KM* 129–31)

The child seals the bond of familial self-sufficiency at the lowest ebb of their fortunes when, at the end of the story, Pinneberg feels so rejected by society that he stands in the cold and dark outside the shack, unable to enter. Characteristi-cally, it is Lämmchen who goes out to him, overcomes the moment of dejection and doubt, and resolves all their troubles in a sentimental embrace: 'The cold had risen to Bunny's heart; it gripped her until she was chilled through and through. Behind her shone the warm red light of the hut window, where the baby was asleep. . . . And suddenly the cold had gone, an infinitely gentle green wave raised her up, and him with her . . . Higher and higher, from the tainted earth towards the stars. And then they both went into the hut, where the baby lay asleep'. (*LM* 441, *KM* 246f) The role of the child as an enriching bond clearly derives from Fallada's own experience at a similar low point in his life, as he later reflects in *Heute bei uns zu Haus*.[9] One critic considers Lämmchen to be 'the classical personification of his [Fallada's] many loving and characterful women', 'an ageless ideal of womanly loyalty and conjugal love . . . No other female figure in Fallada's work measures up fully to the stature of Lämmchen, and no other woman performs more adequately the function of being the guardian of society's lasting values'.[10] He also makes a further general point about the function of marriage for Fallada:

> In Fallada's work an escape from the social, economic and political pressures of our dislocated modern age always lies in a retreat into man's private life . . . It is in this connection that the theme of marriage assumes its significance in Fallada's work. For Hans Fallada a healthy marriage is the very source of

human tranquility and social order. The woman plays the decisive role in the marital relationship: . . . For the socially displaced 'little man' marriage satisfies his need for contacts and helps him to regain some sense of personal and social identity.[11]

It is instructive to compare this view of marriage with the unsentimental manner in which Walter Greenwood handles the theme. Not unlike Pinneberg, Harry has moments of aching for the shelter offered by Helen: '. . . the poignant sweetness of picturing himself shutting the front door and feeling secure against all trespass! He came to regard all front doors with deep respect.' (*LoD* p. 132) Even Larry Meath is not immune from the enticing promise of happiness in marriage: '. . . alluring visions of a clean kitchen radiant with the presence of Sally, rose to his mind. Ineffable home-comings!' (*LoD* p. 152) And Sally herself shares this 'intoxicating picture of themselves in a home of their own'. (*LoD* p. 168) But Sally's dream is shattered on the paving-stones of Manchester, she takes to a degrading life of selling herself, and the novel closes with a squalid, laconic picture of married life that in its sharpness is worlds apart from the blurred sentimentality of Fallada's ending:

> In Mrs Dorbell's house, Helen came downstairs, 'Ah-ah-ing' sleepily. She groped on the tiny kitchen's mantelpiece for the matches, struck one and lit the gas. The glare hurt her eyes; she blinked, stifled a yawn, scratched her head with one hand whilst she stretched with the other. She shivered and shrugged. It was cold. She stooped, raked out the grate and stuffed it with paper, picked up the shovel and trudged to the backyard, pausing by the stairs to shout: 'Come on, Harry, lad. Five an' twenty t'six, Monday mornin' an' pourin' o' rain'. (*LoD* p. 256)

By deliberately repeating this passage from the opening of the novel — when it was Harry's mother waking the household — Greenwood establishes the cyclical nature of these monotonous, cramped lives from generation to generation, with no hint of amelioration or escape.

It has become the fashion among some political philosophers to denounce the nuclear family as an institution that maintains the power structures of industrialized capitalist society and simultaneously offers apparent relief from them. Horkheimer has suggested that the family unit could allow human relations to develop once the authoritarian family based on money has been overcome, and Adorno thought it might function as a refuge from the alienating processes of modern society. Fallada clearly attributes this saving role to marriage in *Kleiner Mann — was nun?*, but it is the increasing alienation of the hero that forms the nub of the novel. Pinneberg is, by his own admission, a mediocre, ordinary person who should even consider himself fortunate not to be worse off as he visits the Labour Exchange:

> Tens of thousands were worse off than him, tens of thousands had no such wife to back them up, and they had, not one child, but half a dozen. Move on, Pinneberg, my man, draw your money and clear out, we really have no time for you; there's nothing whatever unusual about your case. (*LM* 416, *KM* 232)

Pinneberg is by no means a traditional literary hero; his strength as a fictional character is that he represents as a type innumerable other men sharing the same fate and is at the same time a specific individual whose feelings, thoughts and actions we experience directly through the minutiae of his existence. He is the paradigm of the 'Angestellte', that class of salaried white-collar worker in Germany who in the first half of this century had neither the security of State employment, tenure and pensions, like the 'Beamte', nor the sense of class and common interest of the factory worker. With the great expansion of the tertiary service sector in industrial economies there came a massive upsurge in the number of 'Angestellte' as a proportion of the total workforce; over a period when the industrial labour sector doubled in number, the 'Angestellte' increased five-fold. This category of employee — office workers, secretaries, clerks, shop and sales assistants and so on — considered itself superior to the factory-worker and was therefore unready to relinquish its middle-class pretensions when the inflation after the Great War cut its economic base from under it. With scant protection from properly organized trade unions, the 'Angestellte' were — especially in the Twenties — exposed to the wild fluctuations of the economy and, worse still, devastated by the accelerating rationalization of their work. In industry this took the form of machines that replaced men, in offices and commercial enterprises it was ensured both by machines and by other methods that maximized efficiency and productivity.

A penetrating sociological study of the 'Angestellte' in Berlin by Siegfried Kracauer was published in the *Frankfurter Zeitung* in 1929 and as a book the following year, and it had a profound impact on Fallada as he worked on *Kleiner Mann — was nun?*. Kracauer described in general terms, backed up by sometimes harrowing examples, a disturbing picture of this area of the labour market. He explained the demoralizing effects of office rationalization on individuals subjected to monotonous, interchangeable work, as replaceable automata; the marked hierarchical structures in business, with a consequent lack of meaningful communication vertically and distrust on all sides, aggravated by the friction caused by rampant favouritism and connections; the minimally beneficial and protective roles of the arbitration courts and the ineffectual Labour Exchanges; the employee welfare schemes (sport and leisure) whose covert aim it was to polish the firm's image and strengthen staff loyalty; the function of other establishments, 'amusement palaces', cinemas, dance halls to supply the 'cultural needs' of the employees. Kracauer deduced that all aspects of the relationship between a business and its staff were devised to support and confirm the 'pre-established harmony' of free enterprise, and he painted a truly sombre picture of the exploited 'anonymous privates of the white-collar army'.[12]

Pinneberg is in almost every respect an exemplar of the 'Angestellte'. The three jobs he has in succession parallel the intensifying inhumanity of capitalism: he loses his first post in the paternalistic ready-made clothing store of Bergmann because he will not 'demean' himself—'I'm head salesman; I'm not going to carry parcels through the streets' (*LM* 63, *KM* 37), and then at Kleinholz's seed business he is expected to sacrifice his private life — by marrying the proprietor's ugly daughter — as a condition for keeping his job. A pitiful attempt to organize his two fellow 'Angestellte' in some show of unity shipwrecks on the self-interest of each. After this illustration of arbitrary entrepreneurial power and whim, string-pulling by Jachmann, a dubious friend of his mother, obtains a post for Pinneberg as sales assistant in Mandel's department store, and this is where his total abasement takes place. He is prepared to degrade himself even as he enters the building: 'he swore to himself that he would work very hard and do well, be patient and never lose his temper' (*LM* 151, *KM* 85) and he stands obsequiously at his interview with the personnel manager, Lehmann: 'Spiritually, as it were, he stood at attention, hunched his shoulders and kept his head down, so as not to look too tall'. (*LM* 156, *KM* 88) It quickly emerges that personal qualities and individual differences among the staff count for nothing; they are considered purely as robots whose one function is to sell. Pinneberg's assistant departmental manager, Jänecke, voices it: 'I know only one sort of salesman: those whose sales book shows a high total by evening' (*LM* 177, *KM* 99); while Spannfuß, who has been brought in as an efficiency expert and has introduced a fixed sales quota system, underlines this reification of the salesmen when he pronounces: 'Give me your sales book', cried Herr Spannfuss, 'and I will tell you what sort of man you are'. (*LM* 247, *KM* 138). It falls to Lämmchen, dimly conscious of this blatant elevation of exchange-value over use-value of a man's work, to burst out angrily: 'Haven't the weaker got a right to exist? Fancy valuing a man by the number of pairs of trousers he can sell!' (*LM* 237, *KM* 132)

The demands of impossibly high sales quota targets not only set man against man in a fierce competition for survival but also prey on the individual until he cracks and disintegrates under the pressure. This deterioration in Pinneberg is recorded in dismal detail, stage by stage over the months:

> Since the damnable system of quotas had been introduced, everyone's nerve had given way. . . . 'I shall have to sell three hundred marks' worth today,' was in his mind as he awoke, drank his coffee, walked to his work, entered the department, and all day long: 'Three hundred marks'. (*LM* 322f, *KM* 180f)

There are times when Pinneberg manages to achieve his quota and in momentary elation spares no thought for the unfortunate colleagues who have failed, but at others an innocuous remark from Lämmchen drives him into a rage, 'and then he began to curse these slave-drivers that turned men into beasts — they deserved a bomb up their backsides'. (*LM* 248, *KM* 138) While Pinneberg waits one day to be severely reprimanded for lateness — his son's illness is brushed aside as an unacceptable excuse — he overhears a girl being summarily sacked for having an affair with an employee in another department. Both Pinneberg and the girl are vehemently reminded that Mandel's comes before all private considerations:

> 'The Firm makes your private life possible, sir. The Firm comes first, the Firm comes second, and the Firm comes third, and then you can do what you like. You live by us, sir; we have preserved you from anxiety about your livelihood, do you realize that?' (*LM* 374, *KM* 210)

In the dog-eat-dog atmosphere of the store Pinneberg finally succumbs and is dismissed, his backbone broken and morale sapped. Yet he still persists in trying to keep up appearances, though it is now he who stays at home (in the leaky shack), cooking and looking after their child, while Lämmchen goes out sewing in the rich houses. On a trip into Berlin to collect his dole Pinneberg meets contempt from the joiner Puttbreese: 'Why don't you leave off that collar?' sneered the master. 'It's filthy. Out of a job for a year and still going about in a celluloid collar. People like you are hopeless.' (*LM* 417, *KM* 233) Pinneberg is so disheartened he hardly has the courage to go home, and roams the streets in his shabby clothes. He looks at himself in the mirror of a fashion shop, sees a man who has gone to seed, slowly takes off his collar and tie and stuffs them in his coat pocket. When a policeman moves him on roughly from the window of a delicatessen store into the roadway, Pinneberg suddenly comprehends his situation; now he is an outcast, beyond the pale, literally in the gutter:

> . . . he had slipped into the abyss, and was engulfed. Order and cleanliness; they belonged to the past . . . Poverty was not merely misery, poverty was an offence, poverty was evil, poverty meant that a man was suspect . . . he shuffled along in the roadway close to the kerb, . . . [Later] Cautiously he raised one foot and placed it on the pavement. Then the other. He no longer stood in the roadway, he stood once more on the pavement. (*LM* 428f, *KM* 239f)

Fallada has often been reproached by German critics for not making a more explicit political point in *Kleiner Mann — was nun?*. Pinneberg is recognized as a finely-drawn representative of the petty-bourgeois mentality. The gaping discrepancy between unwarranted aspirations and his objective situation leads to his disorientation and vulnerability, but Fallada is censured for not making his hero become aware of the realities and take appropriate political action. These critics would have Fallada incorporate in his novel an unambiguous political stance to demonstrate the false consciousness of the 'Kleinbürger' and persuade them to recognize that their class interest lies with the proletariat. Jürgen Kuczynski was right to describe *Kleiner Mann — was nun?* on its appearance as 'quite unpolitical —yet of greatest political relevance'. Without once purveying a political message or betraying partisanship Fallada recreates through numerous details an accurate political profile of the late Weimar Republic, with its pressures, conflicts, confused thinking and lack of clear direction. There are precise references to the already uneasy situation of the Jews as well as the Nazis' menacing intimidations, but uppermost is the question of Pinneberg's attitude to Communism. He is given an early unheeded demonstration of how to protect workers' rights by Kleinholz's foreman, Kube, and clings to his notions of class when Lämmchen's father tells him unequivocally he would rather have a worker as son-in-law.

Lämmchen, from a working-class background, is shown as having Communist sympathies, yet at the same time she behaves with a petty-bourgeois consciousness. Pinneberg, like so many fellow-citizens, tries to steer clear of political decisions: 'he had thought that this would be an easy way out of the dilemma' (*LM* 238, *KM* 226). When Lämmchen insists they must vote Communist to counter the inhuman practices at Mandel's his vacillation reflects the genuine ignorance, helplessness and self-interest of the ordinary man: 'I always feel I should like to, and then I can't quite make up my mind. At present we've got a job, so we needn't.' (*LM* 238, *KM* 132) In moments of impotent fury — 'Are we never to say what we think? Are we always to be trodden on?' — he almost overcomes his indecision, adding in an undertone: 'Well, next time I shall vote Communist.' (*LM* 320, *KM* 179) But this is only a passing mood, as his later exchange with Puttbreese shows, when the latter tells him to take off his grimy and ridiculous collar. Pinneberg thus has only fleeting insights into his objective situation, which is obscured by empty externals, such as his clothes; one such instance occurs immediately after he has obtained the post at Mandel's, as he walks through the grey masses of unemployed in the Kleiner Tiergarten, reflecting on his temporary good fortune:

> Outwardly Pinneberg did not belong to them; his dress was respectable . . .
> but inwardly . . . these harmless, starving and now hopeless beasts of the
> proletariat . . . These were his proper companions, though just now they did
> jeer at him as a prole in fine clothing. (*LM* 162–4, *KM* 91f)

Throughout *Kleiner Mann — was nun?* Fallada undoubtedly makes very specific and precise political points; but he does not obtrude the authorial voice into the narrative, thus achieving a reflection of time, place and people that is truly realistic.

Walter Greenwood's approach in *Love on the Dole* is more direct and politically overt. His immediate and passionate commitment to the working class almost sweeps aside literary convention and we are effectively presented with a barely disguised documentation of specific historical events. This may in part account for the different reception of the two works in their respective countries: in Britain *Love on the Dole* was understood as a social document and had the effect of stirring the conscience of the nation, while *Kleiner Mann — was nun?* appeared to the German middle class as a graphic and readable fictionalization of their own experiences, hopes and fears. Political elucidation in *Love on the Dole* is stark and uncompromising (in *Kleiner Mann — was nun?* it is submerged and implicit): Larry Meath, the author's mouthpiece, is ever ready to explain the relationship of capital and labour in simple terms, while Mrs Bull, a colourful figure with some earthy political perspicacity, voices the desolate philosophy of the have-nots most pungently: 'National Government, an' Labour nowhere. 'Tain't no use talking socialism to folk. 'Twon't come in our time though. Ah allus votes Labour an' allus will.' [To Sally after Larry's death] 'Ah've seen too much i' my time t' be tuk in by all parson'd like y' t' swallow. Ah've had no eddication but Ah do know that there ne'er was parson breathed wot preached sermon about resurrection on empty belly, an' min's bin empty many a time. S'easy for them as live house an' light free an' a regular wage comin' in . . . Let 'em try clemmin' (going hungry) like us have t' do every day o' our lives. Pay 'em wot they pay them on t' dole an' y'd see plenty of parson's jobs goin' beggin'. Yaach. What's good o' botherin' about us when we've snuffed it? Luk better o' some folks if they'd do us a bit o' good while we're alive,' pause: 'As for that lad o' thine, Sal, lass, don't you wish him back. All me life Ah've lived, lass, Ah've bin waitin' for summat that's never come. Ah don't wish a day of it back agen. There's nowt for the likes of us t' live for, Sal. Nowt. Religion, eh? Pah. Ah've no patience wi' it.' (*LoD* pp. 164, 215) Whether Greenwood shared this forlorn point of view or not, he spent much of his own life canvassing as an active campaigner for the Labour Party, carrying on a tradition inculcated by his socialist grandfather and by his parents, both supporters of the more radical Independent Labour Party. Fallada was in this respect 'apolitical' and, although he had some difficulties initially with the Nazi authorities, he managed to live an inoffensive existence through their twelve years; all his adult life his energies were mainly consumed in drink and drugs, and in grappling with this private incubus.

Nevertheless, despite the manifest differences in their personal political aspirations, both authors pack their novels with a compelling abundance of precisely observed detail and significant motifs that establish a remarkable coincidence between the two. Objectively and subjectively, the context of factory and sales assistant is largely identical in disposition and formulation: the joyless loci of work place, Labour Exchange, dole queue and Unemployment Bureau, dreary hospital; the hostile attitude of public officials and the struggle to obtain minimal rights; the constant fret over money, worrying down to the last coin; the burden of wife and children; extraordinary events (such as Harry's treble win on a horse and a week at the seaside on the proceeds, or Pinneberg's impulsive acquisition of the extravagant dressing-table and his yearning to 'go out in style' just once); the success in an exploitative society of real or 'social' criminals, outsiders and misfits (Sam Grundy, Mr Price, Jachmann, Heilbutt); the uneasy juxtaposition of industrial city and rural land. These shared motifs are set off by some marked contrasts, especially those deriving from the social nexus of the main protagonists. Harry is rooted in a comradely, cohesive community, so that the depiction of his life entails that of many others, while Pinneberg is the isolated individual in the disjunction of the metropolis, he comes from nowhere and has nowhere to go.

Another difference is one of literary form. The self-taught Greenwood applies orthodox patterns of narration but his searching indictment of the society he lives in bursts the outer structure of the novel at many points. Fallada, on the other hand, conforms to the norms of the popular novel: Pinneberg is handled as a literary 'hero' with the consequential effect of this role on the novel — however ordinary or inconspicuous he may be in reality, he nevertheless becomes the focus of *Kleiner Mann — was nun?*, an individual picked out against the rest of society. The clichés of romance are employed to the same end: Lämmchen and Pinneberg, like the great lovers of literature, escape finally into a private whole world of their own over which they have psychological control. It is not without significance that Fallada discarded his original plan for an ending where Pinneberg came home with a prostitute and Lämmchen made coffee for them both. The divergence between Greenwood and Fallada in the design and execution of their novels is apparent and the dissimilarity of their social context pronounced, yet their works are remarkably complementary as literary documents and critical reflections of the malaise of industrial society at one of its major points of crisis in the twentieth century.

Notes

1. Walter Greenwood, *There was a Time*, London, 1967, p. 248. Page references at the end of quotations in the text are to the following editions: *Love on the Dole*, London, Penguin, 1969 (abbr. *LoD*); *Kleiner Mann — was nun?*, Hamburg, Rowohlt, 1950 (abbr. *KM*); *Little Man What Now?* (trans. Eric Sutton), London, 1969 (abbr. *LM*: some translations have been slightly modified).
2. Ibid., p. 216.
3. Ibid., p. 240.
4. Ibid., p. 250.

5. Tom Crepon, *Leben und Tode des Hans Fallada*, Halle–Leipzig, 1978, p. 171f, an imaginative reconstruction of the writer's life based on authentic material.

6. Ibid., p. 172.

7. *Heute bei uns zu Haus*, Stuttgart, 1943, p. 24f.

8. C. L. Mowat, *Britain between the Wars, 1918–40*, London, 1955, p. 481.

9. Op. cit., p. 222f.

10. Heinz J. Schueler, *Hans Fallada. Humanist and Social Critic*, The Hague-Paris, 1970, pp. 50–2.

11. Ibid., p. 117.

12. Siegfried Kracauer, *Die Angestellten. Aus dem neuesten Deutschland*, Frankfurt, 1971 (reprint), p. 100.

The Cult of 'Functional Poetry' during the Weimar Period

J. J. White

Gebrauchslyrik (functional poetry) ranked among the principal types of poetic writing produced during the latter half of the Weimar period, and even the term itself was something of a vogue word in German literary circles in the 1920s. Indeed, it could be argued that such poetry, with its emphasis on some sort of utility to the reader, with its often cultivatedly disenchanted tone and its directness of presentation, was an apt vehicle for the New Sobriety ('Neue Sachlichkeit') which so many writers were then seeking to propagate. Yet whereas 'Neue Sachlichkeit' and such related terms as 'Amerikanismus' and 'Agitprop' have been the subject of a great deal of extensive discussion in recent years, *Gebrauchslyrik* has yet to receive such attention. As anyone consulting anthologies of modern German poetry or literary histories of the Weimar period will know, it has on the whole managed to survive unchallenged[1] into our own time as a much-used descriptive label.[2]

The present essay represents an attempt to examine critically some of the implications behind the term, to look at various types of *Gebrauchslyrik*, in particular Erich Kästner's early poetry, which is rightly acknowledged by many to contain some of the best examples of the genre, and to consider some general features of the cult of the functional in the 1920s.

It was in his second collection of poems, *Lärm im Spiegel* (1929), that Erich Kästner nailed his colours to the mast as a 'functional poet': in a quasi-programmatic 'Prosaische Zwischenbemerkung' (Incidental Remark in Prose). Apart from Kästner's later introduction to his *Lyrische Hausapotheke*, this is one of the most detailed statements made by any writer of the period about the nature of *Gebrauchslyrik*:

> Fortunately, there are one or two dozen poets — and I almost hope to count myself among them — who are concerned with keeping poetry alive. The public is able to read or hear their verses without falling asleep; for they have a spiritual usefulness. They were jotted down as a result of experiencing the joys and sorrows of the present-day world at first hand; and they are intended for anyone who has dealings with the present-day world. Someone coined the term 'functional poetry' for this kind of poem, and this coinage shows how rare real poetry was in recent years. For otherwise it would now be superfluous to refer explicitly to its usefulness. Poems which cannot be used by one's contemporaries in some way are mere rhyming games, nothing more. To be sure, there are skilful rhymes and clumsy poems, but still the latter are to be preferred. To walk on a tightrope of language is something which belongs in the music-hall.
>   Once more there are poems which give a sense of excitement even to the man who has remained unspoilt by literature and which make him smile out

at his empty room. Once more there are poets who feel like ordinary people do and are able to give vicarious expression to these feelings (and views and wishes). And because they do not write just for themselves or for the sake of some cheap originality, they get through to their readers.

The fact that someone puts into words what stirs or worries him — and others along with him — is useful. If there is anyone who finds this idea too facile, let him have it explained to him by the psychoanalysts. It is true, all the same.

Poets have a purpose once more. What they do is a vocation once more. They are probably not as important as bakers and dentists; but only because a rumbling tummy and toothache need more obvious remedies than non-physical complaints. Nevertheless, functional poets may justifiably feel a little happy: they come immediately after artisans in the social hierarchy.[3]

Gebrauchslyrik is presented here as a new movement which arose in reaction to certain self-indulgent, over-decorative forms of writing. Earlier in the passage some barbed remarks were made about the shallowness and conceit of the majority of modern poets ('these poets with their brains blowing in locks in the wind discredit poetry personally' (p. 125)). The terms of the polemical references are so vague that it has been variously assumed that Kästner was primarily attacking neo-Romantic poets such as George and Hofmannsthal, the ecstatic effusions of Expressionism and the more recent versified 'Kitsch' of his own decade. Actually, the target is left deliberately imprecise. Manifesto rhetoric of this kind simply requires some general sense of a new movement or style arising to replace a previous one, conveniently identified as out-of-date and yet still widespread. The reader must feel that the person speaking is not an isolated voice, but representative of something historically important and symptomatic of modernity that is taking place (hence the heroic image of the battle to save poetry's life in the twentieth century). And it must be reinforced by some memorable phrases or catch-words. It is clear from what has been written on Kästner's poetry that the idea of being 'spiritually useful' and of giving 'vicarious expression' to feelings, views and wishes may justifiably lay some claim to such a status. But above all it is the single word *Gebrauchslyrik* with which Kästner is associated, and that to some considerable extent as a result of what is proclaimed in this 'Prosaische Zwischenbemerkung'.

Of course, Kästner is making no claim to having invented the term; on the contrary, the rhetoric of his argument depends on his being seen to be part of something, not just already in the air at the time, but something for which there already existed a familiar label. 'Someone coined the term "functional poetry" for this kind of poetry, and this coinage shows how rare real poetry has been in recent years. For otherwise it would now be superfluous to refer explicitly to its usefulness'. But it would be naive to accept this argument at its face value. The term *Gebrauchslyrik* was not thought up in a purely literary context, as a convenient description of one form of poetry in contrast to a preceding tradition. It was one among a whole series of compound words using 'Gebrauch-' that came into being in the 1920s to capture the functionalism of contemporary culture: such as 'Gebrauchsgraphik', 'Gebrauchsmusik' and 'Gebrauchstanz' (functional

graphics, music and dance), for example.[4] Thus one finds Kästner characteristically publishing early work in the journal *Gebrauchsgraphik*.[5]

One chronicler of the period has gone so far as to propose a linear pattern of
influence in this respect between the various arts: 'Erich Kästner had picked up
Tucholsky's term "Gebrauchslyrik" (on the analogy of Hindemith's Gebrauchsmusik) to describe the neat satirical verses by which he had become known'; and,
going back even further, we are told that 'Gebrauchsmusik, a word coined on the
analogy of Gebrauchsgrafik (or commercial art), involved the exploration of
every available new practical function or outlet for music.'[6]

However, rather than posit any such straightforward pedigree for the idea of
Gebrauchslyrik — with Kästner meaning Tucholsky in particular when he says
'someone coined' the term,[7] and Tucholsky deriving his term from Hindemith
who was influenced by the existing technical term 'Gebrauchsgraphik' — I wish
to propose something more akin to a polygenesis of both the general idea of
functionalism and the specific terms in the various arts. After all, even within the
field of poetry, the notion of being 'functional' was hardly something new by
the time Kästner's *Lärm im Spiegel* appeared. Brecht's collection of poems
entitled *Hauspostille*, with its 'Anleitung zum Gebrauch der einzelnen Lektionen'
(i.e. instructions for use), had been published in 1927. And in the same year *Die
literarische Welt* had printed the text of Brecht's 'Kurzer Bericht über 400 (vier-
hundert) junge Lyriker' (Short Report on 400 Young Poets) in which Brecht
defends his refusal to nominate anyone for the paper's poetry prize — despite a
large field of entries — on the grounds that the works submitted lacked any
'Gebrauchswert' (utility value). 'And precisely poetry must without doubt be
something which one must be able without further ado to test in terms of its
utility value.' Such statements, coupled with Brecht's reference to poems 'which
can be given to people to give them strength',[8] sound very similar to Kästner's
formulations in his 'Prosaische Zwischenbemerkung'. Yet despite the fact that
Brecht's importance for Kästner is as well attested as that of Tucholsky,[9] there
are no stronger grounds for seeing Brecht as the single originator of the idea of
'functional poetry' than there are in Tucholsky's case. In fact, the extent to which
functionalism was 'in the air' can be easily gauged if one turns to Hindemith's
retrospective thoughts on the subject (especially bearing in mind the suggestion
that Hindemith was the one who really launched such a mode of referring to
functionalism).

By the time Hindemith came to give the Charles Eliot Norton Lectures at
Harvard in 1949, he was anxious to defend himself at some length against the
label *Gebrauchsmusiker*. Now whether, as Geoffrey Skelton suggests, *Gebrauchsmusik* had always been 'a word Hindemith himself heartily disliked'[10] or whether
he had gradually realized that he had become the victim of his own slogan is
difficult to determine at this distance from the events. What is clear is that Hindemith did use the word on one documented occasion in the 1920s, but fairly soon
afterwards preferred the phrases 'Haus- und Gemeinschaftsmusik' (music for
home and community) and 'Sing- und Spielmusik' (music to sing and play).[11]
The details of what he had specifically in mind when he considered the utility of
music need not detain us here, but his thoughts about the concept are instructive,
not simply because of the (once more) striking similarities to what Brecht and
Kästner were saying about poetry in the late twenties, but because of the light

they cast on the nature of the contemporary functionalist climate during the Weimar period.

In his preface to *A Composer's World*, Hindemith writes:

> A quarter of a century ago, in a discussion with German choral conductors, I pointed out the danger of an esoteric isolationism in music by using the term *Gebrauchsmusik*. Apart from the ugliness of the world — in German it is as hideous as its English equivalents, workaday music, music for use, utility music, and similar verbal beauties — nobody found anything remarkable in it, since quite obviously music for which no use can be found, that is to say, useless music, is not entitled to public consideration anyway and consequently the *Gebrauch* is taken for granted. Whatever else I had written or said at that time remained deservedly unknown . . . but that ugly term showed a power of penetration and a vigor that would be desirable for worthier formulations. Some busybody had written a report on that totally unimportant discussion, and when, years after, I first came to this country, I felt like the sorcerer's apprentice who had become the victim of his own conjurations: the slogan *Gebrauchsmusik* hit me wherever I went, it had grown as abundant, useless and disturbing as thousands of dandelions in a lawn. Apparently it met perfectly the common desire for a verbal label which classifies objects, persons, and problems, thus exempting anyone from opinions based on knowledge. Up to this day it has been impossible to kill the silly term and the unscrupulous classification that goes with it.[12]

Clearly Hindemith was not forced to bear the label of 'Gebrauchsmusiker' for such a long time simply because someone had happened to overhear him use the term and had published a report on the occasion. The word clung for more general reasons. Hindemith was the victim, not only of the public's need for convenient 'verbal labels', but of a cult of the voguish — in this case, of the functional — which was particularly powerful during the Weimar period. Thematically, Kästner's own works bear ample witness to this cult of the '*dernier cri*', with words like 'Mode' and 'modern', lines like 'Adultery is considered extremely fashionable' ('Paralytisches Selbstgespräch' (Paralytic Soliloquy)), 'I am modern from top to toe' ('Ballgeflüster' (Whispering at the Ball)) and 'So that's the latest style is it?' ('Der Busen marschiert' (The Bust on the March)), poems about fads ('Ein paar neue Rekorde' (A Couple of New Records)) or the latest in social fashions ('Vornehme Leute, 1200 Meter hoch (People of Refinement, 1200 metres high), 'Sogenannte Klassefrauen' (So-called Stylish Women)); the pursuit of voguishness and the ultimate in modernity was in fact as much a part of Weimar society in general as it was a feature of literature and the other arts. Functionalism, be it that of *Gebrauchsmusik* or *Gebrauchslyrik*, was soon fashionable. It caught on rapidly, sometimes despite the protests, at other times with the collusion of artists involved. Articles soon appeared recording the 'arrival' of the *Gebrauchslyriker*[13] and generally giving the impression that 'functional poetry' was a far more homogeneous genre than was in fact the case. One of the chief differences between Kästner and many of the other writers who have been called 'functional poets' is that he consciously presented himself as a *Gebrauchslyriker*, whereas most of them did not.

Kästner, of course, had not named the 'functional poets' he had in mind. Who were they? Certainly, according to the general consensus, he must have been thinking of Kurt Tucholsky and Walter Mehring. As a 'functional poet' *avant la lettre* Ringelnatz is often mentioned. But after this the group rapidly widens to embrace a large number of contemporary poets of various persuasions: Alfred Kerr, Karl Kraus, Bertolt Brecht, Klabund, Mascha Kaléko, Erich Weinert, even Christian Morgenstern.[14]

Various factors need to be differentiated here, if the term is to be properly helpful as a generic concept. Most literary groupings tend to involve demarcation disputes (witness the debates about whether or not Gottfried Benn was ever really an Expressionist). Moreover, iconoclastic movements often entail an undue measure of colonizing for purposes of self-promotion (hence H. G. Wells could be declared a Futurist *avant la lettre* and Bosch seen as an early Surrealist); this surely accounts for the inclusion of Morgenstern and Ringelnatz in the *Gebrauchslyrik* canon. And since, apart from Tucholsky and Kästner, none of the other writers mentioned explicitly championed the cause of *Gebrauchslyrik*, critics have had a certain latitude to include or exclude particular poets without much fear of contradiction. But the major complicating factor is peculiar to the term *Gebrauchslyrik* itself, in that it refers primarily to a specific relationship to the reader rather than necessarily a distinct manner of writing. In now turning to particular examples of 'functional poetry', we shall have to ask the question whether *Gebrauchslyrik* is in fact a matter of common stylistic features or whether, as has been suggested in the case of *Gebrauchsmusik*,[15] it is merely a token label for a functional aesthetic, an attitude to certain literary forms, rather than a technique.

When Kurt Tucholsky launched the term *Gebrauchslyrik* in *Die Weltbühne* in 1928, it was in a review-article on Oskar Kanehl's *Straße frei*, a collection of poems with accompanying illustrations by George Grosz. He quotes two passages from Kanehl to give the reader the feel of the type of poetry he has in mind:

> Ob sie sich hinter Tarifverträgen verstecken
> Ob sie in Arbeitsgemeinschaften
> mit unsern eigenen Organisationen
> im Produktionsprozesse den Profit retten.
> Mit unseren Bonzen Arm in Arm.
>
> (Whether they hide behind tariff agreements
> Whether, in teams working
> with our own organizations
> in the production process, they rescue the profits.
> [They stand] arm in arm with our bosses.)

and

> Nur nicht in euern Kämpfen
> fließt unser Blut.
> Wir sind die
> Bonzen, Bonzen, Bonzen.
> Uns gehts gut.[16]

(But it's not in your battles
that our blood flows.
We are the
bosses, bosses, bosses.
We're alright.)

Oskar Kanehl, a poet better known for his earlier association with the Expression-ist *Aktion*-group, is not usually thought of as a *Gebrauchslyriker*. But then, even if Tucholsky did actually introduce the term, his conception of 'functional poetry' at this time was in one sense more a-historical and in another more political than *Gebrauchslyrik* was for most of his contemporaries (with the possible exceptions of Walter Mehring[17] and Erich Weinert).

Although in Tucholsky's view *Gebrauchslyrik* had always existed ('zu allen Zeiten'), he can still declare that 'the verses of functional poetry are a rhymed or rhythmic party manifesto' and as such ideologically beyond the pale of bourgeois aesthetic criticism. 'Functional poetry' has to be simple, he argues, not in reaction to any earlier literary tradition, but essentially in order to make allowances for the proletariat's educational limitations. For Tucholsky the pressing question is: 'What role does someone who writes such verses play in the proletarian move-ment?' And his answer is: '. . . none other than that of a helper'.[18]

By such a definition, a poem like Tucholsky's own 'Der Graben' (The Trenches, 1926) would surely pass muster as *Gebrauchslyrik*. The tone of the first verse is characteristic of the whole poem:

Mutter, wozu hast du deinen aufgezogen?
Hast dich zwanzig Jahr mit ihm gequält?
Wozu ist er dir in deinen Arm geflogen,
und du hast ihm leise was erzählt?
    Bis sie ihn dir weggenommen haben.
    Für den Graben, Mutter, für den Graben.

(Mother, to what purpose did you bring up your son?
Why did you have your troubles with him for twenty years?
To what purpose did he rush to your arms,
and you softly told him a story?
    Until they took him from you,
    For the trenches, mother, for the trenches.)

The anti-war theme is developed over five more stanzas, ending with the exhor-tation: 'Reicht die Bruderhand als schönste aller Gaben|übern Graben, Leute, übern Graben — !' ('Stretch out a fraternal hand, as the finest of all gifts, across the trenches, men, across the trenches').

It is arguable, however, that Tucholsky's notion of *Gebrauchslyrik* is so wide that it practically becomes synonymous with *Tendenzdichtung* or political propaganda poetry, and no one would hit upon assigning 'Der Graben' to the category of 'functional poetry' without the help of extraneous contextual information.

Despite Tucholsky's role in giving the term currency, his view of *Gebrauchs-lyrik* is untypical. Many of his contemporaries had a more definite view of the genre and also wrote more readily recognizable 'functional poetry' than

Tucholsky did. They tended to write *Gebrauchslyrik* that could be identified as such on first reading, and they did this largely by establishing a functional relationship with the reader by means of a set of signals.

The utilitarian framework within which such *Gebrauchslyrik* was presented could be a matter of a collection's title (Kästner's *Ein Mann gibt Auskunft* (A man gives Information), for instance) or the title of an individual poem (such as the same writer's 'Nächtliches Rezept für Städter' (Nocturnal Prescription for City-Dwellers)). Often writers were indebted to earlier functional traditions. The word 'Postille' in Brecht's *Hauspostille*, for instance, suggests a devotional book, containing a series of exercises for the pious to read. And while on one level Brecht's volume obviously constitutes an ironic playing with the religious associations of the traditional genre, on another the 'Postille'-framework is being effectively used to didactic purpose.[19] The term 'Brevier' (breviary) in Walter Mehring's *Das Ketzerbrevier* (1921) has similar overtones, and in its new context manages to retain its functional associations, while adapting the form to new, heretical purposes. Similarly, the word 'Lesebuch' which occurs in such titles as *Aus einem Lesebuch für Städtebewohner* (From a Reader for City-dwellers) (Brecht) and *Kleines Lesebuch für Große* (Small Reader for Adults) (Kaléko)[20] means a 'reader' or an 'anthology' (as in the expression 'Lesebuch für Anfänger'). And this is precisely what the 'functional poets' meant their collections of verse to be for their readers. Other techniques for signalling the functional mode, such as Kästner's manifesto-like 'Prosaische Zwischenbemerkung' or the instructions for use at the beginning of Brecht's *Hauspostille* or Kästner's *Lyrische Hausapotheke*[21] were rare (certainly, in the latter case, rarer than dismissive references to *Gebrauchslyrik* in critical literature on the period would lead one to suppose).

Yet having, as it were, signalled intent, what did such poems offer? It is my contention that the 'functional poets' of the Weimar period went on to produce a vast spectrum of types of *Gebrauchslyrik* and, what is more, the best writers were able to adapt the paradigm to far subtler and more complex ends than any theoretical programme of *Gebrauchslyrik* would have suggested was possible. This is true even of the works where the functional paradigm is used overtly.

The simplest and most easily identifiable form of *Gebrauchslyrik* proper is what might be called the 'Rezeptgedicht': a poem offering the reader a piece of practical advice, a recipe or prescription ('Rezept' can mean both) to be used when he finds himself in a certain predicament. Kästner's 'Nächtliches Rezept für Städter' (in *Ein Mann gibt Auskunft*) is an example of this type of more overt functionalism:

> Man nehme irgendeinen Autobus.
> Es kann nicht schaden, einmal umzusteigen.
> Wohin, ist gleich. Das wird sich dann schon zeigen.
> Doch man beachte, daß es Nacht sein muß.
>
> In einer Gegend, die man niemals sah
> (das ist entscheidend für dergleichen Fälle),
> verlasse man den Autobus und stelle
> sich in die Finsternis. Und warte da.

Man nehme allem, was zu sehn ist, Maß.
Den Toren, Giebeln, Bäumen und Balkonen,
den Häusern und den Menschen, die drin wohnen.
Und glaube nicht, man täte es zum Spaß.

Dann gehe man durch Straßen. Kreuz und quer.
Und folge keinem vorgefaßten Ziele.
Es gibt so viele Straßen, ach so viele!
Und hinter jeder Biegung sind es mehr.

Man nehme sich bei dem Spaziergang Zeit.
Er dient gewissermaßen höhern Zwecken.
Er soll das, was vergessen wurde, wecken.
Nach zirka einer Stunde ist's soweit.

Dann wird es sein, als liefe man ein Jahr
durch diese Straßen, die kein Ende nehmen.
Und man beginnt, sich seiner selbst zu schämen
und seines Herzens, das verfettet war.

Nun weiß man wieder, was man wissen muß,
statt daß man in Zufriedenheit erblindet:
daß man sich in der Minderheit befindet!
Dann nehme man den letzten Autobus,
bevor er in der Dunkelheit verschwindet . . .

(Take a bus, any bus,
It can't do any harm to change once.
Where to, is all the same. That will be apparent later.
But note, it must be night-time.

In a district you've never seen
(that is crucial for cases of this kind)
get off the bus and place yourself
in the darkness. And wait there.

Take the measure of everything that's to be seen.
The gates, gables, trees and balconies,
the houses and the people living in them.
And don't think you're doing it for amusement.

Then go through streets. This way and that.
And don't follow any preconceived plan.
There are so many, oh so many streets!
And beyond each turn there are more.

Take your time with the walk.
It is, as it were, serving a higher purpose.
It's meant to re-awaken what had been forgotten.
After about an hour the time will have come.

Then it will seem as if you have been walking for a year
through these streets that never end.
You begin to feel ashamed of yourself
and of your heart with its fatty degeneration.

Now you once more know what has to be known
instead of being dazzled by satisfaction:
namely that you are in the minority.
Then take the last bus back
before it disappears in the darkness.)

Kästner offers a recipe to be carried out at night by city-dwellers, with certain success guaranteed ('After about an hour the time will have come . . . Now you once more know what has to be known'). And yet even an apparently straightforward 'functional poem' of this kind, with its simplicity and directness of statement, its notion of a clearly identified panacea with a quick result, is not as simplistic as it might on the surface seem to be.

The 'Rezept'-formula itself is essentially meant figuratively. Instead of the reader literally carrying out the poem's instructions (which would seem a very improbable result for the work to have), he is put in a situation which demands that he *read* about what he should do — in a poem. Thus Kästner's notion of *Gebrauchslyrik* presenting feelings vicariously for therapeutic effect here even extends to vicarious experience of another kind. When Kästner later came to elaborate the 'prescription' idea in his *Lyrische Hausapotheke*,[22] it is significant that all the instructions to the reader about how to use these verses, the 'Gebrauchsanweisungen' (Instructions for Use) tell him simply to *read* specific poems when in certain predicaments ('Man lese, wenn . . .'); there is no suggestion of carrying out the individual poems' demands literally, as there might be in the case of Tucholsky's 'gereimtes . . . Parteimanifest'.

Despite its title, Kästner's poem is not about city-dwellers as a general group, but certain types of city-dweller who need to experience the metropolis from a new perspective. The lines 'And you begin to feel ashamed of yourself | and of your heart with its fatty degeneration' are an indication that a specific kind of person or a particular state of mind will necessitate the *use* of this poem. In the *Hausapotheke*, where the poem is reprinted, the reader is instructed to turn to such a 'Nächtliches Rezept' if he has a tendency to be lazy or when he has had enough of city life.[23] The experience is one of relativization, one which to be effective has to be felt physically, to last some time at night in a strange setting. Something about the kind of reader in need of such a therapeutic jolt is hinted at in some of the small details of the poem. We sense a distinct possibility that he will not take the exercise seriously, and, as if he were a pedant, he has to be told explicitly that it will not hurt to change buses. Moreover, even though the title has told us that this is a '*Nächtliches* Rezept', he has to be reminded that it must all happen at night (as if there were some risk that he will cheat and weaken their impact by carrying out the instructions in broad daylight). Images of being blinded by satisfaction or suffering from some metaphorical fatty degeneration of the heart, or the instruction in the *Hausapotheke* that one should resort to this prescription when suffering from laziness or discontent, suggest that a stultified, perhaps specifically bourgeois insensitivity is being diagnosed as in need of such therapy. In fact, *Lesebuch für Städtebewohner*, the title which Brecht chose for his planned cycle of 'functional poems' about how to survive in the city, could well have served as the title for many of the collections of *Gebrauchslyrik* published during the late twenties and early thirties. There is a frequent link between the idea of people in need of advice and of offering help in the form of useful poetry and the feeling that the city-dweller finds himself in a particular predicament.[24] The exigencies of city-life have simply increased the need for relevant poetry.

The implied addressee of such a 'functional poem' is an important factor, for it could be argued that he often embodies the malaise for which the remedy is being offered and that this makes him as integral a part of the work as the panacea. Kästner's poem conjures up a sense of the blindness of satisfaction and the unhealthy ('verfettet') heart, not just the remedy to be taken. In other words, a poem like 'Nächtliches Rezept' involves a textual strategy for social commentary rather than mere *Gebrauchslyrik* in any literal sense of the word. (No matter how much contemporary poets gestured to the voguish notion of utility, *Gebrauchslyrik* was not in fact very often pragmatically useful or literally employed in the same sense that *Gebrauchsgraphik* was. The functional might be stressed,[25] but the giving of advice often remained a means to other ends or at most remained on the figurative plane. And it was because of this and also because of the very nebulousness of the idea of the reader 'using' what he reads that *Gebrauchslyrik* almost appears to have as many different nuances as there are *Gebrauchslyriker*.)

Bertolt Brecht's 'Verwisch die Spuren' (Cover your Tracks), from the cycle *Aus einem Lesebuch für Städtebewohner* and first published, like many 'functional poems', in a newspaper,[26] the *Berliner Börsen-Kurier* of 1 January 1927, shows again how the simple paradigm can be adapted to complex didactic effects:

Trenne dich von deinen Kameraden auf dem Bahnhof
Gehe am Morgen in die Stadt mit zugeknöpfter Jacke
Suche dir Quartier, und wenn dein Kamerad anklopft:
Öffne, oh, öffne die Tür nicht
Sondern
Verwisch die Spuren!

Wenn du deinen Eltern begegnest in der Stadt Hamburg oder sonstwo
Gehe an ihnen fremd vorbei, biege um die Ecke, erkenne sie nicht.
Zieh den Hut ins Gesicht, den sie dir schenkten
Zeige, oh, zeige dein Gesicht nicht
Sondern
Verwisch die Spuren!

Iß das Fleisch, das da ist! Spare nicht!
Gehe in jedes Haus, wenn es regnet, und setze dich auf jeden Stuhl, der da ist
Aber bleibe nicht sitzen! Und vergiß deinen Hut nicht!
Ich sage dir:
Verwisch die Spuren!

Was immer du sagst, sag es nicht zweimal
Findest du deinen Gedanken bei einem andern: verleugne ihn.
Wer seine Unterschrift nicht gegeben hat, wer kein Bild hinterließ

Wer nicht dabei war, wer nichts gesagt hat
Wie soll der zu fassen sein!
Verwisch die Spuren!

Sorge, wenn du zu sterben gedenkst
Daß kein Grabmal steht und verrät, wo du liegst
Mit einer deutlichen Schrift, die dich anzeigt
Und dem Jahr deines Todes, das dich überführt!
Noch einmal:
Verwisch die Spuren!

(Das wurde mir gelehrt.)

(Part from your friends at the station
Go into the city in the morning with your jacket buttoned up
Look for lodgings, and when your friend knocks:
Do not, oh do not, open the door
But
Cover your tracks!

If you meet your parents in the city of Hamburg or elsewhere
Pass them like strangers, turn the corner, don't recognize them
Pull the hat they gave you over your face
Do not, oh do not, show your face
But
Cover your tracks!

Eat the meat that's there. Don't hold back.
Go into any house when it rains and sit on any chair that's there
But don't sit for long. And don't forget your hat.
I tell you:
Cover your tracks!

Whatever you say, don't say it twice
If you find your ideas spoken by anyone else, disown them [him].
The man who hasn't signed anything, who has left no picture
Who was not there, who said nothing:
How can they get him?
Cover your tracks!

See when you think of dying
That no gravestone stands and betrays where you lie
With a clear inscription which denounces you
And with the year of your death which gives you away.
Once again:
Cover your tracks!

(That is what was taught me.))

In his commentary on this poem, Klaus Schuhmann observes that the work initiates the newcomer into the unwritten laws of the city-jungle.[27] Certainly this is the work's 'functional' strategy, just as in the case of 'Nächtliches Rezept' it was that of showing people how to rediscover a certain lost dimension of their personalities. But again, one should be wary of confusing the *Gebrauchslyrik* framework with the underlying use to which it is being put (and in the case of this poem the complexities are further compounded by a dialectical element not present in 'Nächtliches Rezept', as well as by the problem of exactly who is addressing whom[28]).

Once more the recipe (for how to survive) becomes a form of literary rhetoric. The instructions are, in one critic's words, not in fact meant apodictically in any literal sense, but serve as a means of emphasis.[29] Clearly, there is hyperbole to many of the images, such as those of denying one's parents and friends or allowing the quest for protective anonymity to extend even beyond the grave. The rules for survival are in fact exaggerated comment on the real world: overstating not simply for the purposes of teaching about the hostile world of the city, but because the sense of abnormality imposed by the modern city should lead, not to the conformity which is ostensibly the poem's purpose, but ideally to a reaction against what is being demanded of one. In other words, the functional framework is capable of — and has generally been employed for — more subtle and complex effects than such words as 'Rezept' or 'Gebrauchsanweisung' might automatically suggest.

The use of the 'Gebrauchsanweisung' paradigm in the following extract from Hannes Küpper's 'Nackte Seelen', apparently resulting in a set of directions on how to handle the 'soul' when writing poetry, is a further illustration of the potential of the method:

> Sie [i.e. die Seele] ist kühl und trocken aufzubewahren —
> Und vor Gebrauch, 'nicht' zu schütteln.
> Dagegen empfiehlt es sich, sie jeweils ein wenig aufzuwärmen.[30]

> It should be kept in a cool and dry place —
> And should *not* be shaken before using.
> But under certain circumstances you are recommended to heat it a little beforehand.

The 'Gebrauchsanweisungen', seemingly addressed to a reader on the assumption that he is preparing his feelings for serving in a poem, as if he were opening a tin of food before a meal, once more reveal themselves to be a rhetorical device: this time for presenting an aesthetic and at the same time criticizing a tradition. Because of what Brecht would call its inbuilt 'Gestus' (or 'stance'), the *Gebrauchslyrik* paradigm lends itself admirably to such uses, giving the reader a sense of partaking of the current vogue for the simple, down-to-earth and functional, and yet at the same time creating a variety of effects which transcend any crass utility.

However, it would create a false impression if we were to dwell any longer on examples of *Gebrauchslyrik* where individual poems are couched in terms of recipes, prescriptions, advice to the reader or instructions for use, or where the employment of the imperative or comparable hortatory structures implies an overtly didactic utility. Even in the major collections of 'functional poetry', such as Kästner's volumes up to the *Hausapotheke* or Brecht's *Hauspostille* and *Lesebuch*, such poems represent only a small portion of the poems included. Of the forty-eight poems in Kästner's *Lärm im Spiegel*, for instance, the work which even contains his 'Prosaische Zwischenbemerkung' on *Gebrauchslyrik*, only three belong to this category.[31]

The most popular type of *Gebrauchslyrik* is by contrast the less explicitly functional 'Rollengedicht', a persona-poem describing generic experiences through the first-person perspective of a familiar contemporary type, such as the blinkered 'Bürger', the Depression down-and-out or the cynical intellectual. But the 'Rollengedicht' is by no means limited to a simple monologue approach; such titles as 'Chor der Fräuleins' (The Chorus of Good-time Girls), 'Frau Großhennig schreibt an ihren Sohn' (Mrs. Grosshennig writes to her Son), 'Ansprache einer Bardame' (The Barmaid's Speech), 'Der Scheidebrief' (Farewell Letter) and 'Gespräch in der Haustür' (Conversation in the Doorway), all from Kästner's *Herz auf Taille*, show the range of the form.

The link between the 'Rollengedicht' and a sense of utility for the reader was pointed out by Kästner in his 'Prosaische Zwischenbemerkung'. 'There are other poets, who are capable of natural feelings, and who express these feelings (and views and desires) *vicariously* . . . that someone should express what concerns and oppresses him, and others like him, is useful.' The idea is taken up again in the introduction to the *Hausapotheke* where we are told: 'It is good for us to discover that others are no different, and no better off than us. It is also reassuring, from time to time, to enter into feelings which are the opposite of our own.'[32] As an aesthetic, this may, as has been remarked,[33] hardly be an example of rigorous thinking, but it is a convenient way of linking a large number of potentially useful poems to the *Gebrauchslyrik* idea, and as such it is not without its attractions for the functional poet.

The following first stanzas — from Klabund's 'Ein Bürger spricht' (A Bourgeois speaks), and Kästner's 'Das Lied vom feinen Mann' (The Song of the Elegant Man) and 'Junger Mann, 5 Uhr morgens' (Young Man at 5 a.m.), respectively — show how the 'Rollengedicht', as used by the 'functional poets', combines a sense of poetry about life *as it is really lived* with the therapeutic value of self-recognition (or learning about 'the other half') mentioned by Kästner. In addition, the poems have a certain undeniable 'Gebrauchswert' (functional value) in Tucholsky's sense by dint of the social indictment that they also implicitly contain:

> Am Sonntag geh ich gerne ins Café.
> Ich treffe viele meinesgleichen,
> Die sich verträumt die neuste Anekdote reichen —
> Und manche Frau im Negligé.

> On Sunday I like to go to the café.
> I meet many of my kind
> Who dreamily exchange the latest anecdote —
> And many a woman in a negligé.

> Ich kann, im Kino, auf wen immer warten —
> stets treten Leute stolz an mich heran
> und präsentieren mir die Eintrittskarten,
> als dächten sie, ich wiese Plätze an.

> I can be waiting for someone at the cinema —
> and people always walk proudly up to me
> and present me with their tickets,
> as if they thought I was there to show them to their seats.

> Wenn ich dich früh verlasse,
> tret ich aus deinem Haus
> still auf die kahle, blasse,
> öde Straße hinaus.

> When I leave you early in the morning,
> I walk from your house
> quietly out onto the bare,
> pale, deserted street.

The 'function' of these various 'Rollengedichte' will depend both on the poet's particular choice of persona and on the individual reader's perspective. In the case of 'Ein Bürger spricht', the reader will either recognize the pathetic contrast between thought and action in the class being described (if it is not his own) or he will relish the poor 'Bürger' 's familiar predicament. Of the other two poems partly quoted here, 'Das Lied vom feinen Mann' involves the use of an untypical predicament in order to satirize the amount of importance society attaches to appearances and 'Junger Mann, 5 Uhr morgens', like so many of Kästner's poems, evokes the sadness of illicit urban liaisons. In none of these instances does the 'Rollengedicht' technique simply exhaust it usefulness either in a therapeutic recognition of the familiar or an equally salutary witnessing of life in other quarters. In fact, the 'Rollengedicht' leads to a greater sense of social protest than Kästner's arguments about therapy for the individual reader concentrate on.

If the 'Rollengedicht' satisfactorily fulfilled the requirement of a *Gebrauchslyrik* which generally spoke to the reader about his urban world, about his kind of problems and experiences and in his language, this could also be done impersonally, with an effective 'Sachlichkeit', by means of an epic perspective, as the following situational poem by Mascha Kaléko shows:

> *Ein kleiner Mann stirbt*
> Wenn einer stirbt, dann weinen die Verwandten;
> Der Chef schickt einen Ehrenkranz ins Haus,
> Und voller Lob sind die, die ihn verkannten.
> . . . Wenn einer tot ist, macht er sich nichts draus.

> Wenn einer stirbt — und er ist kein Minister —
> Schreibt das Vereinsorgan kurz: "Er verblich . . ."
> Im Standesamt, Ressort: Geburtsregister
> Macht ein Beamter einen dicken Strich.

> Ein Kleiderhändler fragt nach alten Hüten,
> Offerten schickt ein Trauermagazin.
> Am Fenster steht: "Ein Zimmer zu vermieten . . ."
> Und auf dem Tisch die letzte Medizin.

> Wenn einer stirbt, scheint denen, die ihn lieben,
> Es könne nichts so einfach weitergehn.
> Doch sie sind auch nur "trauernd hinterblieben",
> Und alles läuft, wie es ihm vorgeschrieben.
> — Und nicht einmal die Uhren bleiben stehn.

A Small Man dies

When someone dies, his relatives cry;
His boss sends a wreath to his house,
And those who didn't understand him are full of praise.
. . . When someone dies, he doesn't care.

When someone dies — and he's not a minister —
The union paper writes simply: "He passed away . . ."
In the Registry Office, Department: Register of Births
An official draws a thick line.

A dealer in old clothes asks for old hats,
A funeral dress store sends offers.
The sign in the window says: "Room to let . . ."
And his last medicine stands on the table.

When someone dies, it seems to those who love him
That it can't simply go on as before.
But they are only "left behind in mourning",
And everything carries on as prescribed.
— And not even the clock stops.

This is the language of functionalism: bereft of metaphor, terse, seemingly factual, and yet containing a strong indictment of current conditions. The final lines, 'And everything carries on as prescribed | And not even the clock stops', contrast dramatically with the fact that the reader does pause and think. That is the 'Gebrauchswert' of this poem; like Kästner's 'Nächtliches Rezept', it puts the reader in touch with what he forgets at his peril.

For all their contemporary fashionability, the 'Rollengedicht' and the situational poem were by no means monopolized by the *Gebrauchslyriker* of the Weimar period. In a recent analysis of the genre,[34] Karl Riha shows the 'Rollengedicht' to be a form having its antecedents in literary cabaret and being also used by a number of non-'functional' poets in the twenties. All that the *Gebrauchslyriker*, Kästner in particular, could be said to be doing was adapting a popular form to a new framework. And this is also true of what Riha interprets as a sub-category of the 'Rollengedicht', the 'lyrical autobiography' (for example Kästner's 'Jahrgang 1899', Generation of 1899, or his 'Kurzgefaßter Lebenslauf', Short Curriculum Vitae) where a character surveys his life as a whole, rather than speaking in a particular role and describing a specific predicament.

This tendency to adopt and adapt traditional modes raises the fundamental question of whether *Gebrauchslyrik* is a really distinct mode of writing, with its own style and themes, or whether it is simply a matter of a functional *framework* within which certain kinds of traditional poetry can be viewed with a fresh emphasis. Before trying to formulate an answer to this problem, but keeping the question still in mind, it will be as well to turn to one further connotation of *Gebrauchslyrik* — and that is that primarily it is a matter of a particular style of writing.

In his commentary on Erich Kästner, the editor of the *Penguin Book of Twentieth-Century German Verse* describes his aim as that of writing 'spiritually useful' poetry; he adds: Kästner 'achieves this aim by writing clearly, concisely, wittily, directly'.[35] Is style, then, the key to the functional relationship between the *Gebrauchslyriker* and his reader? Kurt Tucholsky's early definition of *Gebrauchslyrik* undeniably puts a great deal of stress on the quality of the poetry's language, concluding: 'The effect must occur straightaway, it must be immediate, and without digressions'.[36] Kästner's diatribe against the exhibitionism of poetic tightrope artists who really belong in the music-hall, Brecht's self-declared style in the *Lesebuch* poems ('Cold and general with the driest of words'), the cult of the factual statement, of non-figurative language, parataxis, the predilection for the ellipses of conversational speech (for instance, the use of the dash as a common form of punctuation), would all seem to suggest that 'Gebrauchswert' and immediacy of expression are in some way connected in the minds of these writers. Nevertheless, it can be seen that there are substantial drawbacks to such an equation of style and genre characteristics. P. V. Brady has shown that it is appropriate to talk of Brecht's 'obliqueness' in *Aus einem Lesebuch*.[37] Egon Schwarz[38] rightly argues that while Kästner may seem to speak with the idioms of everyday speech in his *Gebrauchslyrik*, it would be wrong to overlook the subtle effects he manages to achieve within that register. And when it comes to another form of *Gebrauchslyrik* which we have not examined in the present context, that in — usually Berlin — dialect, 'unmittelbar' and 'ohne Umschweife' (immediate, without digressions) are hardly an accurate description of the result, for the deciphering of poems in transcribed dialect seldom engenders an immediacy of effect.

The even greater practical problem here, however, is that to discuss 'functionalism' as if it were primarily a stylistic issue would be to end up with a generic literary term that was to all intents and purposes synonymous with 'Neue Sachlichkeit'. And while the history of 'Neue Sachlichkeit' is closely bound up with the cult of *Gebrauchslyrik* during the Weimar period, it is nevertheless clear that *Gebrauchslyrik*, with its particular stress on the function of the poem *for the reader*, with its emphasis on usefulness, is not the same as 'Neue Sachlichkeit'.

The answer to the question of whether the term *Gebrauchslyrik* signifies a group of poems with clearly discernible common features relating to their sense of function (explicit signals of usefulness, a shared stylistic simplicity, specific areas of subject matter etc.) or whether it is simply a convenient label for heterogeneous material and a banner for certain writers to parade behind — or behind which critics can assemble them — cannot be a clearcut one. As we have seen, *some* 'functional poems' do display very particular features which make them part of a distinct group of texts. On the other hand, many do not and only come to be considered *Gebrauchslyrik* because of certain programmatic utterances made by their authors or because of the climate in which they were published. Without the 'Prosaische Zwischenbemerkung', it is doubtful whether the poems of Kästner's *Lärm im Spiegel* would have received such a uniform label as that of *Gebrauchslyrik*. Similarly, if Kästner had not subsequently re-published so many of his early poems in the *Lyrische Hausapotheke*, it is unlikely that the term would have been applied so liberally or for so long to his works. And if Tucholsky, Brecht and Kästner had not given such widespread currency to the notion of literary functionalism (and at a time when the stress was on utility value in so many of the other arts), then it seems improbable that the work of Mascha Kaléko,

Walter Mehring or Erich Weinert would have been seen as representative of such a tendency. All of which is not to undermine the significance of *Gebrauchslyrik* as a literary phenomenon of the Weimar period. At its best, it represented a revitalization of the language of lyric poetry, a cross-fertilization between literature and other forms of culture — not only cabaret and ballad, but, as Bab pointed out, the hit-songs and popular verses of the time — and a re-awakening of poetry's moral concern for the iniquities of trivial day-to-day experience and for the predicament of contemporary urban existence.

NOTES

1. To my knowledge, only one voice has so far been raised in serious objection to the use of the word *Gebrauchslyriker*: by Adolf Endler in 'Provokatorische Notizen über einen Gebrauchslyriker', *NDL*, 11, no. 9 (1963), 96–108, a pointedly Marxist review of Kästner's work, where the term was criticized as an unhelpfully vague umbrella concept, as well as a convenient pose for Kästner to adopt to hide guilt feelings about the legitimacy of publishing his work in the capitalist press.
2. There has been a spate of scholarly publications on 'Gebrauchstexte' in the past decade. See, for example: Horst Belke, *Literarische Gebrauchsformen*, Düsseldorf, 1973; Ludwig Fischer, Knut Hicketier and Karl Riha (eds), *Gebrauchsliteratur. Methodische überlegungen und Beispielanalysen*, Stuttgart, 1976; and Johannes Schwitalla, 'Was sind "Gebrauchstexte"?', *Deutsche Sprache*, 4 (1976), 20–40 and 'Konnotationen in Gebrauchstexten. Möglichkeiten der Analyse im Unterricht', *Wirkendes Wort*, 27 (1977), 171–81. However, these studies belong to the new discipline of 'Textsortenanalyse'. They have tended to focus on the language of various forms of modern non-literary texts such as legal documents, advertisements and reference works. None of them deals with the specific cult of the 'functional' in the literature of the Weimar period. And while it might be illuminating to bring the findings of these specialized studies to bear on *Gebrauchslyrik*, this hardly seems the context in which to do so.
3. Erich Kästner, *Gesammelte Schriften*, Vol. 1: *Gedichte* (Zürich, 1959), pp. 125f.
4. See, for example, the large number of articles published on 'Gebrauchsmusik' and 'Gebrauchstanz' in Hannes Küpper's theatrical magazine *Der Scheinwerfer* during the late twenties.
5. 'Werbung für 1930' and 'Reklame und Weltrevolution' appeared in the issue of *Gebrauchsgraphik* for March 1930 (VII, i and 52–7, respectively).
6. John Willett, *The New Sobriety. Art and Politics in the Weimar Period 1917–33* (London, 1978), pp. 197, 162.
7. See Kurt Tucholsky, 'Gebrauchslyrik', *Gesammelte Werke*, ed. Mary Gerold-Tucholsky and Fritz J. Raddatz, Vol. 2: *1925–1928* (Reinbek, 1961), pp. 1318–22.
8. Bertolt Brecht, 'Lyrik-Wettbewerb 1927', *Schriften zur Literatur und Kunst 1, Gesammelte Werke*, Vol. 18, (Frankfurt a. M., 1967), p. 55.
9. Cf. Erich Kästner, 'Indirekte Lyrik', *Das deutsche Buch* (Leipzig, 1928), pp. 143ff.
10. *Paul Hindemith. The Man behind the Music. A Biography* (London, 1977), p. 16.
11. For further details, see Hindemith's letter of 12 February 1927 to Willy Strecker (quoted in Skelton, op. cit., pp. 85f).
12. Paul Hindemith, *A Composer's World. Horizons and Limitations. The Charles Eliot Norton Lectures 1949–1950* (Gloucester, Mass., 1969), x–xi.
13. See, for instance, Julius Bab, '"Gebrauchslyrik". Mehring und Tucholsky', *Die Hilfe*, 37 (1931), 602–6, and H. Wiegand, 'Neue nützliche Gedichte', *Der Kulturwille*, 7–8 (1929), 158.
14. One of the largest groups of *Gebrauchslyriker* I have come across is proposed in the Penguin anthology of *Twentieth-Century German Verse*, introduced and edited by Patrick Bridgwater (Harmondsworth, 1963), lxii. See also: K. G. Just, *Von der Gründerzeit bis zur Gegenwart. Geschichte der deutschen Literatur seit 1871* (Berne, 1973), pp. 411–27, and Hermann Kesten's introduction to Kästner's *Gesammelte Schriften*, Vol. 1, ed. cit., p. 8.

15. 'All these works were written, as one would expect, in Hindemith's usual musical style, still clearly recognisable however much simplified. The trouble arose when the word *Gebrauchsmusik*, adopted by others, was extended to describe the *style* rather than the function of these pieces' (Skelton, op. cit., p. 16).

16. Tucholsky, op. cit., pp. 1318, 1320.

17. It is indicative of the generally less political connotations of functionalism that Julius Bab, in his review of Walter Mehring's *Arche Noah S.O.S.*, complains that the poet's politics were getting in the way of his efficacy as a *Gebrauchslyriker*: 'die politische Heftigkeit blendet ihn' (Bab, op. cit., pp. 602f.).

18. Tucholsky, op. cit., pp. 1318ff.

19. As Edgar Marsch puts it: 'Die Gedichte verdeutlichen exemplarisch Gesichtspunkte einer klugen, diesseitsbezogenen Lebensweise' (*Brechtkommentar zum lyrischen Werk*, Munich, 1974, p. 115).

20. Although Mascha Kaléko's *Kleines Lesebuch* was published in 1935, it is a clear continuation of the *Gebrauchslyrik* of the Weimar period, just as Kästner's *Lyrische Hausapotheke* (published in 1936) was, to quote John Winkelman, 'of a piece with the volumes published prior to 1933' (*Social Criticism in the Early Works of Erich Kästner*, The University of Missouri Studies, 4, Columbia, Missouri, 1953, p. 10). It would be wrong to assume that the *Gebrauchslyrik* of the Weimar period came to as sudden an end as the Republic itself did.

21. In the case of the *Hausapotheke*, the notion of usefulness even extends to pocket-book size; it is, as the Foreword points out, 'in händlichem Format' (p. 5) — a convenient 10·5 × 17 cm, a 'Taschenbuch' for ready consultation, in fact (cf. p. 7).

22. *Doktor Erich Kästners lyrische Hausapotheke. Ein Taschenbuch Enthält alte und neue Gedichte des Verfassers für den Hausbedarf der Leser. Nebst einem Vorwort und einer nutzbringenden Gebrauchsanweisung samt Register*, Zürich, 1936.

23. *Lyrische Hausapotheke*, pp. 9, 10. Clearly since only some of the volume's poems are listed anywhere in the 'Gebrauchsanweisung' and since only thirty-six predicaments are mentioned, we are only being offered *some suggestions* as to how to use the work, and tongue-in-cheek ones at that, rather than any compendium of advice.

24. Kästner's 'Bei Durchsicht meiner Bücher' (*Gesammelte Schriften*, Vol. 5: *Vermischte Beiträge*, Cologne, 1959, p. 489) refers to the *Hausapotheke* as a work containing 'Gedichte, die sich mit den privaten Gefühlen des heutigen Großstadtmenschen beschäftigen'.

25. As it was most forcefully in 1929 in the first sentence of Brecht's 'Forderung an eine neue Kritik' (*Gesammelte Werke*, Vol. 18, p. 113): 'Die ästhetischen Maßstäbe sind zugunsten der Maßstäbe des Gebrauchswerts zurückzustellen'.

26. Julius Bab (op. cit., p. 604) even argues that newspaper prepublication helped many of the poems to publishing success since readers already knew the poems when their authors' collections appeared.

27. 'Der Text . . . führt in unterweisendem Ton einen Neuling in die ungeschriebenen Gesetze des Städtedschungels ein' (*Der Lyriker Bertolt Brecht 1913–1933*, revised and enlarged ed., Munich, 1971, p. 214).

28. In '"Aus einem Lesebuch für Städtebewohner": On a Brecht Essay in Obliqueness', *GLL*, 26 (1972–3), 162f., P. V. Brady surveys the various possibilities: that it may be Brecht speaking to his reader or one city-dweller speaking to another, or a group addressing an individual or a form of dramatized monologue.

29. Marsch, op. cit., p. 159.

30. The full poem can be found in *Die Neue Bücherschau*, 5, iii (October 1927), 173.

31. Viz.: 'Warnung vor Selbstschüssen' (which begins 'Diesen Rat will ich Dir geben'), 'Bürger, schont eure Anlagen' and 'Hochzeitmachen (Ein altes Kinderspielrezept, modernisiert)'.

32. *Lyrische Hausapotheke*, p. 8.

33. Endler declares, op. cit., p. 102: 'Kästners Poetik ist ein Witz'.

34. 'Literarisches Kabarett und Rollengedicht. Anmerkungen zu einem lyrischen Typus in der deutschen Literatur nach dem Ersten Weltkrieg', in *Die deutsche Literatur in der Weimarer Republik*, ed. Wolfgang Rothe, (Stuttgart, 1974), pp. 382–95. Riha's observation that 'beim Schritt von Ringelnatz zu Brecht und Kästner' and Mehring we see 'eine Wendung der apolitischen in die politische Rolle' (p. 390) is linked to the rise of *Gebrauchslyrik* at this time.

35. op. cit., p. xxvi.

36. op. cit., p. 1319.

37. See especially the first two pages of Brady's analysis.
38. 'Die strampelnde Seele: Erich Kästner in seiner Zeit', in *Die sogenannten Zwanziger Jahre*, ed. R. Grimm and J. Hermand (Bad Homburg, 1970), p. 126. Schwarz argues that although Kästner works within the medium of 'Umgangssprache', it is 'niemals ohne eine kleine Übertreibung, einen parodistischen Anklang, eine blitzartig aufleuchtende Paradoxie, also niemals ohne ein intellektuelles Signal, eine künstlerische Absicht' (p. 127).

Playing to the Audience — Agitprop Theatricals 1926–1933

P. V. Brady

In 1930, on the Friedrichstrasse in Berlin, a young man collapsed in broad daylight in front of a shop window piled high with mouth-watering delicacies. A crowd gathered and soon began to discuss with the young man's companion the irony of the situation: here was an unemployed man, evidently undernourished, prostrate in front of so much luxury. After ten minutes the police arrived and surprised the onlookers by charging them with complicity in an Agitprop performance. The two young men had, meanwhile, slipped away. They were members of a Communist troupe known as Die Ketzer and had staged the entire affair.[1]

This little episode — a later generation might have seen it as a 'happening' — suggests a number of things. First, it suggests a form of enactment closer to real life — deceptively closer in this particular case — than to art. Second, it suggests a form dictated by external pressures — such troupes were in fact under constant threat from the police and tailored their efforts to outwit local police strategy. Third, it suggests not only an interaction of 'actors' and 'audience' but also the absolute priority of 'audience'-response — in other words, success depended on a degree of participation, on the reactions of those who thought that they were witnessing a tragedy.

This third point is important in an altogether different regard. A discussion in the street, unscripted, unpredicted and unrecorded, although it might find a place in a modish aesthetic of found-object serendipity, offers very little hard evidence for the literary scholar. 'Agitprop' — to quote a recent essay — 'resists academic treatment.'[2] The problem is not that no texts exist — they do exist and have been collected. It is, rather, that the element of spontaneity, plainly the very essence of that staged accident in 1930, is a factor to be reckoned with even in texts which have survived. If the declared policy of a troupe is to update its material constantly,[3] then there is little point in achieving, let alone preserving, any kind of textual finality. What survives may at times be no more than the common denominator of performances whose individual life lay in the unrecorded local, topical references introduced into the text and in the explosive interaction — likewise unrecorded — between players and spectators. What survives may, moreover, be of a simple crudity more likely to interest the social historian than the literary scholar, who may be deterred in his search for hidden gems when he reads the advice offered by the central organ of Agitprop, *Das Rote Sprachrohr,* to writers and performers:

> Most troupes will have troupe-poets. Is it right if this work is done by one person? No! It is not right, because that's breeding specialists. It's when a troupe works collectively that it's worth something.

(DA, II, 70)

Why then, given such acute problems of authentication and of literary quality, should the Agitprop movement in the Weimar Republic claim attention? One

110

reason, insufficient in itself, lies in the scale of the enterprise. In 1929 the Communist Party recorded about 180 active troupes (DA, I, 36); between February of that year and February 1930 the Berlin troupe Kolonne Links performed 86 times before a total of around 65,000 onlookers;[4] Die Nieter, a Hamburg troupe, reached some 21,000 in 33 performances during the first two months of 1930;[5] during three weeks of the election campaign in Autumn 1930, 19 Berlin troupes performed a total of 349 times (AF, XVII, 11, 4–5). Numbers of this magnitude prove little, even if they at least point to a certain mass appeal. A more important reason for heeding the efforts of the Agitprop movement lies in the lively discussion which accompanied it. That discussion — declarations of intent, admissions of failure, criticisms of production technique, suggestions of themes — yields in sum a body of writing devoted, from an eminently pragmatic angle, to that somewhat utopian question which occupied radical artists in many genres throughout the Weimar Republic, namely, how to make of art an instrument of social and political change. A second important reason lies, not surprisingly, in the Agitprop works themselves, however imperfectly some at least may have survived. Their interest is best summarized under two somewhat contradictory heads — they are at once traditional and anti-traditional, they look backwards to folk-theatre and popular propaganda-forms and they look forwards in that they respond to many of the theatrical experiments of the day. There is, then, a discussion about Agitprop and there is Agitprop itself. The following pages will consider some aspects of both.

The facts — the spread of Agitprop in Germany between 1927 and 1933 — can be quickly chronicled.[6] In the mid-twenties news was reaching Germany of developments taking place in political theatre in the USSR, notably the 'Living Newspapers' or 'Blue Blouses', small troupes skilled in acrobatics, mime and cameo-sketches and devoting their skills to agitation and propaganda. The German Communist Party, having hitherto encouraged loosely structured 'Red Revues' or 'Political-Satirical Evenings', which were performed on special occasions, set up its own first Agitprop troupe under Maxim Vallentin in 1926. The real momentum was provided in the autumn of 1927 with the visit to Germany of one of the Moscow 'Blue Blouse' troupes. By the following year the effects of the Russian example were being commented on by an anonymous writer in the *Arbeiter Illustrierte Zeitung*:

> Red acting-troupes are shooting up like mushrooms everywhere. 'The Red Rockets', 'The Red Megaphone', 'The Drummers' in Berlin, 'The Riveters' in Hamburg, troupes in Cologne and Leipzig etcetera. They are workers from the factory, especially young workers, often still children . . . They are their own poets, producers, stage-technicians and actors all at the same time. (DA, I, 271)

The troupes, often in fact unemployed workers, played in halls, factories, yards or streets, indoors and outdoors. Sometimes their visit was announced, sometimes whole tours were pre-arranged — plans which, however, were much obstructed by police controls from 1930 onwards. At other times a performance might be of a more unscheduled character, of the kind vividly described in the October 1930 issue of *Arbeiterbühne und Film*:

Outside the factory we organize a quick meeting in the street. We've soon got a barrow or a hand-cart. We've brought our flags. Banners and placards are set up. Two of us dress up as a Nazi and a Capitalist. Somebody else blows a signal on a horn. Work finishes. The first 50 workers appear; 20 stop, 30 carry on. From the next 50, 40 stop and only 10 carry on. We launch into a Nazi-scene. Hundreds of workers are standing around us. Then we play the song of the two metal workers: Severing, with his 30,000 Mark annual pension, and Carl Schulze, made redundant with 12 marks 40 a week benefit. A revolutionary worker speaks. We hand out leaflets. Then we deliver a rousing call to action; 30 minutes have passed. We pack our things and on we move.[7]

Looking back in 1933, in what is one of the most important surveys of the gains and losses experienced by the Agitprop movement, the dramatist Friedrich Wolf saw one immediate gain, a gain achieved in terms of content and almost independent of quality. The Agitprop plays had taken the sentimentality out of working-clas culture, had developed a distanced, less reverential view of bourgeois classics (DA, II, 431ff). Wolf remembers with distaste a time when working-class culture had tended to consist of what non-proletarian tastes dictated, what middle-class socialists thought was good for the working-class. Wolf's point gains in force in view of the marked dependence of pre-war socialist writers on the cultural models of a tradition from which politically they were seeking to dissociate themselves.[8] In the early 1920s the contradiction persisted, and in unexpected places, as is shown by the programme for a commemoration ceremony arranged in 1921 by the Communist Party in Kassel for the 'Victims of the Revolution: Rosa Luxemburg and Karl Liebknecht.' The programme begins with the funeral march from Beethoven's 'Eroica' symphony and then proceeds to mix items more specific to the occasion with two laments by Gluck, a funeral march by Chopin and 'Stumm schläft der Sänger' (The Singer sleeps silently) by Silcher.[9]

Seen against what was offered in Kassel in 1921, the Agitprop movement does indeed seem to have found a certain autonomy, a certain self-sufficiency, and others besides and before Wolf had noticed this. Experiences were now shared by audience and actors, rather than borrowed from elsewhere. Thus the critic Béla Balázs, writing for the unproletarian readers of *Die Weltbühne* in 1930, emphasized what he saw as the distinctive relationship between players and public:

This is why worker's theatre is today the only theatre in Europe which has a unified audience. There are no fortuitous effects here. The sole possible effect is latent, simply awaiting its particular cause. New, barbed points are made — the merest hint suffices. This audience knows all the details. New forms of abbreviation emerge. For these are current, shared matters. New symbols appear. For this public knows what's going on. (DA, II, 120)

Circumstances — conditions of performance as well as the convergent interests of which Balázs speaks — made brevity a singular and much noted virtue of the Agitprop plays. One participant, Hans Käbnick, saw the effect on the troupes:

In place of naturalist longwindedness they have put the briefest summary, the sharpest rapid picture, in place of five-act plays the three-minute sketch . . . They have . . . brought politics itself, not a politically coloured slice of life, onto the stage. (DA, II, 126)

Brevity and pace had been commended as early as 1926 in *Die Rote Fahne,* (DA, I, 250) as the hallmarks of Soviet Agitprop, and when the first troupe visited Germany in 1927 it was their rapid-fire topicality which impressed a critic in *Der Rote Stern* (DA, I, 243). For many, indeed, pace remained a vital element: 'We need more "Tempo", shorter pauses', wrote Alfred Kemenyi in 1930, 'on stage the dynamics of revolution should have the speed of an express-train'.[10]

As long as the pace and crispness of early Agitprop, especially the Soviet variety, are under scrutiny, the result can sound like the familiar rhetoric of believers celebrating in chorus the arrival of something new. But imperceptibly the chorus acquires nuances, as it were, as the native, German products take over. There is criticism as well as praise, alternative ways of achieving agreed goals are discussed. Central to this discussion is the question of form, the question of how far those much-praised snappy scenes might be knit together to achieve a more cumulative effect. The loosely structured 'revue' form could easily become what one critic called a 'bunte Bonbonmischung' (bag of liquorice allsorts) (AF, XVIII, 3,9) in which entertainment defeated the ends of Agitprop. Moreover, the Agitprop sketches could defeat their own ends by creating, in the interests of brevity, the self-perpetuating stereotypes which the central organ of Agitprop, *Das Rote Sprachrohr,* was detecting in 1930 (DA, II, 108). Stereotype form, the article warns, could very easily become stereotype content, a fault exhibited in the predilection for recognizable caricature-types: the journalist with his gigantic pen, the capitalist with his gigantic paunch. The recognizable type had been seen at an earlier stage as an acceptable means of winning an audience at a stroke by acknowledging its *bêtes noires.* By 1930, however, writers on Agitprop were vocal in their dissatisfaction with the pursuit of easy targets. The aim was, as Siegfried Moos, a regular contributor to *Arbeiterbühne und Film,* put it:

> To show the role of capitalism, the role of the bosses in the class-struggle, independently of the thickness of their paunch or the size of their cigar. Artistic effectiveness is not reduced by the accuracy and depth of political content, it is indeed generated by it. (DA, II, 295)

Questioning the effectiveness of propaganda-stereotypes meant asking for a less schematic, less predictable exchange between players and audience. Stock figures and stock situations were, in a sense, abstractions, and to rely on them in order to influence an audience was to beat that audience about the head with ready-made conclusions (DA, II, 285). The audience should, in other words, be left to complete an argument. In criticizing previous practice an unsigned article in the *Illustrierte Rote Post* puts the choice clearly 'Ready-made ideas are being turned out and put on stage; the *conclusion* of an argument is presented *ready-made,* instead of this argument being developed *in the audience itself* (DA, II, 345)'. The argument — especially perhaps when, as early as 1928, the talk is of 'dialectical form' and of 'scenes set off against each other' (DA, I, 331) — begins to have a familiar ring. On their own terms and keeping well within their rather self-enclosed world[11] the Agitprop critics and policy-makers were pursuing lines of argument similar to those which were taking Bertolt Brecht away from Aristotelean theatre and into the Lehrstück. Thus, by the time that one critic, Elli Schließer, is developing, in 1931, the goals for Agitprop, the overlap of terms is considerable: 'We must look for forms which enable us to make visible the connections between class-dynamics. We can do this only with the help of the revolutionary Marxist method of analysis, with the help of dialectics' (DA, II, 286). Nevertheless, and this is why echoes and overlaps matter little, the Agitprop writers were trying to achieve a more structured, more didactic kind of performance within their own resources, within that self-enclosed world. Their interest in bourgeois theatre as a target is less than Brecht's, they have no interest in professional staging and they are aiming at improvements which will still preserve the topicality of reference and the context of workers performing for workers which were the hallmarks of Agitprop. The issue was in broad outline the same for them as for Brecht: what makes and what mars effective political theatre. Their assumptions about text and performance were different.

It is worth emphasizing how very close is the discussion of Agitprop in the years 1928–1933 to the practice of Agitprop. Discussion was not theoretical, since much of it arose through observant reviews of individual performances or through suggestions made with particular troupes in mind. When, for example, three pseudonymous reviews discuss three different troupes on one page of *Arbeiterbühne und Film*, a tally of desiderata can be inferred from the shortcomings that are detected: the limp, unexplosive start, the lack of topicality, the absence of enacted argument, the minimizing of danger, insufficient rapport with the audience (break down the barriers by placing performers in the audience, a reviewer suggests) (AF, XVIII, 3, 14). 'Theory' — the word is too grand — and practice interact too, when material for performance is provided. In *Arbeiterbühne und Film* Siegfried Moos specialized in gathering material around certain topics as a basis for Agitprop performance. His 'Material zu Antikriegsszenen' (Material for anti-War Scenes), for example, is lengthy and varied (AF, XVII, 7, 10ff). It begins with a War poem of 1915: 'Vater ist ein schöner Mann, Mutterle tut weinen. Vater hat 'nen Säbel an, ich möcht' auch so einen' (Father is a fine man, my Mum is crying. Father has put on a sword, I would like one too), and ends with a poem, 'Der Geist des 4. August 1914' (The Spirit of 4 August 1914), by Erich Weinert. Between these are statistics of casualties and of economic costs along with material of a kind that suggests that the anti-war scene might proceed obliquely — quotations in support of war from Hindenburg's 'War does me good; like taking the waters' to a lengthy description of the glory of battle from a recent novel, with evidence of a longer tradition of the death-and-glory theme from St. Matthew. In the following issue Moos offers 'Material for anti-Nazi Scenes' and again the strategy varies, including items, all from Nazi journals, which are provokingly bland: a 20-year-old advertizing for work at minimal wages; a church parade concluding with the Deutschlandlied; an advertisement offering brown shirts for sale.

Those who discussed could also, in effect, be participating. This makes it easier to move from the discussion about Agitprop to the plays themselves, since clearly to those who were involved the two did not inhabit separate worlds. Nor, however, did they always inhabit the same world — there is almost bound to be some degree of tension between party goals and topical targets on the one hand and the nature of popular theatre on the other. The latter — and Agitprop is a species of popular theatre — inherits more than it may appear to admit. It is worth pursuing the ambivalent relationship of Agitprop plays to traditional modes of popular propaganda, not least because it reveals something about the durability of a tradition.

Observers of Agitprop performances occasionally hint at debts which strike a curiously untopical note. Frieda Rubiner, reporting on Moscow theatre long before that theatre had been seen in Germany, notes one historical parallel: she has seen plays which offer 'a loose sequence of scenes, somewhat in the style of the old *commedia del arte.*'[12] Bruno Frei, writing in *Die Weltbühne* of what he saw as a uniquely exciting theatre seems, *en passant*, to look even further back, finding elements of passion-play and an adaptation of the Greek chorus (DA, I, 160). Clearly, if troupes were recommended to try out 'kleine Stegreifspiele' (short impromptu plays) when playing to a village audience (AF, XVII, 7, 9), this amounts to a recipe for traditionalism. Such troupes might never have heard of Greek choruses, let alone *commedia del arte,* but they would be likely to rely instinctively on well-tried simple formulae and topoi. And when the critics begin to deplore the persistence of stereotypes, they are unwittingly placing Agitprop within a tradition.

A simple, early play, circulated by the Communist Party, shows how total the dependence on tradition could be. A short play, entitled *Deutsches Nationaltheater* (German National Theatre) (1924) (DA, I, 151ff) has a herald inviting the audience to watch Germany being destroyed: Stresemann, a priest, a banker, an industrialist and a Junker support the Dawes plan, a lone Communist — in overalls — does not and is beaten up and thrown out. A current issue has provoked a playlet on familiar lines which has a chorus of stereotypes and a concluding piece of violence. Simple confrontation producing violence on stage is the recipe for a more substantial Agitprop play of 1927, *Hände weg von China* (Hands off China), written by Maxim Vallentin for the first Agitprop troupe of the Young Communists (DA, I, 210ff). China is represented by a coolie who hits an imperialist teacher on the head and is himself attacked by a fat European carried in on a rickshaw. Again a priest has a part and those countries involved in the exploitation of China — England, America and Japan — each have a single representative, the England-figure walking around inside a cardboard model of a warship. In this case notes on performance accompany the text and they acknowledge the allegorical dimension of the play by urging actors to elaborate the types. And it is a traditionally structured allegory,[13] having, in its original forms, Venus or Death at the head, which underlies another sketch in which five representatives of coalition parties, masked as apes, are tied to a man in top hat, representing the Chancellor (DA, I, 363). A lost play of the 'Bremen Blaue Blusen', remembered in outline by Paul Dornberger,[14] combined two centuries-old topoi of political allegory: a capitalist lies sick in bed but recovers when given medicine from a bottle labelled 'Strikes forbidden', whereupon a crowd of workers enters, on each of whom capitalist bosses place a saddle and then mount them, only, in a short while, to be thrown to the ground as the workers in concert reject their burdens.

The Agitprop which relies on stereotype figures, the churchman, the capitalist, the politician, the worker, all traditionally accoutred, is simply making visual a complicated situation by identifying the prime movers. It is a tendency common to times of conflict when, as during the Reformation or the 1848 Revolution, popular dramatic forms respond to an extreme confrontation.[15] Agitprop plays can also exhibit emotional stereotypes, that is, they can be as much shaped by an emotion as the bourgeois plays from which they dissociate themselves. The 'happy end', as Siegfried Moos saw (AF, XVII, 6, 3), is a standard feature of Agitprop, as it is in bourgeois theatre. The difference is that in the latter we close with a kiss, in the former with a clenched fist. The convention is described by Knellessen[16] as heroizing *tableaux vivants* with clenched fists and red flags. Victory, or the assertive signalling of the route towards it, is the closing note, and it is preceded by head-on collision — between recruits and a sergeant in one case (DA, II, 246ff), between the compromising socialist and the seasoned revolutionaries in another (DA, II, 204ff). Or again, a different kind of victory climax, and one common to 16th-century pamphlet-dialogues, the defeated figures (industrialist, aristocrat, landowner) speak in turn, each with an eight-line verse (DA, II, 211).

In the earliest German Agitprop plays, moreover, the impression that old tools are being put to new use is further strengthened by the verse that is employed. The reason for verse is simple and familiar — the aim is to strike home, and jingles have a proven efficacy. Instructions in *Das Rote Sprachrohr* to budding Agitprop writers urge them to start with prose but to try to graduate to verse, because it can be more easily learned and can achieve more powerful effects (DA, II, 70). Verse could take many forms: it might be used solely for closing exhortation, it might be mixed with prose, or it might be the sole medium. That the aim throughout was to put verse to very traditional mnemonic and hortative uses is shown by the results and by the impression created on observers: 'Here is a fresh and uninhibited popular art. The simple, but rhythmically extremely powerful rhyming verse reminds one at times of Hans Sachs'[17] (AF, VIII, 6, 6). At this level — more by accident than by design — Agitprop is keeping alive simple traditions of verse rhetoric and of propaganda-symbolism to serve its own simple ends. But, as we have seen, Agitprop-critics were well aware that simplicity can come close to simplification and simplification can have a dangerously defusing effect if it takes the political arguments and the dialectical possibilities out of a problem. It is not least in order to avoid the sense of cosy security that familiar stereotypes can induce that some Agitprop writers resorted to less traditional forms of presentation. A vivid example of a troupe responding to a need for more than simple, familiar polemic is reported of the Kolonne Links troupe by Helmut Demerius.[18] The troupe had chosen to satirize the internal quarrels of the National Socialists by having Hitler, Goebbels, Strasser and others enter, singing in a boat, each having a black-white-red bib round his neck and a chamberpot with swastika on his head. After a struggle over poor ensemble-singing Strasser was thrown overboard. The scene was very popular with audiences, but on one occasion it was suggested afterwards that the scene was too intent on appealing to a simple sense of the ludicrous. The scene was promptly changed by a simple addition — immediately after the comic struggle a member of the troupe, in SA uniform, came on stage, looked round the gathering — who could be sure that he was not a genuine SA man policing the place? — and fired a shot over the heads of the uneasy audience. This, it was implied, was the real, the un-funny Nazi. The original picture was full of echoes — a ship of fools plus Georg Grosz, as it were, who had put chamber-pots on his own targets as early as 1921 in *Das Gesicht der herrschenden Klasse* (The Face of the Ruling Class). The addition questions the tradition, subjects it to a kind of alienation or, better, Verfremdung. Again, a scene entitled *K.O. Ein Boxkampf* (Knockout. A Boxing Match) (DA, I, 262ff), performed by the 'Berlin Rote Raketen', shows another kind of convention being transformed. A boxing-match, itself a familiar component of revues, represents the coalition-parties. First they fight, but then they fight again in formalized slow motion, showing that the fight was pure sham. Once more first impressions are being corrected. And the correction can, so to speak, be simultaneous, as when caricature and reality coexist on stage — a huge cardboard figure of Goebbels along with the real Goebbels in the shape of a gramophone playing a record of one of his diatribes (DA, II, 175).

The innovatory — or, at least, more up-to-date — features of Agitprop go beyond this kind of Verfremdung of familiar motifs. Not surprisingly, the most obvious field for enterprise lies in the use of visual effects. Already in 1925 a slide projector was being recommended as an invaluable tool in the equipment of acting troupes (DA, I, 200). The painter Heinrich Vogeler designed special slides with a blank central area against which the Agitprop players could perform.[19] In 1927 the 'Proletkult Kassel' was using a considerable number of up-to-date effects in its play *Giftgaskrieg gegen Sowjetrussland* (Poison-gas Warfare against Soviet Russia) (DA, II, 226ff). Against an unchanging backdrop, creating a permanent visual dimension for what were in fact 35 individual scenes, the actors remained on stage, changing roles in front of the audience and using film excerpts and slide projections to illustrate the social background. In the same year Rudolf Hartig, writing in *Der Kämpfer*, drew the moral from the recent visit of the Moscow Blue Blouses that proletarian art lay in the maximum use of the pictorial, of stage image, film and photograph and the minimum use of the verbal (DA, I, 243). Much had been learned from influences nearer at hand: Erwin Piscator's collaboration with Felix Gasbarra on the revue *Trotz Alledem!* (In Spite of All), although remote in its complex staging from the Agitprop of a few years later, set an example in the use of visual media which was taken note of. A review in the *Rote Fahne* especially commended the powerful effect achieved by playing part of the review against authentic, chilling photographs of the War (DA, I, 179).

Visual effects need not, however, require machinery. Machinery had, in any case, to be portable and easily packed. It had been much commented on that the Moscow players had achieved a host of effects by means of mime and well-choreographed gymnastics, creating, for example, a locomotive out of their own bodies.[20] The example was followed in Germany: a factory was suggested by synchronized gestures (DA, II, 167), planes crashing were depicted by gymnastic movements (DA, I, 280), actors were instructed to imitate street-noises and factory-noises, preferably without mechanical aids (DA, I, 300). This, it must be emphasized, is not old-fashioned mime but, rather, anti-naturalism, yielding its own variety of realism, in which, ideally, the mimetic skills of a troupe will focus attention on an issue by avoiding any kind of distracting naturalism.

The shift away from traditional form is not only reflected in individual stage-effects. Observers had been quick to note the need for plays which embodied argument rather than circumventing it, plays constructed on complex, 'dialectical' lines. The last example quoted — the troupe imitating street and factory sounds —

is part of such a structure, because in this particular piece, *Hallo, Kollege Jungarbeiter!* (Hallo Young Workmate!) (DA, I, 300ff), narrative scenes alternate with chorus-discussion, combining two contrasting modes to create what has been called a 'Lehrstück' (DA, I, 299). There are many varied attempts to create a form of performance which combine spontaneity with analysis, thereby escaping from the fragmentary superficiality of the earlier Agitprop revues. Thus the *Freidenker–Revue* (Freethinker Revue) (DA, II, 259ff) packs into a rapid sequence of scenes the history of religion, leaving the audience to find cross-references and to draw conclusions, and closing with a sequence of scenes in the USSR depicting ironically the discomfort of one poor Russian peasant who misses his old God. Thus too, on a different scale, *Massenstreik* (Mass Strike) (DA, II, 318ff), a sequence by 'Das Rote Sprachrohr', in which individuals, a chorus, numbered speakers and old-style stereotypes depict the inevitability of strike-action through a sequence of scenes in which prose and verse, dialect and non-dialect, realism and non-realism are combined.

The core of the *Massenstreik* scenes is a mixture of song and speech which seems to have been a speciality of the 'Rotes Sprachrohr', the most renowned Agitprop troupe and the troupe which appears in the Brecht–Dudow film *Kuhle Wampe*. The advantage of this form was that its length could be adapted to circumstances, circumstances which might include police harassment. The chorus could create prose-cameos with improvised touches between the verses of a song, achieving what Elli Schließer regarded as the necessary mixture of generalizing 'Referat' and particularizing 'Blitzszene' (lightning scene) (DA, II, 284). It is a form exemplified by the troupe's *Lied der roten Einheitsfront* (Song of the United Red Front), in which a strophic song is at the same time a rapid sequence of prose-scenes (DA, II, 311ff). A sketch of this kind written by Damerius for the 'Kolonne Links' troupe has the added interest of revealing common ground between an Agitprop-play and a more familiar 'stage'-play. In Damerius' *Einer von Tausenden* (One among Thousands) the songs are taken from Brecht's *Die Mutter* (The Mother) and provide the generalizing element, whilst Brecht's prose text has been rejected in favour of briefer, simpler cameos documenting the particular facts of poverty. The pattern of Brecht's original survives, but the realistic ingredient has been simplified to fit Agitprop-staging.[21]

Dissatisfaction with the somewhat petrified stereotypes of early Agitprop leads also, perhaps unexpectedly, to a kind of cameo-realism in plays around 1930. Again, however, the urge to avoid semblances of naturalism was still strong, as was the desire to present argument rather than conclusions. Thus *Grundeigentum* (Landed Property), a play whose author is named (Thomas Ring) and which was written to be performed in villages by the troupe 'Rote Sensen', keeps close to the facts (the dispossession of small farmers) in a sequence of scenes which form a single action (DA, II, 22ff). Actors were, moreover, encouraged to adopt the dialect of the area in which they were playing. It is the concentration on a single problem, on argument around it and on the detail of the Communist solution which ensure that the assembly of realistically conceived characters does not produce a simple slice of life. In the following year, 1930, the Agitprop organ *Das Rote Sprachrohr* published a text for performance, the *Agfa-Revue*, which, despite its misleading or at least ironic title, achieved the same kind of authenticity in four scenes built around the exploited workers in an IG-Farben factory (DA, II, 73ff). Again characters are individualized and again the resources of a simple stage realism are being used to lend force to both sides of an argument, an argument which involves the audience in the final, fourth scene when audience and players together form a works meeting. Such pieces, in prose throughout, and without the theatricality on which other forms of Agitprop depended, seem to move in a different, more realistic mode. But when scenes follow each other in rapid, provoking succession, as in *Nazis unter sich* (Nazis among themselves) — five sharp sketches with a final change-of-heart (DA, II, 172ff) — one is reminded of the value which the earliest troupes and their observers had attached to concentrated material and 'tempo' of presentation.

Where so much is lost and where the impromptu variations have gone unrecorded, it is not easy to summarize the shared features, let alone the variations, of Agitprop. Certainly it would be wrong to find virtue in what must often have been work of the utmost crudity. Brecht, who found much to praise in the Agitprop brand of simplicity, also warned that a preference for simple black bread over richer fare sometimes quite simply points to a faulty digestion.[22] The facts are that countless thousands saw what, as a total enterprise, is a mixture of revue and didactic-play, of verse, song and down-to-earth prose, marrying traditional fairground, carnival or cabaret elements to the media, film and photography, of the day. What they saw was not devised as purely escapist entertainment, nor could it be translated into an orthodox, professional, theatrical idiom. This much can be acknowledged without needing to concur with those like Béla Balázs, who claimed to find a brand new form of art emerging (DA, II, 119).

Friedrich Wolf, perhaps the dramatist most closely linked with Agitprop-theatre, was critical of the endemic stereotypes but clear about the importance of Agitprop — it 'mirrors most clearly for us the course, the substance and the intensity of the proletarian struggle' (DA, II, 431). Gustav Wangenheim, who adapted Agitprop-techniques for professional actors, preferred to stress what he saw as a powerfully effective brand of popular ('volkskünstlerisch') drama.[23] But it is perhaps Brecht who offers the most appreciative summary of the Agitprop enterprise. The questions asked by those involved in Agitprop about the relationship between revolutionary action and theatrical enactment were often substantially the same as the questions asked by Brecht. It is tempting to wonder how far his own — more enduring — answers were influenced by theirs:

> So-called Agitprop-art, at which some — not the best — noses turn up, was a treasure-trove of novel artistic techniques and modes of expression. Long-forgotten, impressive elements from periods when art was genuinely a people's art re-appear, boldly adapted to new social purposes. Daring abbreviations and compressions, beautiful simplifications — there was often a surprising elegance and crispness and an unwavering awareness of complex issues.[24]

NOTES

1. Ludwig Hoffmann and Daniel Hoffmann-Ostwald (eds.), *Deutsches Arbeitertheater 1918–1933*, Berlin, 1977³, Bd. II, pp. 454–5. This work, the most important collection of Agitprop plays and material, is abbreviated henceforth as DA.

2. Hans-Jürgen Grune, 'Dein Auftritt, Genosse! Das Agitproptheater — eine proletarische Massenbewegung', *Wem Gehört die Welt? Kunst und Gesellschaft in der Weimarer Republik*, Neue Gesellschaft für bildende Kunst, Berlin, 1977, pp. 432–40 (quoted p. 432).

3. The 'Rote Schmiede' troupe of Halle for instance, had a repertoire of about 50 scenes and songs which were, in the words of a member, 'ständig aktualisiert' (constantly brought up to date) (Inge Lammel (ed.), *Lieder der Agitprop-Truppen vor 1945, Das Lied — im Kampf geboren*, Heft 2, Leipzig, 1959, p. 84).

4. Friedrich Wolfgang Knellessen, *Agitation auf der Bühne. Das politische Theater der Weimarer Republik*, Emsdetten, 1970, p. 278.

5. *Arbeiterbühne und Film*, Jg. XVII (1930), Nr. 6, pp. 6–7. The journal, which has been reprinted (ed. Rolf Henke and Richard Weber, Cologne, 1974), is abbreviated henceforth as AF.

6. For further detail, see DA I, 33ff, Grune, op. cit. ('Dein Auftritt, Genosse!') and Gudrun Klatt, *Arbeiterklasse und Theater*, Berlin, 1975. On early attempts at a workers' theatre see Richard Weber, *Proletarisches Theater und revolutionäre Arbeiterbewegung, 1918–1925*, Cologne, 1978, esp. pp. 205ff. First-hand accounts of life and work within an Agitprop troupe are Helmut Damerius, *Über zehn Meere zum Mittelpunkt der Welt. Erinnerungen an die 'Kolonne Links'*, Berlin, 1977 and Daniel Hoffmann-Ostwald (ed.), *Auf der roten Rampe. Erlebnisberichte und Texte aus der Arbeit der Agitproptruppen vor 1933*, Berlin, 1963.

7. The song referred to has survived, its author was Erich Weinert and it appeared as a Bildgedicht, accompanied with photographs of the two, in the *Arbeiter-Illustrierte Zeitung* (repr. Lilly Korpus (ed.), *Rote Signale*, Berlin, 1931, pp. 48–9).

8. Working-class writers 'tended to imitate literary forms created by the bourgeoisie' (Roy Pascal, *From Naturalism to Expressionism*, London, 1973, p. 21).

9. Quoted Knellessen, op. cit., p. 266.

10. *Rote Fahne*, 4.2.1930, in Manfred Brauneck, *Die rote Fahne, Kritik, Theorie, Feuilleton 1918–1933*, Munich, 1973, p. 390.

11. Cf. John Willett's view of the 'quasi-autonomous sphere' of German Communist Party culture (*The New Sobriety. Art and Politics in the Weimar Period 1917–33*, London, 1978, p. 204).

12. 'Neue Bühnenversuche in Sowjetrüßland', *Arbeiter-Literatur*, Jahrg. I (1924), pp. 654–62, quoted p. 655. Repr. in two volumes, Berlin, 1977.

13. The importance of allegory as a vital means of expression in Agitprop-plays was seen in retrospect by Asja Lacis (*Revolutionär im Beruf*, ed. Hildegard Brenner, Munich, 1971, p. 44).

14. Daniel Hoffmann-Ostwald, op. cit., pp. 187–8.

15. On the response to the Reformation see Barbara Könneker, *Die deutsche Literatur der Reformationszeit: Kommentar zu einer Epoche*, Munich, 1975, p. 126. On the response to the 1848 Revolution see Gesine Albert and others, *Berliner Straßenecken-Literatur 1848/49*, Stuttgart, 1977, p. 37.

16. Op. cit., p. 286.

17. Plays by Hans Sachs were themselves in fact performed by a Dresden socialist theatre-club in the early 1920s (reported by Herbert Krauß in Daniel Hoffmann-Ostwald, op. cit., p. 123).

18. Op. cit., pp. 152ff.

19. Recorded by Alf Raddatz (see Asja Lacis, op. cit., p. 95).

20. Cf. Manfred Brauneck, op. cit., p. 297.

21. Helmut Damerius, op. cit., pp. 387–95.

22. 'Einiges über proletarische Schauspieler', *Gesammelte Werke*, Frankfurt am Main, 1967, Bd. 15, pp. 433–4.

23. *Da liegt der Hund begraben und andere Stücke aus dem Repertoire der 'Truppe 31'*, Reinbek, 1974, p. 9.

24. *Gesammelte Werke*, Frankfurt am Main, 1967, Bd. 19, p. 329.

Ödön von Horváth

Stuart Parkes

Ödön von Horváth is of the stuff legends are made on. It is difficult even to re-count the barest details of his biography in a straightforward way. His name is Hungarian; his birthplace, too, was Hungary, although what in 1901 was Fiume in Austria–Hungary is now Rijeka in Yugoslavia. As his father was an official of the Austro–Hungarian Empire, he spent his childhood moving around this vast territory. From 1913 to 1933 he lived mainly in Germany, first in Bavaria (the South German background was a feature of his work) and, then, as his fame grew, in Berlin, where he was part of the lively literary scene that was such a charac-teristic of the declining years of the Weimar Republic. In 1934 he found it advis-able to renew his Hungarian citizenship although he did not settle in that country. In fact, he returned briefly to Germany but within a year he had left it again to live the unsettled life of the emigré, as did so many other writers who were un-willing to remain in Hitler's Germany. He was planning to go to America, when he met his death in Paris in 1938. As he was walking along in a storm, he was struck on the head by a falling branch, a bizarre death that is seen by many as being somehow in keeping with the kind of life that had preceded it. This view is apparently substantiated by the clear evidence that Horváth was a superstitious man and by the fact that before the fateful journey to Paris he had consulted a clairvoyant, who had told him that it would lead to 'the greatest adventure' of his life. A monograph on Horváth even begins with his death and justifies this by saying that there was a 'strict artistic logic' about it.[1] Such a statement is probably best regarded as an excess of what might be called the 'Horváth cult' of the late 60s and early 70s. After his death Horváth's name faded into relative obscurity, although the occasional performances of his plays in the 40s and 50s show that he was never entirely forgotten. The revival that followed the publication of some of his plays in 1961 was so great that he quickly came to be regarded as one of the greatest dramatists of twentieth-century German literature. To what extent he deserves such acclaim is one of the questions that will have to be answered later; in itself this astonishing 'come-back' is another factor that seems to belong to the world of legend.

Horváth described himself as a 'typical old-Austrian' mixture, that is to say the product of a multi-national and multi-lingual Empire. He always maintained, however, that German was his mother tongue, for instance, when he was attacked by the Nazis, who, in an article in the *Völkischer Beobachter* on the occasion of his being awarded the prestigious Kleist Prize in 1931, showed their displeasure by dis-missing him as a Hungarian with nothing at all to say to the German people. This kind of crude criticism need not worry the student of his works; nor indeed should excessive concern with his life or death be allowed to deflect interest from an assessment of his literary *œuvre*. But here, too, there are a number of problems. Speculation about Horváth's person is matched only by speculation about the meaning and quality of his writing. Are his political and social attitudes closer to

Marxism or Christianity? Are his later works written during his emigration from Germany a major part of his *œuvre* or are they to be largely disregarded as of inferior quality? How important are his prose writings, in particular the three novels? These are just some of the questions about which critics disagree. Horváth himself has provided little firm basis for discussion for he made few theoretical statements about his work, unlike his contemporary Brecht. Furthermore, what he did say was frequently expressed in such a haphazard way that some critics are inclined to disregard it almost entirely.

In view of these uncertainties, it seems appropriate to begin an appraisal of Horváth's writing with those works that have received universal acclaim, the folk-plays that were written before he left Germany. The term 'folk-play' or *Volksstück* is taken from an Austrian theatrical tradition, that had been perfected in the comedies of Nestroy in the nineteenth century. What Horváth sought to do was not to revive this old theatrical genre but to adapt it to a changed world. Furthermore, despite what the term seems to imply, he was not seeking to portray the people in the plays in any kind of idealized way. The following brief outlines will show how far removed his plays are from earlier forms of the folk-play.

There are five folk-plays, the first of which exists in two versions. *Revolte auf Côte 3018* (Revolt on Slope 3018; first performed in 1927) or *Die Bergbahn* (The Mountain Railway), as the second version is entitled, is a minor early work. It portrays the hardships of workers building a mountain railway as they are pressed to make faster progress before the onset of winter. Besides showing the exploitation of the workers — the company director in the play is a caricature of a 'wicked capitalist' — the action also concentrates on the engineer, who takes up a position between capital and labour. The technologist's devotion to the completion of his task is presented as a kind of professional fanaticism, a portrayal that is reminiscent of Expressionism.

Italienische Nacht (Italian Night), first performed in 1931, has a clear political theme. It shows how provincial politicians react, or more exactly, fail to react to the Nazi threat, something Horváth saw for himself in the year of the play's publication, when he witnessed a brawl provoked by National Socialists at a political meeting in Bavaria. In the play, the republicans of a small town are intent on holding their Italian celebration, regardless of the presence of Nazis in the town. When the Nazis break up the gathering, the humiliation of the republicans is only prevented by the actions of a group of left-wing activists, who had previously been expelled because they had objected to their elders' political blindness. The play implies that concerted action will be necessary if Nazism is to be defeated; it does not, however, portray any political group in an uncritical way.

That Horváth by no means idealizes the people he portrays is underlined by the title of the third folk-play *Geschichten aus dem Wiener Wald* (Tales from the Vienna Woods; first performed 1931). Instead of the light-hearted atmosphere of a Strauss operetta, the audience is confronted with a series of sordid events. The play centres around a girl, Marianne, who seeks to escape the stifling atmosphere of her home and petty bourgeois environment by breaking her engagement to a neighbour and going to live with the ne'er-do-well Alfred, who has previously lived off older women and various gambling enterprises. The liaison results in a child, which then dies because of Alfred's grandmother, who deliberately exposes it to cold draughts. The death occurs out of town — Alfred's mother and grand-mother are the custodians of a historic tower in a beautiful setting — an indi-cation that Horváth does not regard the country as an idyllic alternative to life in the city.

Another city, Munich, is the setting for *Kasimir und Karoline* (first performed 1932). This play shows the break-up of a relationship against the background of the city's famous Oktoberfest. The recently redundant Kasimir is in no mood to enjoy the event's various attractions. Because of this, Karoline becomes so incensed that she leaves him for another, whilst he turns to Erna, the former girl-friend of a small-time crook, who is arrested during the play. Otherwise there is hardly any plot in the play, whose 117 brief scenes concentrate rather on the characters' personalities and their interaction.

A court case which Horváth heard about from a Munich journalist provided the background to the last of the folk-plays *Glaube Liebe Hoffnung* (Faith, Hope, and Charity; written 1932, first performed 1936). As a preface by Horváth makes clear, it consists partly of a plea for a more humane application of statutes relating to petty offences. Elisabeth has been fined for selling ladies' underwear without a licence. She eventually manages to borrow the money to pay the fine by saying it is for a licence to get a job selling. When her deceit comes to light she is given a 14-day prison sentence. This criminal record also destroys her relationship with a policeman, who puts his career before everything. In despair, Elisabeth drowns herself.

These brief plot summaries show that the folk-plays have many similarities. In fact, a study of Horváth's draft versions reveals that more than one of the plays are developed from the same initial conception. The world of the Great Depression provides the social and political background in nearly every case, whilst the predicaments of the characters, especially the young female ones, are often similar. Even the settings of the scenes do not vary much; cheap furnished rooms and quiet streets regularly recur as favourite locations.[2]

Together with the misery of the Depression of the late twenties and early thirties, Horváth portrays the ominous rise of National Socialism. Although *Italienische Nacht* is the only work with an obvious political dimension, the political events of the day provide an unhappy background to most of the other works. Even *Geschichten aus dem Wiener Wald* with its Austrian setting contains one character, a German law student, with openly fascist views. In *Kasimir und Karoline,* there is a nationalistic doctor, who complains whilst treating the victims of drunken brawls that these are all Germans who have been fighting one another. The policeman in *Glaube Liebe Hoffnung* has been on duty at political demon-strations, which are frequently referred to in the play. The political turbulence of the age is an essential part of the world of Horváth's folk-plays. Even more stressed than the political background are the effects of the Depression, most particularly in *Kasimir und Karoline* and *Glaube Liebe Hoffnung.* Kasimir's anger at being unemployed is evident throughout the play. It expresses itself in bitter condemnation of the prevailing economic conditions and it will not be diverted by the sight of a Zeppelin, which other onlookers admire as a marvel of technology: 'Up there 20 captains of industry are flying around and down here below 20 million are starving. I couldn't give a bugger about the Zeppelin, I know their bloody tricks and I've formed my own opinions'. (I, 256)[3] Elisabeth too, in

Glaube Liebe Hoffnung, is faced with a constant struggle for physical survival. In the first scene, she is enquiring whether it is possible to sell her body 'in advance' for medical research so that she might raise the money she desperately needs to pay her fine. After her imprisonment she is one of the many who wait in front of the Welfare Office hoping for some kind of assistance.

Although the importance of political and social themes in Horváth's folk-plays cannot be overlooked, it is not easy to determine the exact nature of his political views and to answer the related question of whether he is to be regarded principally as a politically committed writer or not. As already indicated, his characters do express political views. In *Kasimir und Karoline,* it is not only Kasimir who is critical of the existing state of affairs; the man Karoline meets at the *Oktoberfest,* Schürzinger, tells her: 'Human beings are neither good nor evil. Of course they are forced by our present economic system to be more egotistic than they otherwise would be, as after all they have to scrape a living'. (I, 258). At the beginning of *Italienische Nacht* the left-winger, Martin, who finally saves the Republicans from the National Socialists, complains: 'the proletariat pays the taxes and the gentlemen of business fiddle the republic' (I, 103). It does not necessarily follow from such statements that the characters are expressing Horváth's own views. In the case of Schürzinger's comment, both the pompous language and the context rob it of any substance it might have as a political statement. He ends by asking Karoline if she understands what he is trying to say: 'D'you understand me?' only to receive the blunt answer: 'No' (I, 258). The credibility of Martin's political views and actions is lessened by the way he treats his girl. He unfeelingly asks her to consort with one of the fascists to gain more information about their plans. When she returns bruised, it is this personal factor as much as wider political considerations that make him go into action to aid the republicans. Kasimir expresses his political opinions in extremely crude terms, as the passage quoted above shows. In view of all these factors, it seems somewhat simplistic to regard the views of any of the characters as in any way Horváth's own.

Despite these reservations, it is clear that, at least at the time of the folk-plays, Horváth had left-wing sympathies. Even if one disregards biographical factors like his association with the German League for Human Rights, a play like *Italienische Nacht* is clearly anti-fascist to the extent that the portrayal of the Nazis themselves scarcely rises above caricature. One Nazi wears an ex-colonial uniform, whilst another is an adolescent seeking to escape from his mother's influence. One of the clearest statements of Horváth's opinions at this time is contained in the novel *Der ewige Spießer* (The Eternal Bourgeois; published 1930), in which it is said of one middle-class character: 'Like all her kind she did not hate the uniformed and civilian criminals, who had conned her through war, inflation, deflation and stabilization, but exclusively the proletariat, because she suspected, without wishing to get it clear in her mind, that the future belonged to this class' (III, 156). In as far as the novel is narrated in the third person by an omniscient narrator, it is tempting to assume that this passage reflects Horváth's own views.

What the plays do not suggest, however, unlike those of Brecht, is any means by which prevailing injustices might be put right. Besides there being no mouthpiece of Horváth himself in the plays, there are no dramatic techniques or external statements that suggest a solution to the political and social problems portrayed. Furthermore, what he does say often suggests that he is not certain whether such solutions exist. *Geschichten aus dem Wiener Wald* is prefaced with the comment: 'Nothing gives so much the feeling of infinity as stupidity' (I, 157), which implies that the events of the play are caused not solely by social factors but also by perennial human weaknesses. The preface to *Glaube Liebe Hoffnung* accepts that there will always be statutes of the kind the play deals with and that conflicts between the individual and society are incapable of solution.

To point out that Horváth does not present easy solutions to social and political questions is not necessarily to criticize him. It is merely to state that he cannot be regarded simply as a socio-political writer. His interest lies equally in the analysis of human character and human relations, neither of which are seen in purely social terms. In general, it is possible to say that the 'folk' of the folk-plays do not appear in a favourable light, irrespective of their social class. The workers of *Die Bergbahn* include the brutish Moser, who savagely beats up a new colleague who has made advances to his girl, whilst the two upper middle-class characters of *Kasimir und Karoline,* the businessman Rauch and the lawyer Speer can only be described as drunken lechers. After having praised the Oktober-fest as an example of democracy, because all social classes mix there, Rauch shows his true nature by ordering away his employee Schürzinger so that he can pursue his designs on Karoline. It is, however, on the lower middle-classes, the Kleinbürger, that Horváth concentrates. He regards this class as the major group-ing within society, claiming that, at least as far as mentality is concerned, the majority of society can be labelled Kleinbürger. In almost all cases, the portrayal of the Kleinbürger is negative. The young male members of the class are nearly always heartlessly ambitious, like Schürzinger, who is willing to hand over Karoline to Rauch if this will further his career, or the policeman of *Glaube Liebe Hoffnung,* who abandons Elisabeth for similar reasons when he learns of her 'criminal' past. His ambition is compounded with an unfeeling sense of duty and with self-pity, which, on Elisabeth's death, soon replaces any sense of sorrow about her fate. He repeats: 'I never have any luck!' (I, 379), when she dies in his presence. The most telling portrait of an older Kleinbürger is the Zauberkönig (magician) in *Geschichten aus dem Wiener Wald,* described by another character as a typical Viennese of the old sort. He is first seen bullying his daughter Marianne about some clothes which have been mislaid — by him, in fact, and not by her as he claims. This incident reflects his whole attitude to women, a mixture of contempt and lasciviousness. Whilst he regards financial independence as a step on the road towards Bolshevism, he takes great interest in female under-clothing during a bathing trip to celebrate Marianne's engagement. When his daughter is in desperate straits after the birth of her illegitimate child, he shows no mercy, thinking only of himself: 'Oh you filthy slut, what are you trying to do to me in my old age . . . It's one disgrace after another — I'm just a poor old man, what have I done to deserve this?!' (I, 232). It is bitterly ironical that when he is willing to be reconciled with Marianne and her child, the baby is already dead. The structure of *Geschichten aus dem Wiener Wald* — the repeated use of the same settings and the frequent repetitions — underlines the unchanging nature of the world of the Kleinbürger. It seems that nothing will improve in the next generation either. When Marianne is accused a second time of having mislaid some clothes, it is her lover Alfred who makes the accusation in much the same way as her father.

Horváth's view of human character, which, as has been pointed out, does not regard people solely as the product of their social environment, appears to owe something to the ideas of Freudian psychology. There is one character in *Italienische Nacht,* Betz, who has half digested some of these ideas. He tells Martin, for example: 'I think you are overlooking something very important in your judgements of the world's political situation, and that's love-life in nature. I've been studying the works of Professor Freud recently, I can tell you' (I, 112). There is, however, no reason to believe that this statement is any more a reflection of Horváth's own views than any other in his plays. At the same time, his own use of such terms as 'consciousness', the 'sub-conscious', 'urges' in his theoretical writings indicates the influence of psychoanalysis. Any discussion of Horváth's conception of man raises the question of whether his plays reflect a contemptuous, aristocratic scorn of his fellow creatures. The presentation of some of the characters, as described above, might seem to suggest this, as do the reminiscences of acquaintances, who refer to his frequent use of the adjective 'tierisch' (bestial) to describe people. In this connection, it can be pointed out that his characters are at their worst when they are supposed to be enjoying themselves, be it at the Oktoberfest or in a Viennese night-club. Critics, too, have accused him of such an attitude, something he was at pains to defend himself against in his own lifetime, saying that he only sought to portray the world as it was.[4]

It would be an over-simplification to describe Horváth as a writer who regards his fellow men without pity as totally stupid and incapable of any decent act. There is one group of characters in the folk-plays that are consistently presented with sympathy as to a large extent the victims of the world around them, namely the young women. This is not to say that they are entirely blameless. Marianne's attempt in *Geschichten aus dem Wiener Wald* to break away from her own environment, which arises from her thwarted interest in rhythmic gymnastics and her unwise love for Alfred, is clearly the result of great delusions. Yet her expression of her predicament in the cathedral when she goes to confession manages to be at the same time almost a parody of the cathedral scene in Goethe's *Faust,* and in its helplessness a sympathetic reflection of a real crisis: 'If there is a God . . . what's to become of me, God? Dear God, I was born in Vienna 8 and went to the local secondary school, I'm not a bad person . . . are you listening? What's to become of me, God?' (I, 217). Towards the end of the play she finds bitter words to express her fate, as she acquiesces in a reconciliation with her father and her former fiancé Oskar: 'I just want to say one thing. When it really comes down to it, I don't give a shit. What I'm doing, I'm doing for Leopold, because none of this is his fault' (I, 247). Similarly, Karoline comes to realize her true situation, after she has let herself be humiliated by Rauch because she felt he might further her social ambitions: 'Often you simply have a sort of longing in you — but then you come back down to earth again with broken wings and life goes on as if you'd never been part of it' (I, 322). Elisabeth, too, before she dies, is able to express her contempt for her former lover, telling him that her suicide is not because of him but because she has nothing to eat. In these moments, the characters achieve a clarity, a lack of self-delusion that contrasts positively with the world around them. This makes them sympathetic, even if their insights do little to improve their material position. In fact, it is only rarely that individual action helps to achieve something good in Horváth's plays. One occasion not surprisingly involves a female character; in *Italienische Nacht,* the wife of the city councillor, despite the callous way her husband treats her, stoutly defends him in the face of the Nazis. Her action, together with the intervention of Martin and his comrades, helps to put them to flight. To find another example of a 'good deed' in a work by Horváth of this period, one has to look to the novel *Der ewige Spießer,* where surprisingly it is a man who does good by finding a job for a girl in danger of becoming a prostitute. The narrative speaks of the importance of such small acts, possibly another indication that Horváth does not see universal political solutions to the problems of the world he portrays.

As has been suggested the portrayal of the Kleinbürger is a major element in Horváth's folk-plays. He is showing the class that, at the time, through its acceptance of Fascist ideology played a decisive role in the history of Germany. It is not surprising that the contemporary dramatist Franz Xaver Kroetz regards Horváth's characters as providing a convincing explanation of why Hitler could come to power. Such cold careerists as Schürzinger and the policeman in *Glaube Liebe Hoffnung* would make excellent National Socialist functionaries.

The merit of Horváth's folk-plays is not simply that they are written about an important social group, it also lies in the nature of its portrayal. Immediately striking in this respect is his presentation of the language of the Kleinbürger. In his few theoretical statements Horváth is conspicuously at pains to explain the nature of his characters' language. He defines it as *Bildungsjargon* (jargon of education), that is to say a linguistic code that has been assimilated by them during the universal educational process but which is external to their real selves. He adds that no dialect should be spoken in his plays, but the standard language as acquired must be spoken as if the character were naturally a dialect speaker. Critics have discussed Horváth's pronouncements at considerable length in view of their somewhat confusing terminology. What he seems to be meaning is a similar distinction to that made in English between accent and dialect. His characters no longer speak a regional language but its influence remains as they attempt to cope with the standard language.

The exact nature of *Bildungsjargon* can be seen from the plays; it is characterized by clichés, a mixture of linguistic levels and occasional solecisms. These are not merely a source of amusement for the audience; their language is a part of the characters' overall predicament. When Marianne in *Geschichten aus dem Wiener Wald* complains about the way she was treated by the police — her desperation has led her at one point to steal — the only response is: 'You can't expect the police to wear kid gloves' (I, 246), an impersonal generalization that allows no sympathy for her previous distress. One of the best examples of a mixture of linguistic levels, again involving generalization, occurs not in a folk-play but in another play of the pre-emigration period, *Sladek, der schwarze Reichswehrmann* (Sladek, the Soldier of the Black Army; first performed in 1929). Sladek makes what appears to be a lofty pronouncement on the role of first love in a person's life, saying 'first love plays a momentous part in life' (I, 502). He then adds 'so I've heard', in this way revealing the received nature of the original statement and reducing it to banality. As Horváth's characters speak largely in clichés, they are incapable of any real communication. They become the victims of a language that constrains all aspects of their life. This explains why Horváth's work arouses such interest in the contemporary writer, Peter Handke, who in his play *Kaspar* presents the socialization process as a series of manipulations by fixed linguistic patterns that force the ideology of society on to the individual.

In the case of Horváth's Kleinbürger, there is of course no awareness of the role of language in their life. It is one of his major tasks as a dramatist to reveal to his audience, which might itself in certain circumstances be carried along on the wave of clichés, what the real significance of the characters' language is. In the case of Sladek's statement on love, the character himself expresses some doubt as to the validity of the statement he has made. Elsewhere, an interlocutor may express what seem to be similar doubts. For example, the Councillor's high-flown phrase in *Italienische Nacht*: 'Our unshakeable desire for peace will repel all the bayonets of international reaction' is greeted by the comment: 'Waffle, you apostle of humanitarianism' (I, 137), by one of the left-wingers. Such objections to others' clichés do not mean that the person making them provides the model of an ideal use of language. In this particular case, Martin's left-wing followers only seem capable of derogatory chants such as 'A fine Marxist' (I, 135), repeated four times as a chant aimed at the Councillor, and a little later: 'Crap! Crap! Crap!' In this context, therefore, criticism of others' clichés is itself a kind of cliché.

One major method through which Horváth reveals the relationship between the characters and the language they use is interrupting its flow with pauses. The stage direction *Stille* (Silence) occurs frequently and Horváth insists that it should not be overlooked. In his theoretical statement *Gebrauchsanweisung* (Instructions for Use), he says of these silences that they show the struggle between the characters' consciousness and their sub-conscious. This is probably something of an erudite over-simplification, as a close study of the play shows that the stage-direction *Stille* is used in a variety of differing contexts. In general, it provides a moment of understanding for the audience, in which it can step back and consider the flow of words at a distance. Thus the silence that follows the line 'then life is a joke' (I, 291), during the singing at the Oktoberfest in *Kasimir und Karoline*, suggests that the opposite is true. Generally, the silences occur within a dialogue. In the 83rd scene of *Kasimir und Karoline*, for example (I, 305), which takes place when Karoline appears to be about to accept Rauch's advances, there are four silences in less than ten lines of dialogue. One occurs when Rauch asks her how much she earns. Her eventual answer is the simple and presumably truthful one that she earns 55 marks a month. The silence helps to underline to the audience that Rauch is exploiting his financial position; if Karoline herself does not realise this, the delay in her answer is psychologically explicable in terms of her mis-placed social ambitions. It is hard for her to admit her lowly financial position. In this way, the silence fulfils a function for the audience, whilst representing the kind of internal conflict Horváth refers to. Elsewhere a silence may simply indi-cate a breakdown in communication. When Marianne tells Alfred the date, the ensuing silence followed by his question: 'So what?' (I, 197), shows that he is unaware of any significance the date may have. Since it is actually the date on which they first saw each other a year earlier, the exchange underlines how the relationship has lost its meaning, at least for Alfred. Thus, in a variety of ways, the silences underline what the language of the folk-plays already shows, the helplessness of the Kleinbürger when they seek to communicate.

In that they without exception fail to provide a linguistic or any other kind of model, Horváth's characters cannot be a vehicle for his critical intentions. Before any discussion of the dramatic techniques he employs for this purpose, it is necessary to consider more closely what these intentions are, beyond the social and political ones already discussed in connection with individual plays. It has been argued above that Horváth's main interest lies in the presentation of character. In this connection he describes his aim as 'unmasking of consciousness' (I, 660). This is another expression that has aroused controversy among critics, some of whom have claimed, for instance, that the term is meaningless, as Horváth's shallow characters have no consciousness to unmask. However, the term is probably better understood as a statement of general critical intent, the desire to reveal to the audience the true nature of his characters, which is nearly always different from the way they see themselves. To do this, Horváth must alienate their self-presentation. His intentions are therefore similar to those of Brecht, namely to prevent the audience from identifying with the events on the stage. The use of silences has already been discussed as an example of a dramatic technique used for this purpose. As such, it differs from many techniques used by Brecht in that the silences are not an external device but a credible part of the events taking place on the stage. Occasionally music is used as an external background to the events on the stage; so for example, in *Geschichten aus dem Wiener Wald*, some of the interpolated waltz tunes provide an ironic contrast to the sordid happenings in the play. Elsewhere music and songs are part of the dramatic context, although they usually have a particular significance. The jolly songs sung at the Oktoberfest in *Kasimir und Karoline* underline the empty futility of the characters' search for enjoyment. An alienation effect is achieved here without recourse to external devices. Even if Horváth does not use the techniques of Brecht's 'epic theatre', it would be wrong to regard him as in any way a naturalist dramatist attempting solely to hold up a mirror to reality. There is, for example, conscious use of symbols in his plays; the white asters in the room where Elisabeth and the policeman temporarily enjoy happiness are a sign that things will not end happily. Furthermore, Horváth is very forceful in demanding that his plays be produced in a stylized way. He sees this kind of presentation as essential if he is to achieve his aim of revealing truth through a synthesis of seriousness and irony.

The combination of factors discussed above gives Horváth's folk-plays their unique quality. Perceptive observations of people in a specific historical situation, together with a technique that allows the audience to be amused, concerned and unsettled at more or less the same time, make up a major dramatic achievement. Finally, the economy of construction of Horváth's plays should not be overlooked. He needs only a few apparently insignificant figures, generally short scenes and almost no interpolated external events to fashion successful plays out of situations of which even the word trivial might seem an exaggerated description.

To dwell at such length on the folk-plays does not mean that Horváth's other plays are of no interest or merit. He wrote far more comedies than folk-plays, concentrating especially on this *genre* after his emigration from Germany. Of the two comedies written at approximately the same time as the folk-plays, *Zur schönen Aussicht* (The Fine Prospect; written 1926) and *Rund um den Kongress* (Round about the Congress; written 1929), it is fair to say that they suffer in comparison, because they lack subtlety and precision. The humour tends to be crude in places, often akin to the most primitive forms of farce. This is especially true of *Rund um den Kongress,* which is a satire on an international congress convened to fight international prostitution. The members of the congress are more interested in living well than attending to the matter in hand. When a girl about to be sold into prostitution appears before them, they show more sympathy towards the unscrupulous trader who is selling her. This criticism of officialdom is balanced by the portrayal of the crusading journalist Schminke — the name means grease paint — whose opposition to prostitution exists only in the realm of theory, and not at the level of individual cases. The play fails because Horváth never gives the impression that he is treating a subject that needs to be taken seriously; on a technical level, it seems a dubious theatrical trick that a representative of the audience has to intervene as a kind of *deus ex machina* before a happy ending can be engineered. Even if one takes into account that the play is called a *Posse* (farce) by its author, it lacks substance.

Zur schönen Aussicht (the title is the name of the hotel where the action takes place) is altogether a more convincing work. It is akin to the folk-plays in that Christine, the main character, is a girl who has suffered and suffers during the play at the hands of unfeeling men. The difference is that she has come into money. This factor alone finally changes the way she is treated; even if it is impossible to speak of a happy end to the play, there is a different atmosphere from the folk-plays where, even if the events do not lead to death as in *Glaube Liebe Hoffnung,* any resolution of the conflicts presented appears temporary and contrived. The socio-political background of the play is also sharply focused. The effect on the characters of the depression becomes clear when they hear about Christine's money. They come to refer to it as 'the good Lord', an indication of the values of the age. One of them, Müller, reflects the political mood of the age in that he combines his belief in male superiority with extreme nationalistic views. Above all, the play is funny, even if it contains elements that are somewhat stereotyped: for instance, the setting in a rundown hotel and the character of the rich but ugly old woman, whose wealth alone allows her to hold sway.

The later comedies lack the focus of *Zur schönen Aussicht.* It seems that in emigration Horváth was intending, or given the nature of his potential audience, was forced to write in a more generalized way. The result of this is a certain degree of confusion. This is the case with *Figaro läßt sich scheiden* (Figaro gets divorced; first performed 1937), whose title shows in itself an attempt to adapt a known literary subject rather than rely solely on personal observation. The play takes up the story of Figaro after the count has emigrated during the French Revolution. Horváth is obviously using the figures of Figaro and the count to write about 'emigration' as such, and the presentation of the boredom and frustration experienced is almost entirely convincing. What this kind of conception ignores, however, is the great difference between the situations of exiles from the French Revolution and those from the Third Reich. Given the nature of Figaro in Beaumarchais' plays, it is also difficult to believe that Figaro would not be on the side of the revolution; despite references to the influence of Susanne, this point is never satisfactorily resolved by Horváth. Eventually Figaro does return to France but he has no sympathy for the direction the Revolution has taken, and when the count returns, he rejects any idea of imprisoning him with the pronouncement: 'Only now is the Revolution victorious by no longer feeling it neces-

sary to lock people up, who cannot help being its enemies' (II, 464). This generalization, in aesthetic terms a rather contrived ending to the play, seems to be a
reflection of Horváth's own views at this period and, as such, represents a considerable change in attitude.

The direction Horváth's views took during emigration, in particular the
influence of Christianity, is very clearly illustrated by his last comedy *Ein
Sklavenball* or *Pompeji* (A Slaves' Ball; second version Pompeii; written 1937).
The setting is the Roman Empire at the time of the coming of Christianity, with
the second version making specific reference to the Pompeii earthquake. Christianity is seen as a liberating force for the slaves in the play, especially in the first
version, but the conversion of their Punic master, the financier K. R. Thago, in
the second version suggests that it is not seen solely as a movement on behalf of the
oppressed. It is difficult to make any connections between the plays and Horváth's
own times; the envy many Romans show towards Thago is, however, reminiscent
of antisemitism. This is somewhat unfortunate in the first version, as Thago
drowns and this is presented as a great day for his slaves. What these later plays
show is that Horváth has not lost his concern for social questions; the major
change is that he sees a possibility of their resolution more through the application
of Christian ideas than through socialistic ones.

The criticisms already made of *Rund um den Kongress* can also be levelled at
some of the later comedies. Two, *Himmelwärts* (Heavenwards; written 1934) and
Mit dem Kopf durch die Wand (Tilting at Windmills; first performed 1934), are
little more than light satires aimed at the world of actors and showing the desire
for fame, the problems of launching a new project and so on. There is one play,
however, where Horváth's use of farce does seem entirely appropriate. This is
Hin und Her (To and Fro; first performed 1934), which shows the fate of an individual without a country, something akin to Horváth's own position at the time.
The main character, Havlicek, has been expelled from the country where he has
lived for many years because he has become unemployed. The country of his
birth will not accept him back because he has been away for so long. The action
of the play takes place on the frontier bridge between the two countries where the
poor man is marooned because of bureaucratic intransigence. This is a situation
that is truly farcical, yet at the same time serious, as not only Horváth's own
experiences but those of millions of refugees and displaced people both in his day
and subsequently show. He also uses the play to satirize the irrational feelings of
hostility that often exist between people of neighbouring countries. Even if all
Havlicek's problems are resolved in a somewhat contrived way — not only does
he help in the capture of some smugglers and thus gain a reward, he is also mis-
taken for the prime minister of one of the countries by his opposite number, who
has come for border talks and is subsequently so embarrassed that he grants
him entry — this does not matter, since the play is about a state of affairs
that is essentially grotesque. Horváth exploits this to the full to excellent comic
effect.

A small number of Horváth's plays do not fit into either the category of folk-
play or comedy. These include the Sladek plays, already referred to (first version:
Sladek, oder Die schwarze Armee; Sladek, or The Black Army; written 1928).
Sladek is a young man who is recruited into one of the illegal right-wing armies
that flourished in the early years of the Weimar Republic. The first version con-

sists of a series of loosely connected scenes which make up a chronicle of the time. In the second version, the events are more compressed. Instead of being imprisoned and finally allowed to emigrate, Sladek is killed during an attack on the private army by regular soldiers. Because of this, the play becomes less of a realistic chronicle. The nature of justice in the Weimar Republic is, for instance, no longer a theme. When Sladek is tried in the first version, it is for the murder of his landlady, which is treated as a 'normal' murder and not as the politically moti- vated one it was. The court is unwilling to accept that there were any private armies, because the people who were behind them, members of the same social class as the judiciary, no longer wish to be reminded of their existence. They now prefer to undermine the Weimar system from within. These antidemocratic forces are heavily criticized by Horváth; it is, however, problematical that the leader of the private army, whose extreme nationalistic ideas make him reject any kind of compromise with the Weimar state, assumes by contrast an heroic stature, because his principles prevent him from entering into the shabby deals of his former backers. Along with Sladek, he becomes a major figure in the plays, more credible than the left-wing journalist Franz, or Schminke as he is called in the second version. He has many of the characteristics of his namesake in *Rund um den Kongress,* putting abstract principle before practical help. Sladek himself is portrayed as the confused victim of the age. He is the archetype of many of Horváth's characters, who, born like their creator at the beginning of the century, have had their life and development strongly influenced by the war and its after- math. He is a weak person, masquerading as a strong one behind the clichés of extreme right-wing ideology, and as such a victim of events beyond his control. Two plays written almost ten years after *Sladek, Der jüngste Tag* (Judgement Day; first performed 1937) and *Don Juan kommt aus dem Krieg* (Don Juan comes Home; written 1936) underline further the differences between Horváth's earlier and later work. *Der jüngste Tag* is close to being a traditional tragedy. A fatal rail crash occurs because of the negligence of an official, who at the same time cannot be entirely blamed because his attention was distracted by the actions of a young woman. The play becomes an examination of the nature of guilt, a guilt the official finally accepts. The setting of the play is vaguely central European and there is no reference to specific historical events. This is not true of *Don Juan kommt aus dem Krieg,* where a literary figure is put in a certain context, the period of inflation after the First World War. The figure of Don Juan is a per- manent human type, as are the various women Don Juan encounters. The play aims at a generalized portrayal of the theme of love. Don Juan searches for love in vain, defeated by his own lack of feeling; that he should finally freeze to death is a sign of his coldness, a negative symbol that recurs in Horváth's later novels. These two later plays have an abstract, almost metaphysical quality entirely missing from earlier works.

That in the last two years of his life Horváth should write two novels is often seen as a remarkable change of direction, brought about by the decreasing num- ber of theatres in which uncensored German plays could be performed. Whatever the truth of this, it must be remembered that Horváth wrote a considerable amount of prose before this time, most particularly the novel *Der ewige Spießer* at the time of the folk-plays. This in turn was preceded by an interesting prose work *Sportmärchen* (Sport Fairy-tales; published 1924), in which sport is seen not as a means of self-fulfilment but as a social phenomenon. In his stories, Horváth satirizes society's exaggerated interest in sport. He is equally satirical in his first novel. This work seeks to show the unchanging nature of a certain type within the bourgeoisie, it again being noteworthy that in his introduction to the novel he speaks of the 'biology' of this type, another sign that he sees his subjects not solely in socio-political terms.

The novel itself consists of three parts, with the events of the first part, the most substantial one, being only loosely connected with those of the other two. In view of Horváth's conception of his subject, the loose construction of the novel is not surprising. He describes the *Spießer* as a type of person who appropriates an idea only to distort and falsify it. The novel becomes a series of potentially endless illustrations of this thesis.

The first part, on which it is proposed to concentrate here, describes how a Herr Kobler becomes a supporter of Pan-Europeanism. There is nowhere any indication of Horváth's own attitude to this political idea, which was a forerunner of the later attempts to achieve a united Europe. The reason for Kobler's conversion to this cause is that the girl whom he meets during a trip to the World Exhibition in Barcelona and with whom he hopes to conclude an advantageous marriage is in fact to marry an American, because her father's firm needs more capital. Kobler has obtained the money for the trip by selling at an excessive price the old car of an ageing female friend and deceiving her about the exact amount of money he has received. The first part of the novel describes the journey to Barcelona and back and the people Kobler meets. As this outline shows, its main character is very much akin to some of the types found in the folk-plays. As the young man who lives by his wits and, if possible, off other people, Kobler is comparable to Alfred in *Geschichten aus dem Wiener Wald*. The other characters, too, would not be out of place in the plays. Kobler's companion on the journey to Barcelona is a journalist, who propounds his idea of Paneuropa between bouts of drinking, a visit to a brothel in Marseilles and coping with his digestive problems. The language the characters use is also that of the folk-plays. An hotelier twice tells Kobler his political credo: 'In these economically depressive times a German should not take his honestly earned money abroad' (III, 173), whilst Schmitz, the journalist, speaks pure *Bildungsjargon,* as when his explanation of the economic role of colonies is interspersed with colloquialisms: 'Believe you me, if the poor old negroes wasn't so shamelessly exploited, that would be the case, because then after all every product from the colonies would be impossibly dear, because then the plantation owners would simply want to earn a thousand times more right away' (III, 209). The novel as a genre provides Horváth with endless opportunities to pursue his satirical aims. There are, however, dangers in this. Without the constraints that the dramatic form imposes, the narrative becomes somewhat self-indulgent, as when the history of the family of the editor of a pocket dictionary is related in excessive detail. The language of the narrative, too, is problematical, often being hardly different from the jargon of the characters. A description of the sea is one example of this:

> Outside was the sea, our maternal source. It is supposed, you see, to have
> been the sea in which many hundreds of million years ago life originated, in
> order to crawl out later on to the land, on which it evolves higher and higher

in that wonderfully complicated way, because it is forced to adapt in order
not to come to a halt. (III, 205)

As a statement of the narrator rather than a reflection of the thoughts of a character, such a jargon-riddled passage serves little purpose. The result of this unrestrained kind of writing, together with Horváth's conception of the *Spießer* as
an unchanging type, is that the novel, although amusing in parts, becomes
repetitive, almost a series of anecdotes around the given theme.

Horváth's two later novels are very different from their predecessor. Both
attracted considerable attention at the time of their publication and the second
one, *Ein Kind unserer Zeit* (A Child of our Time; published 1937), was even
translated into Chinese. Its forerunner, *Jugend ohne Gott* (Youth without God;
published 1937), has as its narrator a teacher in a fascist state, whose attitude
changes from one of passive dislike of the régime, resulting from his wish not to
lose the security of his job, to a hostility that finally leads him to emigrate. The
plot of the novel has many aspects that are reminiscent of a *novella*. The central
incident is a murder that takes place in a schoolboy para-military camp; the rest
of the work shows how the truth about this incident comes to light. The narrator
feels implicated in the events because he delays acting to resolve a quarrel between
two boys, one of whom is the victim of the murder. He sees this projected action
at the time as a way of thwarting God. After the murder he comes to realize the
true power of God and is willing to submit himself to His will. This is another
aspect of his development: from indifference towards religion to awareness of
God. The God that he learns to respect is presented as a terrible, almighty force
with little compassion. The significance Horváth attaches to religion is already
visible in the novel's title, in itself an indication of the growing importance of
metaphysical themes in his later works.

The title also raises the question of Horváth's attitude towards the young
people in the novel, the implication being that their lack of religion has a detri-
mental effect on their character. This is confirmed by the narrator's portrayal,
which is largely negative. They are seen in general as all too willing followers of
fascist ideology. This presentation has been criticized as implying that Horváth
is blaming the children for the horrors of the fascist state, when the fascist state
should be blamed for the nature of the children. Against this, it can be pointed
out that there is one group of children in the novel who have formed a club which
is opposed to the present state and dedicated to truth. Nor are the children's
parents presented in any better light. The teacher has long fallen foul of the
parents of the boy who is eventually murdered, because he has had the temerity to
suggest that negroes are human. A letter from the boy's mother to her son at camp
contains a revealing mixture of sentimentality and brutality:

> Just think, Mandy died yesterday. The day before he was still hopping about
> his little cage so happily and cheerfully and was chirping for our delight . . .
> Father sends you his love. You should just report it to him every time the
> teacher makes remarks like that about the negroes. Father will break his neck.
> (II, 328)

Such a passage suggests that parental influence has been a factor in making the
boys what they are. Furthermore, it would be wrong to assume an exact affinity

between the narrator and Horváth. There is, for instance, an implied rebuke for the narrator when he is reminded of the dreadful fate of the murdered boy, something he admits to have forgotten in his search for the murderer.

Whatever doubts there may be about the nature of Horváth's diagnosis of the ills of fascism, *Jugend ohne Gott* is a gripping story. It is written in a terse style, divided into short chapters and sentences. It does not, however, seek to recount the events that take place in a strictly realistic way. The narrator's interpretation of these events, which is influenced by the changes in his attitudes, provides a major dimension of the narrative, which comes to acquire a symbolic level. The most effective symbol is that of 'coldness', the coldness of the murderer coming to symbolize the coldness of the age. At times, the symbolic elements are less effective; one wonders why Eva, a local girl the boys meet at camp, apparently comes to symbolize both womanhood and nature for the narrator. In general though, the symbolic style contributes to the power of a novel which had few equals at the time of its writing.

Horváth's second novel of the period, *Ein Kind unserer Zeit,* also traces a change of attitude by an individual in a fascist society. This time, the narrator is a soldier, who at the beginning of the novel fully identifies with the ideology of the state. His disillusionment begins after he is wounded during an attack on a neighbouring country and he is eventually forced to leave the army. He finally freezes to death in a park after he has murdered the book-keeper, who was responsible for dismissing a girl he once loved. This girl is now in prison for having an illegal abortion. The change that takes place in the narrator's mind is not solely the result of his being injured; he too experiences a religious awakening thanks to the influence of a nurse who cares for him after his accident. This religious experience is not, however, very deep; nor indeed is his general change of attitude. Although he has reversed some of his opinions, he still expresses himself like the soldier of the fascist state he once was. For example, after regarding the individual initially as worthless, he comes to stress his importance. He adds: 'And whoever says anything different deserves to be exterminated, fully and utterly' (III, 511). This is still the language of a fascist. The limited extent of the change is entirely convincing; the nature of the soldier's death is equally appropriate. Once again, Horváth is using coldness to symbolize the condition of a person corrupted by the influence of an uncaring society.

In view of the nature of the narrator, there is no danger of identifying him with Horváth himself. Only in the last sentences, when he is allowed to speak after his death, does it seem that it is really Horváth speaking. The plea for compassion to the reader 'Do not curse me' (III, 515) is not out of place and belies the view that Horváth is uncaring towards his characters. The final sentence: 'Just bear in mind: he didn't know how to do anything different, he was just a child of his time' (III, 515), is a reflection of the title, which shows that Horváth is still concerned to relate his work to its socio-political background. What he does is to give a generalized picture of a fascist dictatorship. The attack on the neighbouring country, for instance, in which the soldier is wounded, cannot be said to be a description of any specific historical event of the 1930s, but it reflects the nature of a fascist state in that it combines aggression and racialism. Equally significant is that the word *Führer* used in the singular in an early version is used in the plural in the final one. It is principally through the attitudes of the soldier that the picture of fascism is built up. His pride in his uniform results from the poverty and unemployment of his earlier life; the security it provides means that he is not concerned about the people who are making big profits out of supplying the army. Such details give a wider view of the nature of fascism than is found in *Jugend ohne Gott,* where the murder and subsequent events come to dominate the novel.

This is not to say that *Ein Kind unserer Zeit* should be regarded as a contribution to academic discussion on the nature of fascism. Even if there is less emphasis on plot than in the previous novel, it is convincing as a work of art. This is primarily because of the choice of narrative viewpoint. Horváth's use of language makes the soldier come alive as a credible figure of his age. Furthermore, several aspects of the novel are skilfully structured, for example the relationship between the narrator and his father. When he is filled with patriotic fervour, he despises his father for his different political persuasions and for the subservience of his job as a waiter. It does not of course occur to him that he is even more subservient as a soldier. Later when his opinions are changing, his father becomes filled with nationalistic pride at the conquest of the neighbouring country. In general, *Ein Kind unserer Zeit* is less ambitious than *Jugend ohne Gott,* but together they show that Horváth is to be taken seriously as a novelist. Before his untimely death another novel was planned: *Adieu Europa* (Farewell Europe), the title indicating his own intention to go to America. This frenzy of activity is explicable in the light of what he wrote to a fellow writer Franz Theodor Csokor at this time:

> The main thing, my dear good friend, is: work! And again: work! And once more: work! Our life is work — without it we have no life any more. It does not matter whether we experience the victory of our work, or even whether it is noticed. It does not matter a jot, as long as our work is dedicated to truth and justice. (IV, 631)

At the beginning of this survey a number of points were raised, which have not all been fully dealt with. On the question of Horváth's social and political attitudes, it is clear that a change took place in the 1930s, left-wing sympathies giving way to more Christian ones, although the previous social concern does not disappear. A change of style away from that of the folk-plays, possibly an inevitable result of emigration, accompanies this. The result is that the combination of factors that characterizes the folk-plays is lost and with it their penetrative power as a precise analysis of a social class in a specific social situation. The generally held view that the later plays are of less merit is correct.

A final point that requires an explanation is Horváth's sudden rediscovery in the 1960s. One simple reason might be that the discontinuity in German literature brought about by the Nazi era would inevitably lead to some authors being temporarily forgotten. This is not, however, a satisfactory explanation of the phenomenon. The negative reaction to the rare productions of Horváth's work in Germany in the 50s reflects that time, when the main emphasis was on the material rebuilding of the country and anything that smacked of the unhappy days of the depression and the Third Reich was shunned. By the middle 60s this had changed. A new generation of West German writers like Martin Walser and Siegfried Lenz had already written plays about the Third Reich; their dramatic techniques owed much to the influence of Brecht. People were now willing to confront the past again and to accept the kind of critical stance evident in most of Horváth's plays. In the late 60s there followed a spate of regional plays, in which the regions were not glorified as examples of an uncorrupted world but whose major aim was critical realism. Since Bavaria is the part of Germany that has the most clearly defined regional culture, it is not surprising that many of these plays were set there. One of the plays in Martin Sperr's Bavarian Trilogy, *Jagdszenen aus Niederbayern* (Hunting Scenes from Lower Bavaria), deals with discrimination against homosexuals. With his Bavarian connections, Horváth was a forerunner of this development, as was his contemporary Marieluise Fleisser, another Bavarian whose plays were revived at much the same time as Horváth's. An era whose art was marked by a realistic and critical portrayal of social and political questions naturally took a great interest in Horváth's work.

Now, almost ten years after the height of this Horváth revival, it is necessary to consider what the lasting merit of his work is and what general interest it has, especially to the non-specialist in German literature. The folk-plays and novels at least retain their interest as a picture of the age they were written in. At the same time, they are more than historical documents. It is the portrayal of character, particularly in the folk-plays, that gives Horváth's works their significance. A salient feature of many of his characters is their total misunderstanding of their situation; they conceal or seek to conceal this from themselves in many ways but most especially through their language. These attempts to escape the truth often provide the comic elements in Horváth's work. Yet they also reveal the reality of the characters' position, their helplessness in a world where they are the victims of events beyond their control. Because of this, Horváth's work is often marked by a tension between comic and serious elements which gives it its particular power. The contrast between appearance and reality is the source of this tension; it would be a brave or foolish person who would say that the gap between many people's conception of themselves and their real situation was not equally wide today.

NOTES

1. D. Hildebrandt, *Ödön von Horváth in Selbstzeugnissen und Bilddokumenten*, Reinbek, 1975.
2. This is pointed out by Elizabeth Gough in a dissertation, part of which is reproduced in: (ed) D. Hildebrandt and T. Krischke, *Über Ödön von Horváth*, Frankfurt am Main, 1972.
3. All references to Horváth's works are taken from *Gesammelte Werke*, Frankfurt am Main, 1970/71.
4. Horváth states this in an interview with Willi Cronauer which is reproduced at the beginning of his collected works. (*Gesammelte Werke*, Frankfurt am Main, 1970/71).

The translations from Horváth's works are mine, with the exception of those from *Geschichten aus dem Wiener Wald*. These are from the translation by Christopher Hampton. (London, 1977).

Brecht's Plays of the Weimar Period
R. C. Speirs

Whenever a list is made of the 'representative' writers and artists of the Weimar Republic the name of Bertolt Brecht always figures prominently. Yet, when one asks in what sense he was representative of the period one soon encounters problems. If, for example, public resonance is used as a criterion the evidence is contradictory. On the one hand his *Dreigroschenoper* (The Threepenny Opera) enjoyed a degree of success in 1928 which has become an established part of the legend of the 'golden twenties'. Although not quite such a 'smash hit' as the *Threepenny Opera,* his theatrical debut with *Trommeln in der Nacht* (Drums in the Night) in 1922 was also popular with critics and public alike, both in Munich and Berlin. On the other hand, both of these works were untypical of Brecht's twenties writing in certain important respects, and this 'untypicality' may help to explain why they enjoyed far greater success with the public than any of his other plays. If the term 'representative' is used in the sense of being typical of current literary trends, the difficulties in applying it to Brecht do not become any less. In the first place, the literary life of the Weimar Republic was so varied that one cannot properly speak of a period style. In addition to this, Brecht's own literary production and the attitudes to life he expressed outside of literature were so many-sided, complex, even contradictory, that it is difficult to generalize about them. Consequently, the relations of any given work of his to its social and cultural contexts are particularly resistant to short and simple description. Because the subject of Brecht's place in the literary life of the Weimar Republic is such a tangled one, the path beaten through it here is bound to be fairly rough and ready.

Like the Weimar Republic itself, Brecht's first mature play, *Baal* (first draft, 1918), was a product of the First World War. In the first instance this 'dramatic biography' of an anarchic poet with an astounding appetite for life was a reaction to the years of multiple deprivation which the War inflicted on the populations of the combatant countries. Although Brecht was fortunate enough to be spared active service, he could not escape his share of the general misery of the War years. Hermann Hesse's 'novella', *Klingsors letzter Sommer* (Klingsor's Last Summer), written just one year later than the first draft of *Baal,* and read with pleasure by Brecht, took a similar artist figure for its hero and expressed the same intense hunger for experience. Hesse recalled the mood which underlay his story thus: 'Every one of us had the feeling that he had lost and missed out on something, a piece of life, a piece of the self, a piece of development, adaptation and "savoir vivre"'.[1] Brecht's close friend and later collaborator, the artist Caspar Neher, who did see active service, welcomed *Baal* as a much needed source of invigoration: 'Your Baal is as good as ten litres of gin'.[2]

Baal and Klingsor both have a particularly intense hunger for life because they share an unusually keen sense of life's transience. The theme of life's brevity and brutality runs through the whole of Brecht's twenties work as an abiding mark of the existential shock administered by a war in which millions of lives, particularly young ones, were buried in the mud over which the machines of war advanced and retreated. The unifying action of the seemingly loosely constructed *Baal* is that of a 'dance with death', a medieval form to which the experiences of 1914–18 had given renewed relevance. As his name suggests, Baal is a figure with a mythical dimension; he is an embodiment of Eros, the life principle, who is locked in permanent conflict with Thanatos, the force of death. Death presents itself to Baal in myriad forms — in the shape of corpses, of course, but also in the guise of social conventions and contracts, or in such images of transitoriness as fallen trees, wind-driven clouds, drifting rivers or the ever-changing but ever empty skies. Yet Death is not only around Baal but is also within him, both as a process of decay and as the energetic will to consume all that he can of other life before he is consumed in his turn. Baal is an embodiment of the cruel vision of life which Brecht had acquired through the War. Yet this horrifying figure is presented more as an object of admiration than of disgust. Brecht's characteristically aggressive response to what seemed an inherently and ineluctably cruel world was to counter violence with violence, to answer nature's indifference to the individual with unconditional egotism. Thus *Baal* came to be written as a fantasy of mastery over life, achieved through a figure whose vitality and ruthlessness enabled him to turn even the sources of pain (such as transience and the related problem of existential isolation) into sources of pleasure and strength.

Deprivation and existential shock were not the only effects the War had on Brecht. When the War broke out he immediately began, as a schoolboy of sixteen, to write a series of poems, stories and newspaper articles of a patriotic nature, urging his countrymen to accept the sacrifices which would be entailed in fighting for the 'holy cause' of the Fatherland. His 'Augsburger Kriegsbriefe' (War Letters from Augsburg)[3] are documents of an intense youthful idealism which he managed to keep alive for over a year, but which then began to sour into bitter disillusionment. This destruction of a set of ideals, which centred on a religiously coloured conception of service to the community, was the third main injury which Brecht suffered at the hands of the War. *Baal* is a vision of a life lived entirely without the help of any belief in a saving ideal. Baal is an animal who 'dies as all other animals die', a bundle of appetites, drives and sensations, a descendant of the apes (he is repeatedly spoken of as an 'Orang Utang') who is destined to become nothing more than food for worms. Although he sometimes dreams of permanence and tranquility in a 'country where it is better to live', he knows that this is an illusory, unattainable state for a material creature subject to the ravages of decay. As he contemplates the corpse of a fellow lumberjack who has been killed by a falling tree, Baal remarks: 'He has his rest, and we have our restlessness. Both of these things are good. The heavens are black'.[4] For Baal peace exists only in death; until then man is the seat of an unceasing organic process of consumption and decay, and the enjoyment of this process is all the 'meaning' there can be in life. The savagery of this view of life as wholly lacking in any possibility of transcendence needs to be seen both in relation to a war in which the term 'Menschenmaterial' (human material) could be invented, and in relation to the grand illusions which had been nurtured in Brecht before the War began. The harsh cynicism of *Baal* was an act of revenge on the part of a disappointed idealist.

Having once been duped into believing in ideals which were shattered by the reality of the War, Brecht was determined never to be anybody's fool again. The aggressive individualism of Baal, who refuses to be anyone's man but his own, is a magnified version of the recalcitrant attitude which Brecht himself adopted in most areas of life. This youthful 'Widerspruchsgeist' (spirit of contradiction) is reflected not only in the character of Baal, but also in the play's implied relations to its cultural context. The immediate occasion of the composition of *Baal* was Brecht's encounter with the works of the minor Expressionist poet Hanns Johst at a seminar on contemporary drama run by Artur Kutscher, a professor of literature at Munich University and biographer of the dramatist Frank Wedekind (one of Brecht's few youthful idols). Having been ejected from Kutscher's seminar for loudly expressing a dissenting view of the professor's latest protegé, Brecht wrote *Baal* as a counterblast to the 'ridiculous view of genius and amorality' contained in Johst's *Der Einsame* (The Lonely Man), a play which cast the late-Romantic poet, Christian Dietrich Grabbe, in the cliché role of the misunderstood, suffering artist. Johst's theme is the typical late-Expressionist one of the conflict between spirit ('Geist') and life, which makes martyrs of finer souls, such as Grabbe reputedly was. When Johst's Grabbe loses his young wife in childbirth the poet's grief, guilt and resentment make him plunge into a life of apparent debauchery, which is, however, one of secret self-laceration. This 'flagellatory', defeatist response to life's indifference to man's ideals and expectations is the diametrical opposite of Baal's tough acceptance of the world as it is, and his ready indulgence in 'vice' and destructiveness as pleasurable ends in themselves.

Although *Der Einsame* caused *Baal* to crystallize in Brecht's imagination, it was really only the starting point for a much broader attack on the values of the many Expressionist writers whose experiences of the War had led them to proclaim the need for man's spiritual renewal. These Expressionists believed that the sufferings of the War were the birth-pangs of 'the New Man' who would herald in an age of pacifism, universal love, spirituality freed from the shackles of a corrupt and materialist past. Their values represented a secularization of the Christian tradition of rebirth through love, and showed the influence of the Romantic philosophy of Arthur Schopenhauer, who preached the redeeming power of art and of compassion. *Baal*, by contrast, shows the influence of Friedrich Nietzsche, the denigrator of Schopenhauer and prophet of the antichrist. Like Wedekind's Lulu, Baal is an offspring of Nietzsche's Dionysius. Baal and Dionysius both embody the world's eternal sameness ('die ewige Wiederkehr des Gleichen'); both are figures of overbrimming vitality who delight in discharging their energies in violent conflict; for neither is there any possibility of neutralizing the will to power through spiritual transcendence. Baal is an unregenerate Old Adam who mocks the Expressionists' dreams of the New Man. His opposition to the God of the Old Testament is conveyed by his name (the rites of Baal were a constant temptation to the Israelites to deviate from their worship of Jehovah), and his rejection of Christian asceticism is made explicit in his angry reaction to a Corpus Christi procession. In short, *Baal* was a declaration of war not only on the idealistic excesses of contemporary Expressionism but also on the whole Judaeo-Christian tradition which provided the ostensible mainstay of Western society.

Although *Baal* rejected the utopian visions of the majority of the Expressionists, it retained certain distinctly Expressionist features. In conceiving Baal as a larger-than-life, mythical figure Brecht made full use of the Expressionist author's licence to overstep the limits of psychological probability. What unites the play is not a traditional plot, nor the empirical sequence of a biography, but an Expressionist 'vision' of life's 'essence' as a struggle between the forces of vitality and decay. Just like other Expressionist heroes Baal has his moments of ecstasy, although in his case the visions are violent rather than pacific: 'My soul . . . is the moaning of the corn-fields as they roll under the wind. And the sparkle in the eyes of two insects who want to eat one another' (*Baal,* p. 47).[5] Admittedly there is much more earthiness, concreteness and humour in *Baal* than one usually finds in the frequently rather thin-blooded dramas of the Expressionists, but these differences do not detract from the larger similarities. It has been suggested that Brecht's early plays should be considered as belonging, alongside those of Arnolt Bronnen and Hans Henny Jahnn, to a sub-category of 'black Expressionism'.[6] There is some merit in this, as long as the term is not used indiscriminately, so as to obscure the important differences between these authors: Bronnen, for example, wrote the crudest and weakest plays of the three, while Jahnn was more pre-occupied with guilt than Brecht. Nor should the term be taken to suggest that Brecht's early work belongs to a late, 'decaying' stage in the development of Expressionism; it was, rather, an attempt to recover the vitality of earlier Expressionism and to emulate that of such 'pre-' or 'proto-' Expressionist authors as Wedekind or Strindberg, both of whom Brecht still considered in 1918 to be amongst 'the great educators of the new Europe' (GW 15, 4)[7]. The real debt to Expressionism that is evident in *Baal* should not be minimized, for the freedom it gave Brecht from the constraints of Naturalism, and the courage to use symbolic techniques as a means of giving the modern theatre the generality of reference he considered characteristic of 'the major form of drama' in all ages, was to remain a cornerstone of his writing throughout the twenties, and even beyond.

With the outbreak of the 'German Revolution' in November 1918, it seemed possible that various hopes for a radical change in German society might be realized. Some of the Expressionist idealists (Landauer, Toller, Mühsam) even found themselves at the centre of revolutionary political activity when a short-lived 'soviet republic' came into being in Bavaria. In the event, however, the German Revolution achieved neither the dictatorship of the proletariat which was the aim of the Communists, nor the spiritual renewal which was the utopian goal of the Expressionists, but rather the abdication of the Emperor and the creation of a parliamentary democracy. Nevertheless, Expressionist dramas dealing with revolt and revolution enjoyed their theatrical heyday in the first years of the new republic. By 1922, however, both public and critics had grown decidedly tired of plays elaborating the abstract dialectics of revolution. The Expressionists' visionary pathos had come to appear increasingly irrelevant to the day-to-day problems of sheer survival in a country where rampant inflation, unemployment and black marketeering had made the resigned acceptance of man's unchanging fallibility seem more appropriate than any enthusiastic belief in change. The success in 1922 of Brecht's second play, *Trommeln in der Nacht* (Drums in the Night), which ends with the hero taking his cynical farewell of the revolution, reflected this change in the public's mood. Yet there was irony in this success, for when Brecht began to write the play in 1919 his object was to deride the rhetorical, idealistic type of Expressionist play and to insult the bourgeois public who might applaud such plays in the theatre but had no intention of permitting any kind of radical change to occur in reality. By the time the play came to be performed, however, the public's own satiation with theatrical idealism meant that *Drums in the Night* could be received with approval by the very people it had been originally intended to provoke.[8]

Brecht's polemic against Expressionism was conveyed both through the hero's explicit rejection of the claims of an 'Idee' on his loyalty, and through the form of *Drums in the Night.* The clear message of the play was that revolution was no more than a dangerous indulgence in romanticism and therefore quite contrary to the interests of the man in the street. Throughout the course of the action the returning infantryman Kragler is shown to endanger his chances of winning back his girlfriend from the stay-at-home war-profiteer Murk whenever he allows himself to become infected by the mood of hysteria prevailing throughout post-war German society, amongst the panic-stricken bourgeoisie as much as their enemies. In order to be able to perceive and defend his true interests Kragler has to learn to behave in a 'sachlich' (sober, controlled, realistic) manner, accepting that life with Anna (even if she has been made pregnant by Murk) is a better and more humane choice to make than an 'honourable' but fruitless death on the barricades. This anti-Expressionist argument was reinforced by the style and structure of the play. Instead of the abstract settings and symbolic figures of the Expressionist drama, Brecht presented an observed contemporary situation and described the difficulties in adjusting to it of an ordinary soldier, who has endured four years in a POW camp; instead of a loose sequence of scenes illustrating a spiritual development or abstract dialectic, Brecht presented a play with five acts and the conventional plot of one man's struggle with another for possession of a woman. These relatively realistic and conventional features of the play provided a foil for the playwright's travesties of Expressionism. He employed sets painted in the Expressionistic 'diagonal' manner, for example, and an all-too-obviously symbolic red moon, which glowed automatically whenever Kragler appeared on stage, so as to convey visually the 'Expressionist' (i.e. hysterical) atmosphere which Kragler encounters on his return to Berlin. At the end of the play Kragler is made to knock down the artificial moon into an equally artificial river in order to signal his emancipation from the melodramatic, illusory clichés which govern the behaviour of most of the other characters, and which have all but prevented him from achieving happiness. Whereas Kragler eventually learns to follow his genuine feelings instead of the lines of the role assigned to him in the 'Theater' which all around him are playing, his earlier failure to resist that role was signalled verbally by the collapse of his speech into helpless Expressionistic stammering. His incoherence at such points was aggravated by the influence of alcohol. Seen in the context of the concrete struggles of the period, so Brecht implied, the 'drunken' Expressionist manner was merely the voice of impotent hysteria.

To describe Kragler's behaviour at the end of *Drums in the Night* as 'sachlich' is to apply to it one of the key terms in the vocabulary of the 1920s in Germany. Its general sense was 'in control of the emotions', and it was used in all walks of life to indicate that one had in some sense moved 'beyond' the illusions and excitement of the last few years in order to look contemporary reality squarely in the eye. The term 'Neue Sachlichkeit', first coined in 1923 as the title for a proposed retrospective exhibition of paintings produced in the last decade and portraying a concrete, tangible reality, has been seized on by cultural historians searching for a convenient label to apply to the art and literature produced after the demise of

Expressionism.[9] Unfortunately, the term is an awkward and confusing one since almost everyone wanted to describe his own attitude as 'sachlich', but different individuals and groups meant quite different things by it. If there was a mainstream of 'neusachlich' writing, it was perhaps formed by those works which presented contemporary themes, situations and types with a mixture of ironic detachment, satirical edge and sentiment. As examples of this combination of attitudes one might cite the poetry of Erich Kästner or the mid-twenties comedies of Hasenclever, Sternheim, Kaiser, Zuckmayer, and the many other, more minor, dramatists who were only too glad to meet the public's demand for lightweight comedies, confirming their desire to believe that although one might need sharp elbows and few illusions about one's neighbour in order to survive in a tough world, one could still be a person with his heart in the right place.[10] This type of literature expressed a greater or lesser degree of accommodation to the status quo, and as such it conflicted with the radical discontent which was Brecht's dominant attitude to society throughout the twenties. His damning verdict on this allegedly new objectivity was that it was insidious old hat: 'the New Objectivity is reactionary' (GW 15, 161). It is therefore ironical that *Drums in the Night* has a fair claim to be considered the first 'neusachlich' comedy. Like its successors it was contemporary in theme and setting; it attacked the 'Schieber' (profiteers) who were the favourite objects of 'neusachlich' satire; it had a hero who won the day by keeping his head while others all around were losing theirs; it also showed the hero as a man with genuine, good feelings behind the armour-plating of cynicism which circumstances forced him to adopt. That Brecht should almost always have felt it necessary to speak disparagingly about his second play now looks like a reaction of exasperation to the ironic twist of history that transformed what was originally conceived as an angry rejection of the hollow and cliché attitudes struck in the revolutionary period, into a herald of the sentimental-cynical attitude that became the new cliché in the years of Weimar's stabilization.

America was an object of great fascination to the general public and intellectuals alike in the Weimar Republic. It epitomized the new, the modern world of technology, skyscrapers, booming cities, business efficiency, a fresh, uncomplicated and unsentimental attitude to life, jazz, films, cocktails, professional boxing, all of them things which elicited responses ranging from excitement to abhorrence. Initially, Brecht could think of America only with enthusiasm, as an alternative to the dullness, decrepitude and impoverishment of life in post-war Germany (GW 20, 10; GW 68–9). However, by the time he came to write his third play *Im Dickicht* (In the Jungle), later entitled *Im Dickicht der Städte* (In the Jungle of the Cities), which he set in Chicago, he had developed a more complex and ambivalent vision of transatlantic civilisation as exemplifying with particular clarity the historical process of urbanization, what Brecht called 'mankind's migration into the great cities'. Although Brecht had read Upton Sinclair's novels portraying the brutality and squalor of American life, and even drew on this knowledge for the milieu of his play, *Im Dickicht* was much more concerned with the existential effects of city life than with providing an indictment of its social and material inequities. The setting of the action was 'a cold, unreal Chicago',[11] and the point of view from which the characters' behaviour was observed was one of 'Relativität' (relativity or relativism). (GW 15, 70). This was a somewhat pretentious term, similar to Nietzsche's concept of 'perspectivism', and was used by Brecht to describe the effects of human individuation. He saw each individual as isolated from all others by his unique personal disposition. Although a person's psychology might be grasped intellectually by another person as the 'typical' product of various circumstances, actual subjective experiences were incapable of being shared: 'every man is the best one in his skin', i.e. each man's life is his own, private affair. The main interest of the play lies in its particular application of the themes of subjective relativism and isolation to the conditions of modern urban life.

The jungle image in the title of the play expresses the young Brecht's conviction that, though they live in cities, men are still driven by the same instincts as their ancestors, the apes. The chief of these instincts is the will to power which, in the animal world, issues in the struggle to master a hostile environment, but also in competition with other animals of the same type. In man this will has operated unusually successfully thanks to his superior intellect; its visible achievements are the forms of civilization through which man exploits the rest of nature, and within which individuals can assert their supremacy over other individuals. However, man's intellect is an ambiguous distinction, since it can undermine the achievements of the will by making men aware of the imperfections in their creations or, worse still, by prompting man to ask what the ultimate object of all his activity is. The resultant boredom with material achievements is what gives rise to the wild 'metaphysical struggle' that forms the main action of *In the Jungle*. The two principal characters are an ageing Malayan called Shlink, the unscrupulous owner of a successful timber-business, and a young white man[12] named George Garga, who ekes out a living for himself and his family (recently immigrated into Chicago 'from the plains') by working, sporadically, as an assistant in a dingy lending library. Shlink initiates the fight with Garga by offering him money in exchange for a literary opinion, because, having spent a lifetime achieving power and security, Shlink is suffering the effects of his own success: boredom, alienation, a diminished sense of being alive as a result of the habitual insensitivity he has cultivated in the struggle to rise in the world. He therefore devises, as a last challenge for his still restless will, a struggle to gain possession, not of something tangible, but of another man's mind and feelings, hoping that the intensity of sadomasochistic excitement will provide him with one 'last sensation' (D. 137) before his death. Garga in turn accepts Shlink's challenge because, as a poetry-loving idealist who dreams of escape to a Gauguinesque simple life in Tahiti, he is profoundly disaffected from the world of work, duty and material success.[13] Yet, despite their common desire to defeat one another, the fight peters out in stalemate because the isolation and inaccessibility of the private self make it seem pointless to go on. Whereas victory for an ape was a relatively simple matter of leaving his enemy bleeding in the undergrowth (D. 93) Shlink and Garga can find no way to measure their respective spiritual strengths, nor can they even know when a 'blow' has truly struck home, nor sense how much pain each has caused the other. Thus the outcome of the fight reveals the 'treacherous' nature of the process of evolution: the mind, having enabled man to civilize nature, ultimately deprives him of the satisfactions of simple, instinctual behaviour by seeking out new, unattainable goals which leave the will to power frustrated. The alienation of man from man in the last stages of the fight takes the general process of man's alienation from nature yet one stage further. The cold, hard, inimical city, itself an image of the process of 'de-naturation', provides a fitting backdrop for Shlink and Garga's harsh insights.

The escape by Shlink and Garga from a life of deadening routine shows that, as far as Brecht was concerned, the Expressionist mood of revolt had not simply been superseded by the cynical or sentimental compromises of 'neue Sachlichkeit'. Certainly, Brecht's sympathetic presentation of Kragler's 'sachlich' choice of his bed in preference to the barricades, remains in evidence in his approving attitude to the willingness of Galy Gay, the hero of *Mann ist Mann* (A Man's a Man, 1926), to transform himself into a 'human fighting machine' in order to save his own skin. On the other hand, Brecht's continuing attraction to irrational, self-destructive revolt is equally apparent throughout the twenties; it can be seen in his adaptation of Marlowe's *Life of Edward II*, in *The Threepenny Opera* (in Macheath's recklessness) or in Jim Mahoney's rebellion in *The Rise and Fall of the City of Mahagonny.* Yet it is not only this variability of standpoint from play to play that makes it pointless to divide Brecht's early work into Expressionist and post-Expressionist or 'neusachlich' phases: for there are sharp conflicts of perspective and value within each individual play. *In the Jungle,* for example, mixes cold, ironical contemplation of the irrational tendencies in modern man with excited participation in the characters' impulses. This ambivalence is reflected in the style of the play. The struggle between Shlink and Garga is presented through the imagery of the jungle, the boxing ring, the Wild West and the Chicago underworld, imagery taken from such forms of popular culture as the adventure novel, the sports arena (a source of images exploited also by many other writers of the time), and the thriller. Brecht, a lifelong addict of detective stories, was also working on scripts for film-thrillers just before he began writing *In the Jungle. In the Jungle* interprets these forms, the 'mythical amusements of the great cities beyond The Pond' (GW 17, 948), as providing outlets for the aggressive energies built up in man by the frustrations of modern urban existence. But as well as having a cognitive, 'estranging' function, the violent imagery also invites vicarious involvement in the idiosyncratic struggle. Although Brecht would have been horrified at the thought, the mixture of cold analysis and rational excitement of *In the Jungle* is strongly reminiscent of the work of Gottfried Benn, an Expressionist poet of right-wing persuasions whom Brecht detested; ambivalence about the role of the intellect in human evolution is a further important area of agreement. Similarly, Brecht's *Edward II* at times betrays a sympathetic understanding of the savage excitements of war that is closer in spirit to the work of Ernst Jünger (another right-wing writer) than to anything one finds amongst the writers of the Left with whom Brecht's name is habitually linked. Brecht's early tendency to take a very long view of human history, and to describe it in terms of conflict between such general categories as 'brain' and 'instinct' or 'appetite' is also comparable with Spengler's approach to history in his *Decline of the West,* one of the most popular books of the twenties. The continuing influence of Nietzsche is probably the main reason for such similarities of preoccupation. Even allowing that there are also important differences between Brecht's writings in the 1920s and those of Jünger, Benn or Spengler, the perhaps surprising areas of overlap should not be ignored — even if they do make Brecht's place in the literary life of Weimar harder to define.

Brecht's next project after *In the Jungle* was an adaptation of Marlowe's *Life of Edward the Second of England* (1924). Although this may seem a rather out-of-the-way undertaking to engage in at that time it can be related to the contemporary context in three main respects; as one of a number of historical plays, as an adaptation of a classic text, and as a play about a son's revolt against his father. The producer Leopold Jessner had given the contemporary German theatre a lead in developing a bold, up-to-date approach to the staging of revered classic plays. Using Expressionist techniques of stage design and acting he made *Richard III*, *Macbeth*, and Schiller's *Fiesco* into vehicles for powerful statements about issues of pressing concern. Brecht, following Jessner's lead, went even further in asserting the right of the present to imprint its own concerns on works handed down from the past. Characteristically provocative, he advocated an attitude of ruthless 'vandalism' towards the classics (GW 15, 176–84). His own adaptation of *Edward II* exemplifies his determination to have regard only to the 'Materialwert' (usefulness as raw material) of the earlier author's work: he removed or simplified long sections of the plot, transferred functions from one figure to another, radically re-interpreted the central characters' motives, so as to fashion out of Marlowe's chronicle with its concern for the supra-personal issues of kingship, a lurid, ballad-like vision of life as a sado-masochistic tussle between 'pathological' individuals. This use or abuse of history to confirm an author's own optimistic or pessimistic, political or apolitical vision of the world was widespread at the time: Fritz von Unruh's *Louis Ferdinand, Prince of Prussia*, Ernst Toller's *The Machine-Wreckers*, Hans Henny Jahnn's *The Coronation of Richard III*, Alfons Paquet's *Banners* and *Tidal Wave* all belong to this type of 'historical' drama. Brecht's individualistic view was shared to a considerable extent by Jahnn, although the latter's Richard III broods on evil and guilt in a way that is quite foreign to Brecht's wholly amoral, blood-lusting Edward. As well as representing an affront to the Expressionists' tragic accounts of the role of 'Geist' (spirit) in history, *Edward II* was yet another example of Brecht's malicious pleasure in taking a pattern of action used by the Expressionists and adapting it for his own purposes. Here he used the theme of a son's revolt against his father as the starting point for a life of insurrection against all forms of authority and convention. His hero is motivated not by indignation at paternal corruption and a desire for a better world, but by existential resentment at the world's resistance to his will and by his sheer appetite for battle.

The comedy *Mann ist Mann* (A Man's a Man) is a parable about the instability of personal identity. Brecht completed it (in 1926) at a time when Pirandello's plays were being much performed in Germany, but this was more coincidence than consequence, since Brecht had had the theme and the basic shape of the plot in his mind as early as 1919. In his original conception the action had a more obvious, immediate relation to the contemporary situation in Germany, in that the characters who induce the protagonist to abandon his old identity and accept a new one were at that time to be a group of 'Schieber' (black marketeers), whose business flourished during the chaos of the immediate post-war period. By 1926 Brecht had re-situated the plot in a Kiplingesque (but quite fantastic) India, where three British machine-gunners inveigle Galy Gay, a peaceful and ingenuous Irish stevedore (who conveniently happens to live in Kilkoa!) into joining the British Army under the assumed identity of Jeriah Jip — the name of the original fourth member of the crew who went missing as a result of an unofficial raid on a native temple. The effect of this distancing of the action was to accentuate the generality of the play's social and philosophical concerns: again Brecht's tendency was to carry on the symbolic tradition of Expressionism rather than follow the 'neusachlich' trend towards naturalism, reportage or, at least, the drawing of characters/ types from contemporary German life. The unstoppable advance of the British Army through India and on to Tibet was chosen to symbolize the rapid spread of modern civilization across the face of the globe. The essence of this civilization is conveyed by the crowded troop train which eventually carries Galy Gay-alias-Jeriah Jip towards the Tibetan border at the inhuman speed of one hundred day's marches per minute.

However, it is not only modern, mass society that is seen as a machine in the play. So also are the individuals who have to serve its purposes. Thus the stevedore Galy Gay is transformed into the soldier Jip just as a car might be re-fitted or re-built ('ummontiert'). Yet the levers by which the transformation is effected are natural ones: the marauding soldiers play on the hero's appetites and instincts (principally that of self-preservation) in order to make him change his social persona. In fact, the machine of society develops from the machine that is nature. Society as a whole, like each individual in it, is governed by the mechanisms of appetite: it is the lust for 'gold' that brings the Army of the Queen to India, and it is no less important for the Army's advance that the appetite of its tanks for petrol be satisfied than that the needs of its soldiers for food and drink be met. As with the relation of the cold, hard city to the jungle in *In the Jungle*, so the machine that is society does not represent man's perversion or falsification of nature in *A Man's a Man*, but rather a final revelation of the inherently mechanical quality of life. Consequently metaphors taken from the animal sphere ('elephant', 'mammoth') and from the mechanical sphere ('passenger train', 'car') are used interchangeably to characterize the behaviour of Galy Gay throughout the play. In one symbolic set-piece the interrelatedness of these apparently distinct spheres is neatly captured in the image of the mechanical elephant, which plays a crucial role in the transformation of the hero. The point of all this symbolism is to deny that man has any possibility of escaping or transcending his material determination. The mechanical transformation of Galy Gay is a fierce parody of the spiritual 'Wandlung' (transformation) described and aimed at by the idealist Expressionists. At the same time, the intensity of the imagery is quite unlike the shallow, optimistic similes in which 'neusachlich' writers would liken modern man's toughness to that of his machines. For an artistic use of such imagery comparable to Brecht's one needs to turn to the visual arts (e.g. Georg Grosz's 'Republican Automatons').

It has been suggested that *A Man's a Man* reflected two particular phenomena of the 1920s: the introduction of 'Taylorism' into German industry (i.e. the use of time-and-motion studies and conveyor-belt production methods to increase efficiency) and the advent of behaviourist psychology. 'Taylorization' may have influenced the writing of the play, but it would be wrong to place too much emphasis on this. In the first place, the First World War had already demonstrated the power of machines in the modern age, and the increasing uniformity and anonymity which their use entailed. Secondly, *A Man's a Man* is much more concerned with the machine age as a metaphor than with the immediate experience of working in modern factories.[14] As for Behaviourism, there is no evidence that Brecht knew Watson's theories before the 1930s. In fact, since *Behaviourism* was not translated into German until 1930, it is doubtful whether Brecht *could* even have been influenced in 1926 by the new psychology. Quite apart from this, although Brecht applies the model of a machine to human behaviour, he does not eschew the vocabulary of the inner life (hopes, fears, instincts) which it was the aim of Behaviourism in its strict, scientific sense to make redundant.

Where the twenties flavour of *A Man's a Man* is very evident is in the form and style of the play, which show the influence of the silent film farce. Brecht once described the play as 'a comedy just made for the screen' (GW 17, 973) and noted that it should have 'light, tipsy, functional decor, flimsy and provisional. Chaplin'.[15] The basic pattern of the action is that of the chase in which a 'little man' is pursued by bullies on whom he eventually turns the tables; this primitive type of plot could be found in one film comedy after another. Brecht even seems to have attempted to simulate the mechanical quality that life acquired when seen through the lens of an early cine-camera, by introducing an element of stiff stylization into the speech, and sometimes even into the movements of his characters. As usual, however, Brecht's use of a 'low', popular form was anything but naïve. In his hands slapstick farce became a symbolic form, expressive of man's condition as a stand-up, knock-down clown, pushed this way and that by the determining forces in nature's circus. On the other hand, the light, popular form also suited his preference for laughter rather than tears as a response to this vision of life.

Every one of Brecht's early plays made use of music and song to leaven the dough of the spoken word. For *A Man's a Man,* for example, he had composed a song of the same title and had also prescribed that Widow Begbick's daughters play jazz to entertain the customers in their mother's canteen — but also, of course, to provide Brecht's own audience with yet another form of 'Spaß'. But the works in which the characteristic jazz idiom of the 1920s figured most prominently were the operas on which he co-operated with Kurt Weill — *The Three-penny Opera* (1928) and *The Rise and Fall of the City of Mahagonny* (1929). These two pieces were very different in character. The first, which proved to be the theatrical smash-hit of the period, was a quickly dashed-off adaptation of John Gay's *The Beggar's Opera,* designed to make some money for Brecht and Weill and to meet E. R. Aufricht's need for something new and popular with which to launch his re-opening of the 'Theater am Schiffbauerdamm'. This 'lightweight minor work'[16] looks at the world from the cheerfully cynical perspective of picaresque characters who would like to have some romance in their lives but recognize that they cannot afford to entertain any illusions.[17] The hero, Mackie Messer (Mac the Knife), runs his gang of hoodlums with all the ruthlessness of a hard-headed businessman, but allows his heart to rule his head when he insists on dallying with his whores in Turnbridge despite the fact that there is a warrant out for his arrest. This small indulgence in bravado and vanity almost costs him his life in a world where treachery can be bought for a small sum. However, having made his cynical point about human baseness clearly and repeatedly, Brecht (like John Gay before him) finally allows sentiment and good-humour to win the day by having the queen grant the dashing young hero[18] a pardon, which brings him down from the gallows and into the waiting arms of his Polly. Although this parodies the conventional happy ending of operetta, it nevertheless has the effect of gratifying the expectation of a happy ending which is nourished in the audience throughout by the comic tone of the piece (effectively neutralizing most of its satirical potential), and by its presentation of the desire for romance as something quite understandable even if it cannot be realized. This mixture of sentiment and cynicism, which was perfectly matched by Weill's half-parodistic use of popular music, made *The Threepenny Opera* Brecht's most straightforwardly 'neusachlich' work — and paid off handsomely in box-office returns. The bitter-sweet flavour of the opera clearly hit the mood of a public determined to keep a cheerful face despite hard experiences; but this general appeal may also have been enhanced by the refreshing change it offered from the diet of sickly Viennese operettas that theatre and film impresarios were still offering to the public in large quantities.

Unlike *The Threepenny Opera, The Rise and Fall of the City of Mahagonny* did not enjoy immediate and broad popularity. Not only was it a much more demanding composition in musical terms, but it also presented the public, as *The Threepenny Opera* did not, with a devastating vision of the malaise of contemporary society. The city of Mahagonny, situated in a mythical Wild West somewhere between Alaska and the gold fields, exposed the aggressions and discontents underlying the surface of economic and political 'stabilization' in the Weimar Republic. The opera's analysis of the fundamentally anarchic character of all human relations (which is accentuated, but not created, by the conditions of life under capitalism) poured scorn on the notion that *any* modern civilization can escape destruction by pandering to and exploiting the appetites of its members. While the masses of Galy Gays will be willing for a while to accept a life of mechanical routine in exchange for the satisfaction of their modest appetites, sooner or later men with a more intense hunger for unconstrained happiness and with less easily lulled aggressions will rebel against the human ugliness mirrored in man's creations, and will bring down society in chaos. *Mahagonny* resembles nothing so much as a blasphemous *Messiah*, since it draws extensively on biblical stories to tell a story of the Hell man creates for himself on earth (rather than the story of God's providential care for his Creation). The opera is an anarchist's dream of revenge on the civilization of the great cities, a fantastic re-enactment in a modern idiom of the fall of Sodom, Gomorrha and Babylon, with the playwright taking the role of a gleeful prophet of doom. Yet, although the destruction of Mahagonny is accomplished through the martyrdom of its 'Messiah', Jim Mahoney, 'a simple woodcutter from Alaska', the opera does not end on a note of revolutionary hope, but in virtual cacophony, as the citizens march around in confusion chanting the dirge, 'Can't help a dead man. Can't help you or me or no-one'. Even by the time Brecht completed *Mahagonny* (1929) the existential pain which had been the main stimulus for his imaginative work throughout the twenties had still not been replaced as a motive for writing by an optimistic commitment to revolutionary change.

There was a lively strain of political theatre in the Weimar Republic, beginning with Erwin Piscator's short-lived 'Proletarian Theatre' in Berlin (1920–21). Brecht's name is habitually linked with this aspect of Weimar's theatrical life, yet the evidence concerning his involvement with it is slight, and the evidence about his attitude towards political theatre contradictory, but indicative of reserve or even hostility rather than approval. The materialist-anarchic direction Brecht took after his disaffection from the cause of German Imperialism meant that he was more likely to be generally sympathetic to the political Left than to the Right. His personal 'bolshiness' was much in evidence during his short period of military service as a medical orderly (he was regularly to be seen hatless and wearing yellow gloves in barracks!), so that his comrades thought him the right man to elect on to a local 'soldiers council' during the period of the revolution. According to Brecht's own retrospective account, however, he lacked both political convictions and enthusiasm at the time (GW 20, 25). It is true that he wrote theatre criticisms for the *Augsburger Volkswille,* the organ of the Independent Socialists, in 1920, and in this capacity he urged local trades unionists to support a production of Hauptmann's *Rose Bernd,* a play which he represented as having more 'revolutionary' implications than it really possessed. On the other hand, his notebooks from that period express scorn for the 'little revolutionaries, those who abolish the Kaiser and introduce Communism' (GW 20, 7) and strong antipathy towards Bolshevism, not because of 'the disorder actually achieved there [i.e. in Russia], but the order actually aimed for' (*Diaries,* p. 45). *Drums in the Night,* which puts the case for the individual's rejection of revolutionary self-sacrifice devastatingly well, could be read not only as an attack on Expressionist idealism, but also on the partisan enthusiasm of the political theatre which was just emerging out of Expressionism as Brecht revised his manuscript.

In 1926 Brecht wrote to his collaborator Elizabeth Hauptmann that he was 'fathoms deep in *Capital',* yet in that same year he replied to the repeated assertions emanating from the Left that art should become a weapon in the class struggle with the observation that 'proletarian art is as much art as any other kind: more art than proletarian. It may be useless, and it is quite certain that it *is* useless during a struggle, but art does not care about that' (GW 15, 66). The years 1926–29 are perhaps the most puzzling of his whole career. On the one hand he was involved to a greater or lesser extent in a number of Piscator productions (*Rasputin, Die Abenteuer des braven Soldaten Schweyk, Konjunktur*); he was learning to use Marxist terminology through his discussions with the sociologist Fritz Sternberg; and he was working on several plays (*Fatzer, Weizen, Der Brotladen*) which were concerned with the problems in the relation of the individual to the collective or with the mechanisms of the capitalist economy, but all of which remained fragmentary. On the other hand, his theoretical writings in this period were critical of Piscator's 'old-fashioned' (i.e. emotive and naturalistic) deployment of his own technologically advanced staging techniques, while Brecht's completed creative works (none of which were produced by Piscator despite his desperate need for suitable texts) show no evidence of commitment to the proletarian cause before the middle of 1929 (i.e. up to and including the *Lindberghflug*). The lack of any political commitment in Brecht's twenties work is matched by the tenuousness or even hostility of his relations with literary groups or trends throughout this period. It is reported, for example, that he took an active part in the discussions held by the 'geistesradikale' (intellectually radical) 'Gruppe 25' (1925 Group), yet his name does not appear on any list of signatories to the group's public pronouncements on matters of public interest.[19] Independence had become his watchword after his early fateful commitment to the Imperial cause, so that, no matter how much he might be persuaded that the coming age would be a collectivist one, any fresh commitment was extremely difficult for him to make. Hence the relatively long period of his 'courtship' with Marxist ideas; hence also the radicalism and completeness of his commitment when the catastrophic events of 1929 forced a decision on him. It was not only as a good Latinist that he knew the truth of the tag *Hic Rhodus, hic salta.*

When Brecht began to write plays of a revolutionary tendency his work was certainly influenced by his forerunners in the field of political theatre, but it also continued to have a marked individuality. Although he made use of Piscator's technical innovations (the split stage, projections, film, the moving and rotary stages, loudspeakers) he laid more stress on enabling the spectator to gain a complex, dialectical understanding of social processes, than on his political passions. However, such distinctions were not hard and fast in every instance; *Saint Joan of the Stockyards*, for instance, was both analytic and agitational. Similarly, when he began to write short didactic pieces ('Lehrstücke') he did not conform to the 'Agitprop' practice of dramatizing topics of immediate political controversy, but preferred to aim at a deeper and more lasting form of political (and aesthetic) education. His 'Lehrstücke' were written to train their performers in the dialectical mode of thinking rather than to indoctrinate a passive audience with ready-made political slogans.

What I have emphasized in this account of Brecht's dramatic work in the 1920s is his non-conformism — what he himself described as his 'Widerspruchsgeist' (spirit of contradiction). Although certain features of his plays can be thought of as 'neusachlich' and others as 'expressionistic', their peculiar mixture of cynicism and passion, realism and stylization means that the individual plays mostly cannot be taken as exemplifying either trend. It also means that one cannot speak of a clear development in his work from Expressionism through 'Neue Sachlichkeit' during the twenties. This long period of recalcitrant individualism may be seen as the precondition for the radicalism and innovatory character of his eventual conception of political theatre. Had he aligned himself with the reformist, compromising 'sobriety' of 'Neue Sachlichkeit', it is unlikely that he would have become free to develop in a revolutionary direction at the beginning of the 1930s. Equally, had he been drawn into an early commitment to revolutionary politics, as the erstwhile anarchist Franz Jung had been, he might well have gone through the same process of disillusionment and disaffection from the Communist movement.[20] On the other hand, if fewer Germans had shared Brecht's dislike of compromise, there might have been no need eventually to make radical political choices for the red or the brown. Although it expressed itself in an individualistic manner, the cult of irrationalism in Brecht's early plays, up to and including *Mahagonny,* was part of a wider irrationalist tendency running through large sections of Weimar society. Before 1929 Brecht refused to contribute positively to the development of Germany's first democratic republic; indeed he cannot escape some small share of the blame for stoking the fires which eventually destroyed it.

NOTES

1. *Klingsors letzter Sommer* (Zurich, no date) p. 276.
2. *Baal. Der böse Baal der Asoziale: Text, Varianten and Materialien* (Frankfurt am Main, 1968), p. 99.
3. There is a compilation of these early texts in Frisch and Obermeier, *Brecht in Augsburg* (Berlin/Weimar, 1975), p. 225 et seq.
4. *Baal* (Potsdam, 1922) p. 53. An accurate view of Brecht's early work can only be gained if one uses the first published versions of the texts; the versions contained in the standard editions contain revisions which reflect Brecht's later point of view.

5. In the two earliest, manuscript drafts of the play these lines are introduced with the stage direction, 'arising ecstatically, full of sun', *Baal: Drei Fassungen* (Frankfurt am Main, 1969), p. 55, p. 119.

6. The phrase is taken from G. Rühle, *Theater für die Republik* (Frankfurt am Main, 1967), p. 25.

7. References in this form are to Brecht's *Gesammelte Werke,* 20 vols. (Frankfurt am Main, 1967).

8. Brecht frequently spoke disparagingly of *Drums in the Night,* claiming that he only wrote it to make money. Yet diary entries from the time when he was revising the manuscript indicate that he put much more into the play than he was prepared to admit to others.

9. H. Lethen argues that the term 'Neue Sachlichkeit' should be restricted to work produced in the years 1924–32; see H. L., *Neue Sachlichkeit 1924–1932* (Stuttgart, 1970). Lethen's reason for this is his desire to establish a causal connection between this cultural trend and the socio-political effects of the Dawes Plan, which reputedly encouraged the 'Americanization' of German industry. Yet the terms 'Amerikanismus' and 'Asiatismus' did not appear for the first time in this period, but had been circulating since before the War, in German debates on the country's cultural identity. Equally awkward for any attempt to link artistic and social change closely is the fact that the Mannheim exhibition of 'neusachlich' painting in 1926 was already able to draw on more than a decade of work.

10. For surveys of the comedy in this period see E. Schürer, 'Die nachexpressionistische Komödie' in W. Rothe, *Die deutsche Literatur in der Weimarer Republik* (Stuttgart, 1974), and R. Grimm, 'Neuer Humor? Die Komödienproduktion zwischen 1918 and 1933' in *Die deutsche Komödie im zwanzigsten Jahrhundert,* ed. W. Paulsen (Heidelberg, 1976).

11. *Im Dickicht der Städte. Erstfassung und Materialien* (Frankfurt am Main, 1968), p. 134.

12. Brecht's choice of a white American and an Asian as his chief characters suggests that he intended to allude to the generalizing cultural debates still current in Germany at that time. His treatment of these 'types', however, is characteristically ironic, for he has the Westerner become increasingly passive in the course of the action while the Asian becomes increasingly frenetic.

13. The theme of escape from Europe to the South Seas is found in a number of plays written out of the mood of depression that followed the War; see H. F. Garten, *Modern German Drama* (London, 1964) p. 174.

14. Interpreters of the play are fond of quoting the lines, "Technology steps in. Standing at a vice or at a conveyor belt the big man and the little man are equal, even in stature" (GW 1, 340). Yet these lines were not part of the 1926 version, but were added subsequently by Brecht to increase the immediacy of the play's socially critical implications.

15. Note in the Bertolt Brecht Archive, BBA 150/44.

16. According to Ernst Robert Aufricht, Brecht himself described the piece in these terms to him; see E. R. Aufricht, *Erzähle damit du dein Recht erweist* (Berlin, 1966), p. 64.

17. According to the first published version of the opera (Vienna, 1929), the following text was to be projected on to a screen during the overture: "This evening you are to see an opera for beggars. Because the conception of this opera was as grand as only beggars may dream of, and yet the production had to be cheap enough for beggars to afford it, it bears the title *The Threepenny Opera*". Thus the very staging of the opera was to reflect symbolically the discrepancy between aspiration and reality.

18. The notion that Macheath should be presented as a portly, staid member of the middle classes resulted from Brecht's afterthoughts about the piece, which he decided should be given greater clarity as an allegory of the bourgeois way of life. His original conception, by contrast, was of Macheath as a young gentleman, idolized by the ladies (GW 17, 989).

19. See K.–P. Hinze, 'Gruppe 1925. Notizen und Dokumente', *Deutsche Vierteljahresschrift,* 1980, Heft 2, pp. 334–46.

20. See Horst Denkler, 'Der Fall Franz Jung. Beobachtungen zur Vorgeschichte der "Neuen Sachlichkeit"' in *Die sogenannten Zwanziger Jahre,* ed. Grimm and Hermand (Bad Homburg, 1970).

Johst's *'Schlageter'* and the end of the Weimar Republic

J. M. Ritchie

In his commentary on Hanns Johst's play Günther Rühle describes the Schlageter case as one of the 'most neuralgic events of the Weimar Republic'.[1] As far as the history of the German theatre in this period is concerned Johst's *Schlageter* was also the first play to proclaim the Third Reich. Hitler himself had singled out Schlageter as a hero on the second page of *Mein Kampf* and in the last pages of the same book described the occupation of the Ruhr by the French as a great, decisive and fateful hour in Germany's history, seeing it as the first real opportunity to strengthen the German people's will to fight. Johst had been interested in the Schlageter affair since 1923, but did not start to write the play until 1929 under the influence of the widespread Schlageter memorial services and of the interest Hitler took in the story. At that time he was also influenced by his reading of Möller van den Bruck's *Der preußische Stil.* The final version of the play was completed before the foundation of the Third Reich, but Johst's publisher had advised against publication during the Weimar Republic, fearing that it would be banned, and it did not appear in print until after the Nazis' assumption of power. Because of Hitler's known interest, both in Johst's work and in Schlageter, it was not surprising that he asked that *Schlageter* be dedicated to him, which it was, 'with loving dedication and unswerving loyalty'. The première took place on 20 April 1933 in the Berlin State Theatre for Hitler's first birthday as Reichskanzler, and almost exactly ten years after the execution of Schlageter by the French at four o'clock in the morning of 26 May 1923 on the Golzheimer Heide outside Düsseldorf. The National Socialists had taken over the reins of government only a short time before, on 30 January 1933. They also took over control of the theatre with remarkable speed. On 4 February 1933, only four days after the birth of the Nazi regime, Johst was given a position with the National Theatre together with the Intendant Franz Ulbrich, who in fact put on *Schlageter* as his first production. The theatrical overlord for Prussia was the new Ministerpräsident Hermann Göring. In this first patriotic, national drama Albert Bassermann played the part of the general, Veit Harlan that of Friedrich Thiemann, while the daughter Alexandra was played by Emmy Sonnemann, whom Göring later married. The performance of the play was clearly intended as deliberate opposition to the 'decadence' of the Weimar Theatre, in which, according to Johst, there was nothing but: 'Ladies underwear, sex, drunkenness and mental illness. Drama was the most blatant seat of decadence, materialism and bias'.[2]

Present at the first performance, in addition to prominent National Socialists like Dr. Goebbels and Staatskommissar Hinkel, were invited representatives of the new literary cadre which was to take over from the rejected intellectuals of the Weimar Republic; men of the stature of Emil Strauß and Peter Dörfler, Will Vesper and Hans Friedrich Blunck, Wilhelm Schäfer, Jakob Schaffner and Magnus Wehner. At the end of the performance there was no applause. Instead, after a brief silence, the audience rose as one man to sing the first verse of

153

'Deutschland, Deutschland über alles', followed by the first verse of the Horst-Wessel-Lied. Only then did an explosion of applause come, forcing author and actors to take curtain call after call, which they did giving the new Nazi salute. This was clearly more than just a theatrical success; it was a national event. *Schlageter* became compulsory school reading and went on to be performed throughout the land, although for party political reasons it was taken out of the repertoire as quickly as it had been taken up. Plays of this kind, dealing with the real history of the early Nazi movement, could too easily come into conflict with the requirements of day-to-day party politics. By the end of 1933 the whole question of the occupation of the Ruhr was once again a particularly delicate one in the diplomatic and political manœuvring between Nazi Germany and France; hence, despite or because of its effectiveness on the stage, a play like *Schlageter*, dealing with real people and real problems, had to be dropped in favour of the cloudier mysticism of the Thingspiel. Plays of that kind, however, did not appeal to Johst and he did not attempt them. *Schlageter* marked the end of his theatrical career. It was the last play he wrote, and by the end of that same year, he had left his post in the State Theatre after internal squabbles, to become President of the Reichsschriftumskammer, President of the Deutsche Akademie der Dichtung, Reichskultursenator and first holder of the NSDAP prize for Art and Science. His career henceforth was to be that of the highest cultural official in the National Socialist hierarchy and not that of a dramatist or writer.

If the Schlageter case can be described as one of the most neuralgic events of the Weimar Republic, Johst's own career to this point also appears paradigmatic for the period, because of his development from Expressionism to National Socialism.[3] As is now well known, he was by no means always the rabid nationalist and denouncer of Weimar decadence: on the contrary, he was steeped in all the attitudes which right-wing circles most deplored, and only gradually made his pilgrimage from avant-garde literature to National Socialism. His development in fact has led critics to ask the general question, whether there was something about Expressionism which made its exponents especially susceptible to extreme views, and as far as Johst himself is concerned whether the seeds of National Socialism were already present in his earliest works, or whether his later views meant a conscious break with his past? Certainly National Socialist critics did everything in their power to distance their cultural leader from any suggestion of earlier contamination, though for their purposes Johst's early career was disappointing. For health reasons he had never served in the army and hence had never himself gone through the baptism by fire he was later to present as so fundamental a German experience. Far from harbouring strong desires to be a soldier, it seems to have been his ambition to be a missionary, and his early literary efforts, characterized by a cloudy religiosity, were strongly anti-militaristic, not to say pacifistic. In his first published work *Die Stunde der Sterbenden* (The Hour of the Dying, 1914), he was far from welcoming the War in the jingoistic language of his contemporaries; on the contrary, war was denounced, and the main tenor of this one-act play is a longing for brotherhood. War and militarism are equally denounced in the satirical playlet *Morgenröte* (Dawn), published in Franz Pfemfert's *Aktionsbuch*: and other works of his from this period have also been adduced to demonstrate the fundamental pacifism of his beliefs at this time. The essence of Johst's early work has been summed up as follows:

The fundamental themes and motifs always turning up in expressionist writers in connection with the quest for the New Man: feelings of isolation, longings for the brotherhood of man transcending national frontiers, the question of the meaning of sacrifice and with it the challenging of traditional values; and the will to redemption, expressed through Christian symbols.[4]

Yet the step from this to *Schlageter* is not really so great: certainly the readiness for sacrifice is common to both; and for the rest, as L. A. Willoughby (an early commentator on the significance of Johst) put it, the main change was the turning away 'from self to otherness, from the individual to the community'.[5] *Schlageter* was only the final step, identifying this community of thought and feeling with National Socialism.

Between 1914 and 1929, when he started to work on his Schlageter play, the steps on the path towards final acceptance of the National Socialist solution were many, and still had to take him through various forms of Expressionistic excess. Hence his 'ekstatisches Szenarium', or group of ecstatic scenes, *Der junge Mensch* (The Young Man, 1916), seems at first sight yet another typical outburst of longing for brotherhood, yet the transformed New Man's words: 'I will embark upon action' could, to some extent, be understood as an expression of Johst's first steps in the direction of his later National Socialism. Certainly Johst himself was to interpret his play in that way, when he linked the political action of the Schlageter group with this Expressionistic concept of the 'young man': 'In the witch's cauldrons of my bosom all this crystallised and these young men were right as far as I was concerned; these outcasts were "young people" in my eyes.'[6] The two dramas that followed, *Der Einsame* (The Lonely Man, 1917) and *Der König* (The King, 1920), show the next stage in Johst's quest for the New Man. Adolf Hitler was reputedly fascinated by the latter of the two, while the Grabbe-drama *Der Einsame* on the other hand attracted the particular attention of Bertolt Brecht, who saw the production of the play in the Munich Kammerspiele in 1918, took part in the discussion of it at the Kutscher Seminar and felt impelled by it to write his own counterblast *Baal*.[7] It was probably Johst's romanticized vision of the poet against which Brecht reacted so strongly. However, there may also have been other elements which he found objectionable; not only the heroic mythologizing of the drunkard dramatist and his quasi-religious 'passion', but also the antisemitic dismissal of Heine: 'He's a Jew! Need I say more about the pig?' Significantly, as has since been shown, it may have been Johst's image of Grabbe which encouraged the Grabbe-renaissance of the Nazi period. In his next play *Propheten* (Prophets, 1922) Johst once again shows, this time through Luther, a German leader figure seeking a true German belief. That this should mean the rejection of reason and the blind acceptance of faith is taken for granted. To Melanchthon's words: 'Knowledge is power!' Luther replies ('in a hard and triumphant tone') 'Belief — absolute power'. In this play too the Jew is rejected as an object of hatred and contempt. In other plays, for example *Wechsler und Händler* (Merchants and Money-changers, 1923) and *Die fröhliche Stadt* (The Happy Town, 1925), Johst is quite clearly dealing with the same problems, except that by this time he is doing so against the caricatured background of the Weimar Republic; yet it was not until 1927, when he wrote *Thomas Paine,* that he began to develop fully his basic theme of the new German leader, though it needed an incredible distortion of the historical facts to turn the publicist, republican democrat, enlightened thinker and author of *The Rights of Man* into a parallel to Hitler. The result was not successful, and it was only when he dramatized the near-contemporary story of Schlageter and his execution before a French firing squad, that he enjoyed complete success with the now equally successful National Socialist Party. It *is*, therefore, possible to trace a consistent progression in his work.

At first sight the figure of Albert Leo Schlageter does not seem to possess the qualities which go to make a great national hero. As Weiskopf puts it: 'The real-life Horst Wessel was a hooligan and a pimp; only in later legend was he transformed into a lofty figure of pure light. Leo Schlageter was a similar case'.[8] After an army career as an artillery officer he took part in various Freikorps activities as a member of the 'Organization Heinz', one of those bands of soldiers which had grown accustomed to war and could not stop fighting, either against the 'external enemy' in the Baltic and Upper Silesia, or against the 'inner enemy' whenever revolting workers needed to be shot down during 1921–2. He took part in acts of sabotage against the French as leader of the 'Sprengtrupp Essen', blew up a railway bridge, killing some French soldiers, was captured by the French, tried before a military court and executed for spying and sabotage. There seems to have been no doubt that there was treachery and betrayal among the German group; indeed, Schlageter may not only have been betrayed by his own comrades, he almost certainly betrayed them in an attempt to save his own skin. Needless to say, treachery is only tangentially a subject for discussion in the play. Indeed, it is quite clear from reactions at the time that all sides in the Weimar Republic needed a 'national' hero and, despite the unpromising nature of the human material, Schlageter had to serve. The Weimar Republic was even exposed to the phenomenon of National Bolshevism, in the incredible alliance between Communists and right-wing Nationalists, when the Communist leader Radek, in a speech to the Expanded Executive of the Communist Internationale, praised the Nazi martyr, and thus initiated, at least for a few months, the so-called Schlageter–Kurs (Schlageter Policy), bringing Communists and Nationalists together to make common cause in their fight against the French. Political confusion and party expediency were commonplace features of the Weimar Republic, but no greater confusion could have been caused than by the spectacle of 'the strange phenomenon of Communists and Nationalists sharing the same platform, writing in the same newspapers, and even conceding some merit to each other'.[9] What Radek was attempting to do was to react realistically to the confusion in the minds of workers caused by the appeal of nationalism as a solution for economic and political problems. That it was not only simple workmen, or unscrupulous Communist politicians, who were prepared to see in Schlageter some kind of national saviour, can be deduced from the eulogistic manner in which one of the greatest thinkers of the age, Professor Martin Heidegger, Rektor of the University of Freiburg, addressing the Schlageter memorial service at his university on 26 May 1933, ten years after the execution, delivered a rhapsodic eulogy evoking a 'vision of the future rise of the people'. From this, and other such eulogies, one begins to appreciate the reasons why Schlageter became a mythical hero in his own time. Firstly, as Hitler's words in *Mein Kampf* indicate, it was the historical period in which he lived that was important, namely the immediate post-War period under the grim shadow of the Treaty of Versailles and all it meant. The particular event with which Schlageter's name is associated was the occupation of the Ruhr valley by French troops in the spring of 1923, and that meant the illegal presence of a foreign invader on the sacred German soil. Particularly disturbing too was the apparently craven reaction of the republican government to this situation, namely to advocate a policy of passive resistance. It was the soldier Schlageter, who adopted a policy of active resistance and died in this situation, that Johst took as the hero of his play, making him symptomatic for the rise of National Socialism and the resurgence of Germany. Schlageter's lonely death is linked with the rise of National Socialism and 'the people's new beginning':

> Using a known historical figure of the recent past, Johst successfully dramatised the struggle of the Nazi party's fight for power. It brings this struggle to life and effectively preaches the message that the Nazis had preached so loudly and often so violently since the beginning of the movement. The beliefs and spirits which motivated these men find dramatic expression in this play.[10]

Now the play itself must be examined to see whether it does indeed, as has been claimed, contain all the major issues which the Nazis exploited on their road to victory throughout the course of the Weimar Republic. Johst describes his play simply as a *Schauspiel* (drama), indicating perhaps that, despite the death of the hero, the mood is not tragic; on the contrary the open ending, engaging the audience as it does, was clearly intended to suggest a greater and more glorious future, when Schlageter's death makes Germany awaken. The *dramatis personae*, with its limited range of characters, also indicates that we are not to be presented with a vast historical pageant, nor is there any indication in the play of the War itself. On the contrary, the play is set in the post-War period in a largely middle-class setting of domestic interiors in which the university, politics and the army are represented, but workers, foreigners and others are excluded. There are no judges or court officials, hence there is to be no court scene, which is just as well given the kind of damaging evidence which might have been brought forward against Schlageter. Any conflict in the play will be shown as existing within the republic itself, and not as resulting primarily from any external enemy. In the first scene, Schlageter the returned soldier is presented as a student, his speaking manner is the characteristic post-Expressionist style of the Weimar Republic, namely matter-of-fact, *sachlich*. The language is the slang of the soldier-student and accordingly witty, snappy and anti-literary. Significantly, Schlageter is attempting to study book-keeping and economics, something exposed as deeply suspect, if not indeed ultimately responsible for Germany's present parlous state of affairs. National Socialism is now commonly decried as a concealed agent of capitalism, but this and other scenes clearly indicate its latent frustration with the economic pressures of the modern world. Schlageter is being invited to identify the subjects of his study, economics and book-keeping, as false solutions, and return to being a soldier again. His comrade, the flyer and professor's son Friedrich Thiemann, puts the anti-intellectual case: 'Action! Not a glimmer of theory'. Collective decisions arrived at 'round the green baize table' are rejected in favour of a life of camaraderie and action with real comrades like 'der lange Lulatsch' and 'der ewige Emil'. Peace means a life among 'careerists, petty-bourgeois, leadswingers, bourgeois graduates' — war means being together with 'Some of the best, old front-liners, flyers, comrades'. In the old days — 'one look, and we understood each other!' In peacetime: 'We twitter past each other . . .' Certainly many German plays before this had dealt with the plight of the returned soldier, but this time the 'superannuated imperial officers put out to grass' are returning to a Germany which is no longer the same; the Empire has crumbled and a new state, a republic, which has no time for them, has taken its place. Schlageter describes himself as not liking to make long speeches, but of course he does and in doing so he presents his view of history, rejecting all literary and academic views of what front line experience may have meant for his generation. The Emperor has departed and Ebert has taken his place as Reichspräsident, the War has at least finished and peace has come. In the same way, as he sees it, the pen must succeed the gun. Thiemann, on the other hand, argues for the exceptional role of the soldier, as one who does not simply hold a position, but who takes up a position. Using almost the words and images of Johst's own earlier play, *Luther,* the soldier is compared with the prophet. For the time being, however, Schlageter resists this injunction to be like Luther, but it is this decision, based on feeling and conviction, not reason or logic, which he will eventually take. 'Liberal writers, psychology institutes, lecture-rooms, etc.' are, according to this view, not the source of enlightenment; it is feeling, faith and conviction one must turn to. That the situation here being presented is no isolated, individual one is further made clear by Thiemann, who speaks of 'our generation', as one where the young people at a very early stage went off to fight a war of whose causes they were unaware, a war which simply used them. Presenting the War in this way not only avoids all possibility of assigning the blame for the War, it also helps to explain and motivate the resentment which the younger fighting generation is now said to feel against the older generation, whom they find filling positions of power and authority on their return. Significantly this resentment is directed not only at company directors and captains of industry, who have done well out of the War, but also particularly at politicians, opportunists and party officials. For the time being, however, Schlageter insists on sticking with his studies, although, according to Thiemann, examinations and qualifications are useless in view of the general unemployment situation. Schlageter is still no 'prophet', no statesman, but merely, as he describes himself, 'a peaceful farm-boy from the Black Forest'. Thiemann has forcibly presented the Nationalist case, but as in an Expressionist play Schlageter still has to go through a transformation, see the light and find the true path. The play, despite all the anti-intellectual discussion of the first scene, is essentially a quasi-Expressionistic *Wandlungsdrama* (transformation drama). Significantly too, it is this point in the debate which contains the phrase which was to become one of the most famous of the period and be often (wrongly) attributed to various Nazi party leaders. Thiemann has already used the contemptuous words 'aesthetic soft soap', before he finally explodes with the words: 'when I hear the word culture I slip the safety-catch on my Browning'. These anti-culture sentiments do not stand in isolation, but are spoken in the context of some of the concepts most fundamental to National Socialism. Thiemann rejects *all* ideas as mere 'Weltanschauungssalat' (world-view salad), especially ideas like liberty, equality and fraternity. This is what he is reacting against when he rejects culture. These ideas come up in connection with reflections about the nature of 'the German', as compared with other nations and races, the Russians, the French, the English, the Jews, and the suggestion emerges that the deepest significance of the German lies in 'Kampf' — struggle. Imperialism, Catholicism, Marxism, Liberalism, Fascism, Bolshevism, Parliamentarianism; his answer to these complex issues is the gun: 'Kämpfen!! Soldatsein!!!' (fighting, soldiering). The multiplicity of exclamation marks, indicating how the words are to be spoken, is almost Expressionistic. Thinking a thought to its conclusion for Thiemann means *blood*. The laws of life are not intellectual ones of the spirit, but violent ones of the blood: 'We are flesh and blood, and the laws of life are therefore not spiritual, they are bloody! Is that understood'. Towards the end of this scene Schlageter himself takes a greater part of the debate and it is he, who in quasi-religious, mystical manner, relates this concept of the blood to that of sacrifice. Peoples are governed by the same principles as individuals, rulers too must be capable of sacrifice, able to stand the sight of blood. When the German emperor was no longer capable of this, the soldier was released from his silent, holy service. Rule by divine right, the secret mystery of responsible rulership faded, and all that was left was democracy: 'Der Rest ist Demokratie'. No more explicit rejection of the Weimar Republic could be found than this. It is Schlageter too, who adds the final key-word to the complex of blood and sacrifice which will take the place of republic and democracy, namely *Volk* (the People). He will carry on as a nameless civilian and complete his studies, but he does so without any belief in the majority parties which at present dictate the accepted beliefs of the time: 'world community and humanity . . . world commerce and Europe . . . international understanding and so forth . . .'. Such false beliefs can for him only lead to catastrophe and total bankruptcy. Instead of the 'majority', what he demands for Germany is one united people. Despite the quasi-religious language which is so characteristic of Johst's style, this combination of blood, *Volk* and sacrifice is now clearly a long way removed from Christianity and very much closer to National Socialism.

Act one, scene one of Johst's play *Schlageter* is entirely taken up with two men in one room talking. The issues adumbrated are important ones, nevertheless such a long, static scene does not make for gripping drama. Scene two brings on Thiemann's sister Alexandra and with her the possibility of some love interest. She is a modern German girl, who works for a living with her typewriter and is able to quote the latest (inflationary) rate of exchange, 22,000 Marks to the dollar, as a further reminder of the difficult times the new Republic is going through. As opposed to the frontline soldier's viewpoint of her brother, she is able to present the home-front perspective, and she proves as capable as her brother of making long speeches, when she accuses Schlageter's generation of being 'half-heroes', who have been too ready to become republicans. This is one of the few points in the play where reference is made to the Jews, and to that extent the play is atypical as a National Socialist work. In any event her spirited words force the reluctant Schlageter to formulate his feelings. Where before her brother had failed to extract much from him, he now launches into a long speech about the position of the returned soldier as foreign body in the new Republic. His voice becomes charged with mystery as he conjures up a vision of these returned soldiers gradually putting on their uniforms again, to be not imperial or republican soldiers, but comrades — Germans. The scene has developed into a love scene; it is one in which Alexandra makes him declare his 'passion', but the love declared in such mystical, quasi-religious language is a love for Germany, which goes far above and beyond any love he may begin to feel for Alexandra.

Act one finishes with the promise of real action on the news that the French are occupying the Ruhr. Thiemann's comrades assemble with plentiful supplies of TNT and it seems to be common knowledge that the republican government of Cuno and Ebert intend to follow a policy of passive resistance: in other words, as good republicans, they will behave like 'statesmen, European slaves, fellahin, and reparationists'. Schlageter, however, still expects any active resistance to be undermined by the politicians in Berlin, the seat of republican government, which will denounce them as 'Landsknechtspöbel' (freebooting rabble) and 'Fememörder' (self-elected executioners). What is required in his eyes is 'Aktion nach innen' (an internal campaign), the extermination of the 'Weltverbrüderer von 1918' (world fraternity-mongers of 1918), the destruction of parliamentary democracy and the creation of a truly German government. To this extent he sees clearly enough and is gradually emerging as a leader. However, he is still fumbling for the truth, seeking some deeper sense beyond the blind romanticism of the bomb. 'Helotry, officialdom, serfdom and self-seeking patriotism'; these, it is true, have to be destroyed, but his conscience needs a higher authority, he is a soldier who needs to obey.

If the first act of the play fully expresses the nationalistic sentiments and resentments at work in the Weimar Republic, the scene changes in Act Two to the office of the President and to more explicit ridicule of the Weimar Republic itself, which is characterized in the very first words by its constant elections and lack of political conviction. According to the President the vote is merely something one exploits to improve one's own personal position. He himself, his large hands betraying the worker who has miraculously risen to this position of power, is characterized by lack of self-confidence in dealing with the clever young academics and the authoritative aristocrats who surround him. His comrade Klemm, a quick, slippery, self-made man in the new 'American' manner, is the ruthless climber who always knows where his own best interests lie. These are the men who have made the revolution that has resulted in the republic, and of the two Klemm is presented as the more unpleasant for his naked enjoyment of the power his position brings, whether with business or with government circles. Politics and politicians in the republic, in other words, are presented in terms of the worst kind of opportunism. Klemm, the unscrupulous republican politician, has placed spies in nationalist circles and knows therefore of the action planned against the policy of passive resistance. He sees the problem entirely in party political terms as an impasse between nationalist extremists and French-supported separatists. His solution is treachery. As he sees it the universities are the breeding ground for trouble, therefore he suggests that Schneider should use his own student son to betray his comrades. The scene which follows is perhaps the most improbable of the whole play, because it involves a secret meeting between an unnamed General and Schlageter in the President's office. Yet despite its improbability the intention of such a scene is clear, namely to contrast the despicable manœuvring of the republican politicians with the true German worth of the soldier. For the politician tactics are everything, for the soldier duty is everything. What emerges from the discussion with the general (modelled on Generaloberst von Seeckt as the wise adviser and fatherly friend), is a further clarification of Schlageter's position. As far as he is concerned the French occupation of the Ruhr has demonstrated that socialistic talk of understanding between nations and the common brotherhood of man was all so much swindle, and from this he claims that the nationalists have the *right* to rise up, create a radical national government and reject the November 'system' completely. The action will be directed against the false republican government in Berlin, the German people will awaken and seize power. Passive resistance is rejected as a weak collective decision arrived at round the green baize table, which is all very well as far as it goes, as a rational, diplomatic solution, but Schlageter wants leadership. He appeals to the General's conscience, his conscience as a German, he calls for a policy of life, temperament, emotional impulse. At this point the general turns the tables on Schlageter and accuses him of seeking a source of command so that he can abandon himself to blind obedience. He distinguishes between the pure will to radical nationalism, which motivates Schlageter's comrades, who are answerable only to their own conscience, and 'absolute revolutionaries of the Third Reich'. Schlageter is finally forced to recognize that he can expect no support from official Germany and accepts his isolation.

The striking feature of this episode is that it is impossible to accept the arguments presented as in any way a logical progression, persuading Schlageter in the direction of a particular course of action. On the contrary, the characteristic element of this scene, as indeed of the whole play, is that Schlageter is not persuaded by reason or logic: on the contrary, he is suddenly and *intuitively* filled with the mysterious conviction that he must sacrifice himself for the greater cause, Germany. In the first act he had rationally considered his own personal strategy for survival in the post-War world. Now instead he is filled with the mystical conviction that he cannot pursue his own personal life when the fate of the nation is at stake. Like so many Expressionist heroes, he has an illumination and accepts his mission. To a certain extent this places the General in a bad light, because despite his obvious sympathy for the cause, he cannot give the straightforward answer he is asked for. Instead he seems to be exploiting Schlageter's sacrifice for political ends.

The final scene of act two takes place between the President and August. Here, as in an Expressionist play, there is an obvious generation gap between father and son, between the socialist father who has made his way in the world, and the sophisticated young student who, at the university, has come into contact with an entirely different type of person: 'The reactionaries . . . the barons . . . the privy counsellors . . . have got their heads screwed on'. The young man argues that the new Germany has gone beyond class-warfare, strikes, socialism, the internationale and has found another solution to the problems of the time, namely *Volksgemeinschaft* (community of race). August, the representative of the postwar generation, which has no personal experience of modern warfare, artillery barrages, flame throwers or tanks, is a revolutionary like his father was before him, but a right-wing not a left-wing revolutionary. He too believes in Schlageter's 'national arousal', and comments particularly on the possibilities of a Putsch. Nor is he alone; he consciously speaks for his generation: 'Young people like us who stand alongside Schlageter, do so not because he is the last soldier of the World War, but because he is the first soldier of the Third Reich!! (*Curtain*) II, 8.

In real life Schlageter became a member of the NSDAP in the autumn of 1922 and was said to have been a founder member of the Berlin branch; however, as far as the play is concerned Schlageter has so far done nothing to justify this description of him as the first soldier of the Third Reich. However, such rational considerations have nothing to do with the theatrical effectiveness of these last words of act two. Father and son are poles apart. They represent entirely different intellectual, ideological and political positions and there is no way they can communicate on a rational basis. Only the father's experience of French chauvinism will bring old and new revolutionaries together.

The third act of the play returns to the scene of the first and to the language, jokes and songs of soldiers and students, only now the talk is of how far they are prepared to go 'to bring the soul of the people to boiling-point'. Their talk is of 'responsibility', which may mean killing not only Frenchmen (contemptuously referred to as Schangels), but also Germans on the train as hostages. There is still no Nationalist Socialist salute at this stage, so they speak the single word 'Deutschland', as they give their pledge with a solemn handshake in a scene reminiscent of the Rütli-Schwur in Schiller's *Wilhelm Tell*. In the scenes that follow Schlageter, who has now accepted his responsibility to the group and to Germany, is built up as the leader figure, the Führer. First of all August Thiemann comes to warn him that there are spies among them, but Schlageter has a faith that is stronger than such trials, stronger than party loyalty, namely a belief in Germany: 'Die Partei Deutschland!' Though Schlageter denies that he is in any way exceptional: 'I am just a good comrade, a man who hears in comradeship the heartbeat of his Fatherland'. It is this very value he places on *Kameradschaft* that makes him the leader all the others will blindly follow. This impression is reinforced in the following scene by the appearance of the faithful batman Fischer, so that in this respect too the play follows the remote model of Lessing's *Minna von Barnhelm*; indeed to a certain extent Alexandra even takes over the role of Minna for it is to her that the returned soldier appeals for affirmation of his belief in 'Dienst' and 'Treue' (service and loyalty). He appeals to her to give the command which failed to come from official circles. Clearly there is an implied conflict between his private wishes and desires, his love for Alexandra and his need to be faithful to something even higher, namely the Fatherland, and once again the stress is on 'responsibility'. In the past they were the pupils, now it is their duty to teach; they are the schoolmasters of their country. All that remains for Alexandra and Schlageter is a sentimental scene of lovers' parting, as the police close in on the conspirators. Schlageter's 'mad love' takes him away to what he considers his duty to Germany. Alexandra is left behind as the ever-faithful German woman, smiling through her tears. For a play replete with such brutal values there is no lack of sentimentality.

The main feature of the play so far is that it is all talk and no action. We hear what the group intend to do, but we do not see them do it. The audience will not see a French railway bridge being blown up or a train being derailed, nor hear the screams of the French soldiers dying. As has been pointed out, the play is not so much directed against the external enemy, the French, as against the internal enemy. The constant image is of a sleeping Germany, which has to be awakened and united by this act. The play is therefore a typical example of civil war literature:

War literature has to be put alongside the Civil War literature, which from about 1930 on supported national-socialist policies, by carrying the national war-halo over onto the militant National Socialists and stylising the Civil War into a war of national decision. In this way the place of the external enemy was taken by the 'Reds', especially by the Communists. Works which set the pattern were K. A. Schenzinger's *Hitlerjunge Quex* (1932) and H. H. Ewers *Horst Wessel* (1932), as well as H. Johst's drama *Schlageter* (1933).[11]

Accordingly the fourth act takes the action not to the court, which is to decide the fate of the captured German activists, but to the Professor's drawing room, where the *effect* of the court's decision will be shown on a representative group. From the start the possibility of justice for the young men is doubted, for they are to appear, not before a German Civil court, but before a French court martial in Düsseldorf! The French are supposedly famous for their chivalry, but the suggestion that they may well treat the incident simply as the fanatical behaviour of silly young men is immediately repudiated. However, it is not so much the French that the accused have to fear. Germany is after all at peace with France, and the original charge against the accused has come from the German side. Unfortunately Germany is not united; as the Professor puts it, there is no feeling of solidarity, and this means that the French can rely on the support of the Marxists inside Germany. The intention to point the accusing finger at the Marxists comes across quite clearly. The Professor, in fact, makes a long speech in which many of the problems of the Weimar Republic are raised. From a *European* point of view it will seem right, according to the Professor, to stop this kind of behaviour, but in the course of the play such 'Europäische Gesittung' (European thinking), has already been countered by the strictly German national viewpoint. Anything European and international is bad — everything German is good! In the same way the German is said to feel helpless, because the course of justice has been removed from his domain: 'Foreign law, a law alien to the soil in our own land!' In addition to this the professor makes reference to the general state of Germany, which is suffering disastrous inflation to the point where the Mark is soaring in the exchange rate to two million against the dollar. In the face of such figures collapse is inevitable, corruption is widespread and established moral concepts crumble.

In view of the previous violent rejection of culture it is perhaps surprising to come across a discussion of the key German concept of 'Bildung' (education) at this point, but the professor is a teacher of the young and he turns to the general question of education and the concepts he has inculcated over the years, above all love of Germany. Germany seems to have sunk so low, and he has these young men on his conscience, because it is teaching by him and others like him that has brought these young men to their present dilemma. From this long speech it is once again apparent that the Schlageter case is by no means a simple matter of a few fanatics who blow up a railway bridge. On the contrary it is intended as the symbolic crystallization point of all the problems of the Weimar Republic, as seen from the nationalist point of view. Schlageter's situation is presented as typical of a whole generation, which has been filled with 'idealistic', heroic notions of dying for the Fatherland, and which has had to return from the War to the 'vacuum of a Germany bled dry and pulverized'. Significantly it is the true German woman,

Alexandra, who replies to the professor's self-castigation, with words which were to be among the most powerful and emotive in the National Socialist arsenal. *Einsatz* (commitment to action) is what one expects from the young, from the soldier at the front (wherever it is!), and this cannot be expected of the older generation. Nevertheless representatives of the older generation *can* be expected to hold on, to endure, and never give up. In the years to come the German people under Nazi rule were to hear constant appeals for *Durchhalten* (endurance). It is she, too who introduces the stab-in-the-back concept. The home-front must not weaken and destroy the efficacy of the front-line fighters, and, though the war is long over, Schlageter and his comrades are still front-line fighters.

In addition to such 'endurance and stab-in-the-back ideas' one further concept emerges in the course of this discussion, which is a deliberate echo of Hitler speeches and National Socialist literature, namely the concept of the 'will'! Speaking as a general who has constantly had the responsibility for sending men into battle, His Excellency agrees with everything that has been said so far, recognizing that they are all matters of common concern. He talks of 'men of the German life-spirit' and denies that there can be any questioning of the free will behind their sacrifice. Alexandra too refers to the 'will' in this peculiarly German-nationalistic sense: 'the free will has been fighting from 1914 till now', and the scene closes with the same proclamation from the true German mother, Frau Thiemann, who exclaims: 'Father, my boys went of their own accord, and are still volunteers!'

Where, before, the play had brought the improbable meeting of Schlageter and the General in the President's own office, it now continues with the even more unlikely entry of the President into the very home of such nationalist sentiments. But however improbable such a scene might be, the intention is obvious, namely to mark the change. When the old socialist's eyes are opened, he sees the errors of his past ways and enters into union with his former opponents. National harmony must be demonstrated to be possible between Marxists and Nationalists as a result of the action of Schlageter and his comrades. The President is a proletarian and a socialist, he too has served in the army for four years at the front and has come out of the World War like many others believing in 'peace and reconciliation'; but now he is beginning to doubt such slogans and swears that, if his son is harmed, he will become a 'revolutionary' again, and destroy the government. This brings the old socialist almost exactly into line with the intentions of Schlageter and his activist group. Once again in the play doubt is cast on the divisive role played by socialists and Communists inside Germany, and when the frantic father asks who is to blame for the dreadful situation, the General (who now addresses him as a soldier like himself) points the finger at the socialists. A clear distinction is made here between *Kameraden* and *Genossen* (military, as against political, comrades), which the President immediately appreciates. The socialist idea, that there are comrades on each side of the national frontier, is explicitly rejected by him. International understanding between nations has failed and he accepts the need for a united people against the common foe: 'We must stand united, like our sons . . .' At that point the telephone rings and the sentences are announced — all the prisoners get long prison sentences except Schlageter, who is condemned to death. National and socialist political parties can therefore still work *together* on behalf of the prisoners, but nobody can save Schlageter, who is singled out for solitary death.

In the scenes that immediately follow, further demonstration is given of the depths to which Germany has sunk. The arrests continue, the leader of the Organization Heinz, for example, is reported to have been arrested by German police, and a visual example of the activities of the German police against their own kind is given by the arrest of Schlageter's batman, Fischer, on the premises. A Frenchman somewhere lifts the telephone and Germans arrest Germans. Alexandra conjures up a dreadful picture of a still disunited Germany, in which instead of acting together all still fight against each other. The General, however, immediately conjures up the counter-image of an awakening Germany with fresh columns of marching men ready for a new start. The Expressionistic concept of Aufbruch is here used in an entirely different context; indeed, the play, which till now has been so naturalistic, assumes general Expressionistic features, for it suddenly moves from the figure of Alexandra screaming in her madness, to the vision she sees of the trucks which drive Schlageter to his place of execution: 'The last image follows the scene like a vision'. After the Expressionistic gesture of Alexandra, with her fists clenched above her head, comes the symbolic stance of Schlageter bound with his hands behind his back 'as if with the whole world on his shoulders'. Lighting effects are added to sound effects to reinforce the impact of the final scene, as Schlageter is forced to his knees by a rifle blow, while the firing-squad fill the back horizon like a black wall and priest and lawyer stand to one side. Schlageter, with his back to the audience, turns slightly to the left, before uttering his last words:

> Germany!
> One last word! One wish! Command!
> Germany!!!
> Awaken! Take fire!!
> Burn! Burn furiously! (iv, 6)

Again he has left the realm of normal prose behind and the punctuation indicates the Expressionistic nature of this ecstatic utterance. His last words are more than a wish, they are an order to Germany to awaken, to burst into flames. Meanwhile the fire that he tries to ignite in Germany is matched by the order to fire which is given by the commander of the firing-squad. Again significantly and symbolically the flash from the guns passes through Schlageter's heart into the darkness of the theatre to be reflected and picked up presumably by the audience. What appears to end in triumph for those who have brought about the death of Schlageter will lead to the ultimate triumph for Germany herself, when as a result of Schlageter's sacrifice she does awake!

From an analysis of the conclusion of Johst's play some idea of Johst's artistic intentions can be deduced. Johst developed a theory of the open end, making the audience an integral part of the whole. According to this theory members of the audience would abandon their distanced position as mere observers of events on the stage and would sympathize with, and actively become involved in the action, in a manner which is the exact opposite of Brecht's later theory of alienation: 'The full rigour of attitudes to be adopted, the demands made upon the spirit, the logical carrying out of the decision arrived at, the metaphysical creative final act, all this must take place within each member of the audience'.[12] As Johst's *Schlageter* shows, this does not mean that the play culminates in the proclamation of party political slogans or direct references to specific causes. The play will not be a crude work of propaganda of that type, although such works did exist. Instead the theatre, by its formal quality, should offer an emotional event appealing not to reason and logic, but to 'deeper' spiritual realms, capable of releasing energies for action, in a certain direction. The play becomes an 'experience', whereby the attitudes which the hero represents are transmitted to the audience: 'The theatre we want has to be theatre of *experience*. Only then can it be more than mere pantomime, dancing, and scenes on the stage. Only then can it be elevated formally into truly cultic expression of mass feeling'.[13]

It has been possible to show the development of Johst from Expressionism to National Socialism; and *Schlageter* itself retains, as has been seen, many of the characteristic features of the author's avant-garde beginnings, especially the final, visionary scene of the play. The question still remains of the extent to which Johst was expressing deeply held beliefs. F. C. Weiskopf has doubted this and accused Johst of 'Konjunkturwitterung' — intellectual opportunism, in the same way as Johst accuses republican politicians of opportunism:

> He is an opportunist through and through, though that is exactly what makes him capable of producing literature, which, faithful to basic national-socialist principles, places feeling above reason, clouds of words above clear concepts, the blood above intellectual perception.[14]

This kind of reaction is understandable, but it is perhaps unjust, for there is little doubt that Johst did believe in what he was doing. As his confessional work *Ich glaube* (I believe) indicates, he did try to work out a consistent theory of theatre as cult, community and national experience, and his development over the years does show him going back from his own Expressionistic beginnings to the Greeks, 'Sturm und Drang' drama and Kleist in order to build up a consistent, though conservative 'Ethos of Limitation' culminating in heroic, mythologising drama of the *Schlageter* type. In effect, however, what he was trying to do proved impossible. He attempted to go beyond naturalism to create larger-than-life drama, yet his play is a curious mixture of naturalistic dialogue and symbolic intention. He tried to go beyond reason to myth, yet his whole play, while denying logic, is built up of one discussion scene after another. He tried to create drama which would culminate in the metaphysical act, yet his play is a denunciation of *Bildung*, culture and all theory and philosophy. Johst accused the theatre of the Weimar Republic of Cultural Bolshevism in its neglect of the hero, yet in his own traditionally constructed four-act play, he failed to create a traditional hero who arrives at insight into his own fate and acts in a convincing manner. On the contrary, Schlageter is strangely passive:

> One thing has to be established right from the start: Johst's Schlageter figure offers no genuine dramatic hero. For that . . . it is too passive in conception. In this play too the real action is moved outside the play itself, and what we experience is just emotional and intellectual discharges.[15]

What remains is far from being a great play (even National Socialist critics were aware of its many weaknesses), yet it is representative in many ways, not only of the fact that some Expressionists did move from Left to Right, from pacifism to adulation of the front-line soldier, but also of the ways in which the apolitical aspirations of Expressionist intellectuals for sacrifice and belonging could be perverted by the frustrations of the Weimar Republic into cultural suicide:

> This play is a revealing document for German history at that time, one which by the literary context in which it stands, unfortunately also proves how much tradition of idealistic thinking, twisted and shrivelled into its opposite, National Socialism could draw on.[16]

NOTES

1. Günther Rühle, *Zeit und Theater. Diktatur und Exil 1933–45.* Berlin, 1974, p. 734. The text of *Schlageter* is now most easily available in this volume pp. 77–139. All references will be to this text.
2. Günther Rühle, *Theater für die Republik 1917–1933,* Frankfurt am Main, 1967, p. 1155.
3. Helmut F. Pfanner, *Vom Expressionismus zum Nationalsozialismus,* The Hague–Paris, 1970; Peter H. Bumm, *Drama und Theater der Konservativen Revolution.* Munich, 1971.
4. Walter Riedel, *Der neue Mensch, Mythos und Wirklichkeit,* Bonn, 1970, p. 68.
5. L. A. Willoughby, *German Life and Letters,* I, 1936–37, p. 73.
6. Günther Rühle, *Zeit und Theater,* p. 740.
7. Dieter Schmidt, *'Baal' und der junge Brecht,* Stuttgart, 1966, pp. 27–30.
8. F. C. Weiskopf, 'Liebesdienst und Lobgesang. Zu Hanns Johsts Schauspiel "Schlageter"', *Neue Deutsche Blätter,* Monatschrift für Literatur und Kritik, 1. Jahrgang 1933–34, Heft 1–6 (Reprint Berlin, 1974), p. 315.
9. Warren Lerner, *Karl Radek. The Last Internationalist,* Stanford, 1970, pp. 120–123.
10. Richard S. Kemmler, *The National Socialist Ideology in Drama: A Comprehensive Study of Theatre and Drama during the Third Reich,* New York University Ph.D. diss. 1973, p. 74.
11. Uwe K. Ketelsen, *Völkisch-nationale und national-sozialistische Literatur in Deutschland 1890–1945,* Stuttgart, 1976, p. 70. See also the same author's *Von heroischem Sein und völkischem Tod. Zur Dramatik des dritten Reiches.* Bonn, 1970.
12. Hanns Johst, *Ich glaube!* p. 17.
13. E. W. Möller, 'Wandlungen des deutschen Theaters', *Hochschule und Ausland* XIII, 1935, p. 48.
14. F. C. Weiskopf, op. cit., p. 318.
15. Heinrich Bachmann in *Germania,* Berlin, quoted from *Das deutsche Drama in Geschichte und Gegenwart,* ed. Dr. Richard Elsner, Berlin, 1933, p. 261.
16. F. N. Mennemeier, *Modernes Deutsches Drama 2,* Uni–Taschenbücher 425, Munich, 1975, p. 109.

Walter Benjamin — Towards a new Marxist aesthetic

Hugh Ridley

> For it is an irretrievable picture of the past which threatens to vanish with
> each present age which has not seen itself as the intention of that picture.
>
> W. Benjamin, *Theses on the Philosophy of History*, v

There is a problem in approaching Benjamin's writings parallel to the more general question of how to approach the Weimar period itself from the distance of fifty years and across the *cordon sanitaire* of the English language. If the Weimar Republic is seen as a cabinet of literary curiosities, a well into which the historian lowers his bucket in anticipation of fullness, Benjamin may well disappoint as often as he fulfills the promise. His aphorisms, the choice essays on Paris and Berlin, on Kraus and Goethe, on collecting — these will attract the eye as trophies and contribute to a sense of the richness of Weimar culture. Yet they can also disappoint for Benjamin's irritating habit of reading well-known authors 'only when they are out of fashion', his interest in what can seem the small rather than the major objects in cultural and political life, in short his elusive and oblique approach to the age. To make Benjamin a trophy of Weimar culture becomes a problematic undertaking. If on the other hand Weimar is seen as a time of intense social, political and intellectual turmoil, and the debates which it threw up as having a relevance to the present which is neither that of the collector nor that of the antiquarian historian but a relevance which comes from the Weimar Republic's struggle to overcome problems which we have yet to solve, trying out intellectual and cultural forms which our own age sees in no sharper focus:—if this is how Weimar is seen, then Benjamin's place will be that of one of its most interesting citizens.

These general reflections cannot be avoided, for they are at the centre of Benjamin's own work. As someone involved in assessing and recapturing the essence of a past whose relevance to the present he never ceased to doubt, Benjamin repeatedly compares methods of approach in a way relevant to our own approach to him. In a 'Fragment on methodological questions of Marxist literary analysis', for instance, he compared two approaches to a literary tradition (he is, as so often, talking about a proper understanding of Baudelaire's work), using the metaphor of a camera:

> The bourgeois scholar looks into the camera like a layman, delighted at the colourful pictures he can see in the viewfinder. The materialist dialectician operates with the camera. His business is to reach certainties. He may examine a greater or smaller section of the picture, choosing a harsher political light or a more gentle historical lighting, and finally he lets the shutter flash and takes the picture. When he has taken out the plate, the picture of the object as it entered the social tradition, concepts take over and

168

develop the picture. For the plate can only contain a negative, since it is taken from an apparatus which puts shadows for light and light for shadows.[1]

This simile well expresses Benjamin's methods. It shows the selection of material objects of contemplation (as often as literary works or ideas), the sharpening of focus and concentration which is so characteristic of his Paris studies, the refusal to accept the surface appearance of reality and the determination to demask by intellectual activity that underlying material reality of which objects are expressions. Benjamin once commented on the 'shameless solidity' which the luxury goods of a consumer society display, so self-important in their status as objects that 'every shaft of light from the mind breaks harmlessly on their surface'.[2] Such objects were a challenge. He set himself the task not simply of attacking the false consciousness of previous ages but also the deceptions and confidence tricks which 'normal' external reality contained. To treat Benjamin as a trophy in the cabinet of Weimar curiosities would, in his own analogy, be to refuse to press the shutter.

Only within the last fifteen years or so has Benjamin been regarded as worth mentioning in any cultural history of the Weimar Republic. His impact during the 1920s was hardly such as to attract the historian's attention at that time, and the process of his rediscovery has been part of the rethinking of that period of cultural history. His post-doctoral dissertation on German tragedy in the Baroque was withdrawn before examination, when the appointed examiners found its level of discourse, hovering between mysticism and materialism, incomprehensible: a judgement which many later readers have accepted. His work on Goethe's *Elective Affinities* did nothing to appease the academic and literary establishment, and closed for good the door into university teaching. His other works of the Weimar period, mostly short articles and reviews, many of them published in the *Frankfurter Zeitung,* found readers and still deserve close attention, without having appeared at the time to be the seeds of major work. As Benjamin became closely involved with Marxist theory, through acquaintance with the works of Georg Lukács, and with its practice through his friendship with Asja Lazis, the effect was hardly to enlarge the circle of his readers. The Left stood on the brink of great schism, not merely between Stalin and Trotsky but also between the various camps within the Party's artistic and cultural movements, particularly as the proponents of Socialist Realism began to wage war on the avant-garde movements of the Left. Benjamin's involvement with the left-wing of Weimar culture brought him little status save as a friend and footnote in Brecht's biography and as yet another name in the list of exiles in 1933.

Benjamin's work first emerged from the shadows in the mid-1950s, as his friends T. W. Adorno and Gershom Scholem began to piece together the scattered essays into a complete edition. George Steiner has recently commented on the tensions inherent in Scholem's presentation of his former friend;[3] Benjamin's relationship with Adorno, Horkheimer and the Institute for Social Research (the so-called 'Frankfurt School' which went into exile in 1933) has been the subject of much discussion. Benjamin's disagreements with the Institute have remained since the mid-1960s the subject of controversy and polemic, not unconnected with an increasingly critical focus on the Weimar Republic itself. Ever since the periodical *alternative* set out in 1967 to rescue Benjamin's ideas — and, it was claimed, his texts — from the misleading interpretations of Adorno and his circle, the Adorno-Benjamin debate of the 1930s has been anything but a historical curiosity. Particularly with the Frankfurt School's dissociation from the cause of the student revolt of 1968 (which led many of that generation to criticize Adorno's work more generally as involving political passivity) a new generation came to discover in Benjamin a political activist blurred by Adorno's presentation of his friend and by the first full-length study of his work, Rolf Tiedemann's *Studien zur Philosophie Walter Benjamins* of 1965. Benjamin's relationship to Brecht came to be one of the focus-points of this revaluation, not least because of a growing awareness that Brecht too was in danger of 'political neutralization'.[4] This shift of emphasis cut across the tradition of Benjamin's previous reception. Scholem had regarded Brecht's influence on Benjamin as 'disastrous', while Adorno, as he admitted to Benjamin in a letter of March 1936, saw it as his task 'to hold your arm steady until the sun of Brecht has once more sunk into exotic waters'. It was felt by the late 1960s that Adorno had been holding Benjamin's arm too long. Especially following the first publication in 1966 of Benjamin's outspokenly political essay from the early 1930s, 'The Author as Producer', a number of critics have made the relationship to Brecht central to their reading of Benjamin's work. In so doing, these critics — Helmut Lethen, Heinz Brüggemann, Helga Gallas and Michael Scharang[5] — have created a Benjamin picture paradigmatic for the generation of 1968 and of great interest to a particular picture of Weimar culture.

This process is not a question of the politicization of, so to speak, an accidental case. The majority of the issues which it highlights are those which emerged in Benjamin's own debates with Adorno in the 1930s. They involve among other things the relationship between Benjamin's somewhat esoteric early works and the outspokenly Marxist essays of the 1930s, and the place of theory within Marxist praxis. Benjamin reception thus has implications for an overall Marxist aesthetic and literary method. It is also noticeable that recent criticism in Germany has been driven to Benjamin by the striking affinities between their own situation and that which Benjamin himself confronted, and it is in a genuine search for answers that they have read his work. Among the circumstances which have made this generation so open to Benjamin's work I may briefly mention: the search in the 1960s for a West German literature capable of coming to terms with the experiences of the German working-classes; the efforts of the student movement to find links with the working-classes and to rescue their socialism from mere intellectuality; finally — and most controversially — a sense that the experiences of the Weimar Republic were relevant to a Federal Republic tending (on the evidence of the Emergency Laws, the Grand Coalition and the like) towards a form of authoritarianism which intellectuals needed to combat decisively.[6] Many of these student attitudes were, of course, merely articulations of much more widely held opinions, and this too has helped to keep the Benjamin debate hot longer than if it were merely for consumption.

It is for these reasons, therefore, that this essay will focus on Benjamin via two of his most directly political essays — 'The Author as Producer' and 'The Work of Art in the Age of its Mechanical Reproduction'. Although the publication of neither work falls inside the Weimar period they are, as I hope to demonstrate, an unmistakable part of the legacy of Weimar.

I

'The Author as Producer' takes as its motto a call to 'win over intellectuals to the working-classes'.[7] It poses the question of commitment not by analyzing the *content* of the committed work ('how does a work regard the relations of production of its age? does it agree with them? is it reactionary? or does it aim to overthrow them? is it revolutionary?' (p. 97f)), but by focussing attention on what Benjamin calls the 'literary technology' of the work: namely 'the function which the work has within the literary relations of production of an age' (p. 98).

The writer is a producer. Like manual workers he applies his labour to the production of objects, which others then buy and sell. He thus supplies a production and distribution apparatus which he neither owns nor controls.

The central insight of the speech is hardly new. It recognizes the writer's place in that capitalist literary system which had been documented in Balzac's *Les illusions perdues,* and in those many other passages in the nineteenth-century novel where some struggling author in his garret confronts the mechanism of the 'literature industry' of high-technology publishing with its market, the newly literate masses, and its commodity, literature. Yet, whereas Balzac and the others had juxtaposed to this sphere of alienated and devalued literature a realm of pure art, Benjamin does not indulge in nostalgia. He views the writer's recognition of his standpoint, as one producer among many, from the point of view of political commitment, and therefore positively, as a proletarianization of the intellectual which goes beyond economic insecurity or political sympathy to an identity with the working-classes in their relationship to capitalism, on the basis of which meaningful commitment is possible.

In developing this idea — negatively in his critique of the left-wing intelligentsia of the Weimar Republic, positively in his hints of a new aesthetic — Benjamin reaches some of his most interesting formulations.

The relationship between the intellectual and the public had always been a problem for the Weimar Republic. At the end of the 'Kaiserreich' (Second Empire), in the figures of artist heroes such as Gustav von Aschenbach, the theme of the isolation of the artist had become a commonplace. The Expressionists set out to change this, and to reform society either from the messianic bandwagon of the Poet-Hero or by the indiscriminate 'ins-Volk-gehen' (intellectual slumming) of intellectuals with a bad conscience, desperate to be like the 'negroes, acrobats, soldiers and aviators' of Werfel's celebrated poem. They were followed by numerous intellectual groups on the Left queuing up to organize the world in accordance with principles of reason and intellectually perceived justice. Kurt Hiller was perhaps the most famous of these intellectual and all-too-ineffectual leaders. 'The fact that intellectuals adopted an advocacy position', a modern commentator remarks, 'in no way guaranteed that they would have the desired (or any) social effect'.[8] Benjamin saw this earlier than most (his comments anticipate Caudwell's attack on Shaw's vision of 'a bureaucracy of intellectuals'[9]) and provided a much needed revision of unmediated intellectual socialism.

Benjamin believed that the consistent failure of intellectuals' commitment to socialism was due to their blindness to the question his speech raised. They did not realize that their commitment to socialism would change the basis of their life as professional writers. So they went on merely supplying the existing apparatus of literary production with new material and never thought to 'refunction' the apparatus itself. For that reason, Benjamin argues, their revolutionary ideas remained without effect. He notes 'the ability of the bourgeois apparatus of production and publication to assimilate and indeed to propagate enormous quantities of revolutionary themes without calling into serious question its own existence and that of the class which owns it' (p. 105). We see here an important moment in the attack on the pluralism with which bourgeois society tolerates even revolutionary ideas and neutralizes them by including them in the process of consumption. (Böll has recently made some similar remarks on this as a feature of the Federal Republic.) Benjamin's aim in 1934 was not merely to interpret this condition, however, but to change it.

His essay next turned to consider another area of allegedly revolutionary activity in Weimar: the artistic movement known as New Objectivity ('Neue Sachlichkeit'). In attempting to come close to those realities of industrial society which the traditional arts were unable to convey, the writers of the late 1920s had turned to documentary, to photography and *reportage,* aiming at a radical objectivity in their presentation of the dehumanization and misery of German society.[10] Once more Benjamin argues that, because these writers changed only the internal style of their work, without considering the work's place in the literary production relations of their day, the consumption of their works was able effortlessly to turn a revolutionary intention into a counter-revolutionary effect. It is Benjamin's general thesis 'that however revolutionary a work's political intention may be, it may in fact have a counter-revolutionary effect for as long as a writer's solidarity with the proletariat stems from the opinions he holds rather than from his recognition that he is a producer' (p. 102). One work in particular, Regner-Patzsch's book of photographs *Die Welt ist schön* (It's a lovely World), managed 'to make even poverty an object of enjoyment', although its aim had been the reverse (p. 106). Technical brilliance of photography, far from unmasking poverty, had been turned into an object of consumption by the unchanged apparatus of literary production. In an age surrounded by coffee-table books, leather-bound versions not simply of 'great literature' but also of committed writers like Orwell and even the works of Mao Tsê-tung, we can perhaps appreciate the force of Benjamin's argument.

The essay is uncompromising. It takes for granted that all literature works for or against specific class-interests, and though it has none of the fervour of the literary executioner it certainly divides writers into sheep and goats. Before dismissing such a tone (as Adorno did), or jeering at Benjamin for his failure to create a new literary production apparatus (as Fritz Raddatz still does),[11] we need perhaps to remember the age in which Benjamin was writing. The spectre of National Socialism is behind almost every line, for Benjamin is determined to expose the half-way houses of intellectual compromise which were being occupied by his fellow writers. Unlike Adorno, who admitted even in October 1934 that he 'would have had no political objection' to remaining in Hitler's Germany,[12] Benjamin was convinced of the necessity of a totally alternative system. Benjamin left no room for inner emigration, no preservation of a spurious independence and autonomy for the writer, since it weakened the battle-lines in the fight against fascism. His essay is the equivalent in criticism of Brecht's statement for poetry that in such a dark age even 'a conversation about trees' is a crime 'because it involves silence about so many crimes'.

It was Brecht who provided Benjamin with a model for the new style of intellectual activity. Benjamin was very early to appreciate the salient features of Brecht's 'epic theatre', and his formula for Brecht's commitment is particularly interesting for being defined not within the limited terms of political tendency (the message and content which the plays try to 'get across' to a consuming spectator) but in terms of his literary technology, that rewriting of the relationship of audience and dramatist which transforms the theatre's function, 'turning consumers towards production; in short, making spectators collaborators' (p. 110). Benjamin's view of Brecht thus preserves that essential critical element in his Marxism which in the 1930s kept him distant from Stalinism and in the 1960s made him ripe for the New Left.

Benjamin's other model for the author as producer was Sergej Tretjakov, a Soviet playwright and essayist, who had combined Futurist ideas with wholehearted and practical support for the Revolution. Tretjakov had spent many months in the late 1920s working on a collective farm, with the tasks of 'calling mass meetings, collecting money for the purchase of tractors, persuading landowning peasants to join the collective farm, inspecting reading-rooms, setting up wall-newspapers and editing the collective farm's newspaper, reporting to Moscow newspapers, introducing radios and itinerant cinemas, etc.' (p. 99). In these activities Benjamin saw a practical example of the refunctioning of the intellectual's role which his ideas involved. He was also aware, as Tretjakov was, of the attacks such a radical stance would provoke. It is very easy to portray all these activities as being beneath the dignity of a creative writer, and belonging more properly within the activities of an 'educated bureaucrat'. Critics have also attacked Tretjakov for anti-intellectual attitudes, a facile *sacrificum intellectus.*[13] Yet Tretjakov was convinced that the concerns traditional to intellectuals — the concern for truth, for human values and the critical approach to reality — could only express themselves in the new social forms which he had adopted. In 1934, far from 'flattering' the Soviet authorities by reference to Tretjakov's work,[14] Benjamin was already showing how far his view of intellectual commitment diverged from that of the Communist establishment. It was clear that the literary authorities were backing away from radicalism in literature (no doubt in part withdrawing their approval from any kind of critical intellectual tradition within Marxism), and were anxious to revert to a situation in which writers wrote books and readers read them: that 'semi-shopkeeper mentality' which Lenin had decried[15] and from which revolutionary writers like Tretjakov had tried to escape.

II

These developments in the Soviet Union, which were ultimately to lead to Tretjakov's disappearance in one of Stalin's purges, point back to what had been the original starting-point of Benjamin's speech: his discontent with the state of Marxist aesthetics. This is therefore the place to sketch the relationship between his views and the developments which preceded them.

It is well known that Marx and Engels did not bequeath to their followers a seamless and all-embracing aesthetic philosophy. From their various comments on literature, notably on Lassalle's play *Franz von Sickingen* (1859); from Engels' late letters, culminating in the celebrated letter of 1887 to Margaret Harkness which championed objective realism in preference to committed socialist literature; above all from the theory of base and superstructure enunciated in the *Critique of Political Economy* (1859), critics had to piece together their own picture of a Marxist aesthetic. Franz Mehring and G. V. Plechanov, writing at the turn of the century, developed the first relatively systematic aesthetic method, showing the economic determinants of the literature of the past and evaluating on that basis its usefulness to the socialism of their day. Mehring in particular had only a limited interest in formulating a programme for the development of socialist literature. He believed that literature would play a much smaller role in the emancipation of the proletariat than it had in the emancipation of the bourgeoisie. 'If the German bourgeoisie had its heroic period in the realm of art', he wrote in the essay 'Art and the Proletariat' in 1896, 'that only happened because the economic and political battlefields were closed to it'.[16] The implication was that these battlefields, rather than art, would be crucial in the struggle of the German proletariat.

Perhaps as a result of such scepticism, neither Mehring nor Plechanov developed a fully rounded aesthetic theory. Their analysis of literature was dominated by questions of content, and any discussion of form either took place in traditional Kantian terms or was regarded as inappropriate, for Mehring resisted such discussion as 'brushing dust from the butterfly's wings'.[17] Predictably, the SPD was more anxious to catch up with the bourgeoisie in matters of art than to overhaul its critical methods. Thus before 1917 Marxist aesthetic theory merely oscillated between utilitarianism and the cult of pure art.

After the October Revolution there were in the Soviet Union several movements attempting to reformulate a Marxist aesthetic. Trotsky's *Literature and Revolution* (1924), which continued the view that no particular proletarian class-literature should be expected in the early years of the Revolution, gives a view of the breadth of effort being made. On the one hand Bogdanov and the 'Proletkult' movement attempted to develop an exclusively proletarian literature, 'pock-marked' in quality but appealing to the masses by means of its 'class passport'. Other movements, notably those around Majakovsky, were attempting to find a revolutionary style in art which would correspond to the political and social revolution which was taking place. These movements were less concerned with the class from which writers came, than with writers' revolutionary consciousness. It is clear that Benjamin followed developments in the Soviet Union very closely (that was anything but unusual in Weimar Germany), and that his concept of the author as producer owes much to both Tretjakov and to Boris Arvatov, another member of the circles round Majakovsky.

Developments in Germany after 1919 had been more strongly coloured by the concept of committed 'party literature' than in the Soviet Union, yet a vigorous debate about Marxist aesthetics became established.[18] This was possible partly as a result of the gradual dimming of the hope of immediate revolution, partly too because of the fact that so many writers and intellectuals had found their way to the Party by the early 1930s; and partly too as part of the re-emergence of a more philosophical tradition in Marxism, brought about by the publication in the 1920s

an entirely new departure in the history of art. Just as the development of printing transformed every aspect of the written word, from the social function of its authors to the style of their works, Benjamin argues, so developments in technology since 1850 have triggered off an earthquake in all aspects of aesthetics. Previous methods of reproduction actually enhanced the qualities of the original work of art, underlining its physical uniqueness (*one* original, many copies), its personal nature as the statement of one man, and its genuineness. By contrast, technical reproduction destroys just those qualities of a work of art which have always been regarded as essential to it, qualities which Benjamin summarizes as the 'aura' of the work of art. He derives the word from the origins of works of art (and the aesthetic theories associated with them) in cult and ritual (p. 480). (A comparison, for instance, between the values contained in and expressed by an icon in its original location and those of a technically perfect copy offered for mass sale makes Benjamin's argument clear.) It underlines also that the content of works of art is not absolute and timeless but a product of the work's place in the 'living social context' of each age.

The effects of technology do not stop at the reception and transformation of existing works of art. Benjamin's essay shows the increasing effect of technology on the production of new works and on the theories and justification which accompany them. From those moments in the mid-nineteenth century when literature turned away from an aristocratic public towards a new mass public, determined to study ordinary people's lives 'at work' (as Freytag claimed) rather than the leisure of the few; from such moments a development had been running which would sweep aside all the aesthetic assumptions of previous ages. The dynamic for change lay on one hand indisputably in the socio-economic base, with the change from rural to city life, and the increasing division of labour under industrial capitalism. These changes affected art by altering both the reality art described and the general mode of perception of reality. But technological advance also came to influence artistic production and reproduction directly, and in the new medium of the film and photograph Benjamin identifies a culmination of this development, and he believes that only in understanding the new medium can a new aesthetic be formulated.

The debate about film occupied an important place in Weimar intellectual life, and Benjamin's essay represents a vehicle through which this debate was transmitted to the post-war cinema world. In particular film's effect on the narrative forms of the novel and on the drama, its affinities with the newly emergent white collar culture of the cities, its ability as a medium to supply equally the requirements of realism and fantasy, had been discussed since the first experiments of the Lumière brothers in the heyday of Naturalism.[23] Benjamin was not alone in his observations of the correspondence between the techniques of film and the experience of urban life: Döblin and others had commented, for instance, on the speed with which sense-impressions changed in the city and on the ability of the film to mirror this speed. Benjamin repeatedly discusses the place of shock in the life of the city and in the technique of the film, but his conclusions are more radical, however, than those of his contemporaries. At a time when it was still customary for critics to debate whether or not the film was an art-form (Brecht's review of the film-debate in his *Dreigroschenprozess* (1932) analyzed this attitude), Benjamin argued that the existence of the film had thrown into question the very concept of art itself. Any idea of art which starts from the individual creativity of the artist is defunct (for the film is a collective endeavour); any approach to art which starts from individual response and reception is nullified by the collective reception of the film; any idea that art is concerned with a separate and distinct realm of experience must succumb to the particular closeness to reality which characterizes film and photograph.

Not that film is in itself automatically realistic. Already in 'The Author as Producer', as we saw, Benjamin had been critical of documentary styles which imagined that the photograph as such showed everything. The truth about the world is not visible on the surface like paint, and, as Benjamin's analogy of his work with a camera showed, it takes more than a view-finder to understand the world. Nevertheless Benjamin was insistent that *as a medium* film was politically progressive. It was no coincidence that the historical emergence of photography in the nineteenth century was 'contemporary with the dawn of socialism' (p. 481).[24] Benjamin's argument was to show that the destruction of 'aura' is the equivalent in art-history of that shift from the cult of the individual to that of the masses which marks the victory of socialism (pp. 479–80). In his famous study of the great Soviet films of the 1920s Béla Balázs, too, had underlined the correspondence between the aesthetic and political tendency of the film. He had claimed that, while great films were also possible under capitalism, socialist films were great 'because the spirit which is dominant there [in the Soviet Union] does not contradict the spirit of the film. The tendency of the camera is their tendency.'[25] Benjamin's understanding of the film, though similar, was based on German experience and came from his reflections on Brecht's encounter with film in the early 1930s: first with the version of *The Threepenny Opera* which the Nero film-company made of Brecht's stage-success, and secondly with the film *Kuhle Wampe,* which Brecht made directly in collaboration with Slatan Dudow and Ernst Ottwalt. It is unmistakably Brecht's experience which is expressed in Benjamin's essay, as two brief examples will show.

The film *Kuhle Wampe* (1932) deals with the unemployed of Berlin, and in one of its early sequences it portrays the suicide of Ani Bönike's young brother, who is unemployed. In a series of largely silent montage sequences the film follows the young unemployed as they ride round the city, vainly looking for work. We see Bönike only as a member of that group, lost in the crowd; it is his pedalling rather than his face which is the lasting image. When he returns home to the endless argument with parents who blame him for failing to find a job, Bönike throws himself from a window, having first carefully unstrapped his watch.

In 'A small contribution to the theme of realism' Brecht tells of the censors' objections to this scene.[26] They complained, Brecht tells, on the grounds that the scene was political rather than individual in its message. 'Your film sets out to portray the suicide as typical', the police authorities informed Brecht, 'as something not simply convenient for some (morbidly inclined) individual or other, but as the fate of a whole class.' Brecht describes the uncomfortable feeling that he had been 'caught out' by this description, the intention of the film guessed far better by its enemies than by many of Brecht's colleagues on the Left. The policeman art-critic had pinpointed the exact purpose and weight of the scene, which wanted to exploit the ability of the film *as medium* to reject the apparatus of interior and individual motivation and reach out beyond limited psychological statements to those with the widest social import.

Brecht's reflections on film — based partly on the American films which were so popular in Weimar, and partly on his immediate experiences of filming — naturally led him to see great similarities between the techniques of the cinema and the theory of 'epic theatre' which he was evolving at the time. Benjamin, as the earliest champion of Brecht's theories, took these ideas over in the 'Art-Work' essay. In Brechtian language he suggests that the action of viewing a film, by 'uniting the attitudes of criticism and enjoyment' (p. 497), gives the spectator a new relationship to the work. Instead of passively accepting reality as it is, the spectator 'tests' reality through his reaction to the film (p. 488). Under 'the inspired leadership of the lens', he penetrates the surface of reality, smashing open by the lens' new perspectives, the oppressive environment of 'our pubs and city streets, our offices and furnished rooms, our stations and factories' (p. 499). The film actor, unable to put himself over to the audience as an emotional entity (for the film is shot in separate sequences, cut and edited), finds his work revealed as a process of communication. He makes of gesture and movement tools of analysis and communication, rather than simply ways to express internal feelings with which the spectator then has to identify. The spectator therefore not only benefits from the observational and liberating capacities of the camera lens, he also finds his way to a testing and questioning approach to human relationships and behaviour.

In arguments of this kind Benjamin was doing more than recording the influence of technical change upon the production of art. He had found in Brecht's work not merely an example of effective criticism of the society of his day, but a prefiguration of a future socialist aesthetic. In this spirit Benjamin had announced, in the preface to the 'Art-Work' essay, that his examination of developments in the superstructure would, like Marx's account of the socio-economic base, contain both analysis and prognosis. He discusses the new technology of film therefore both as a revolutionary weapon of criticism operating 'under the existing conditions of production' (p. 473) and as an anticipation of a newly-based socialist aesthetic. The temptation of this approach lies, of course, in the closely related assumption that, because technology was the basis of the new aesthetic, technical progress might itself bring about politically desirable ends, and of itself work for socialism. There were, for instance, those at the beginning of the nineteenth century who believed that progress in mechanical reproduction of the printed word (this was the time of the invention of the rotary press) would of itself defeat the apparatus of censorship and political control.[27] In their day, contrasting the reactionary political controls with the dynamic and uncontrolled release of printed freedom, it was easy to think that technical progress in itself was the handmaiden of democracy. Technology as a political utopia haunted socialism throughout the nineteenth century, and into the 1920s — as Helmut Lethen has so convincingly shown. There are moments in Benjamin's essay when he clearly was searching for political hope under the wings of technological progress. He had watched Brecht's theories emerging from the practices even of the capitalist film industry and believed that the 'genuinely revolutionary' qualities of photography could triumph against all odds.

These optimistic moments in Benjamin's essay were based on the experience of Weimar culture. They related much less closely to the situation of the mid-1930s than to the declining years of Weimar. (Similarly, we might say of 'The Author as Producer' that, whatever impact Benjamin hoped for among French intellectuals, its real public was the pre-1933 German Left.) Developments in the cinema in the mid-1930s had raised questions to which the 'Art-Work' essay did not offer specific answers, notably of course the development of talking pictures.[28] In addition, although Benjamin's essay assumes (with much justification) that the National Socialists were pursuing a restorative cultural programme which would emphasize traditional aesthetic ideas, some developments in the German cinema were much more radical. At a time when Riefenstahl was making films such as *The Triumph of the Will* which, unlike so many of the costume historical dramas later to emerge from the National Socialist cinema, seemed absolutely modern in their techniques and orientation, it is striking that Benjamin should be so confident that the aesthetic principles evolved by his essay were 'totally unusable for the purposes of fascism' (p. 473). On first reading, the remark may seem to betray something of the misplaced optimism of Weimar.

It is important to consider this question. If indeed Benjamin were seriously wrong about fascism and its art, or if his work merely echoes the glossy fallacies of the stabilization period of Weimar, his theories — particularly where they impinge on the realities of politics and history — would have fallen at the first fence. Such an interpretation of Benjamin's claim has appealed to those critics anxious to play down his political significance,[29] but there are at least two central arguments invalidating that interpretation, and these we need briefly to consider.

We need to remember that this essay was linked to 'The Author as Producer' no less strongly than to the Paris study. It is not intended as a discursive 'prolegomena to the history of art' (Benjamin's own description of what his essay was not meant to be),[30] or as a philosophical thesis on the relationship of base and superstructure. It is a manual for the committed artist, telling him the weapons at his command, their use and their effects. What happens in the National Socialist film, or in the talking films of Hollywood, is not a 'natural' development of the film as medium, but a deliberate extension of the technique of film with particular aims in mind. Benjamin knew the film-theories of, for instance, Ernst Jünger. He saw that the destruction of the traditionally individualist intellectual position was an essential part of the practice of German fascism, just as he knew that Benn had celebrated the death of bourgeois art ('There will never again be art in the sense of the last five hundred years')[31] before throwing himself headlong into Hitler's reconstruction of Germany. Without the destruction of the autonomous individual, 'total mobilization' was impossible and thus technically 'progressive' artistic movements would be manipulated in the direction of fascism. Socialist tendencies were not contained neatly within an historical process which was conveniently eroding bourgeois values: they had to be brought out of the historical process, and only a committed position, not a contemplative one, could do that.

For this reason, Benjamin came increasingly to focus on what Bloch (in his defence of modernism against the Socialist Realists) called the 'art' of inheriting the past. Benjamin's 'Theses on history', written very shortly before his death in 1940, were concerned above all to attack the notion that history is inexorably moving in a particular direction, and that socialism needs only to sit back and wait for history to shower it with inevitable rewards. Indeed Benjamin attacks the

SPD for just this passivity in the face of history, both before 1914 (for instance in the debates about 'super-imperialism') and again in the period of stabilization under Weimar. He argues that history needs to be reinterpreted and reordered in the service of present causes, that it does not naturally lie in any one direction but must constantly be 'brushed against the grain'.[32] Benjamin's argument epitomizes what Nietzsche had called the 'critical' approach to the past. By 1940, with the spectacle of war, the Nazi-Soviet pact, the persecution of the Jews and Stalin's purges, it is hardly surprising that Benjamin did not feel impelled towards historical optimism. But this does not mean to say that the undoubted optimism of the 'Art-Work' essay participated in the crudely progressive cult of technology of the 1920s. Not even in 1936 did Benjamin have any illusion that he might be 'swimming with the stream',[33] any more than in 1934 he had seriously believed that Tretjakov's model of intellectual activity belonged in the mainstream of Soviet developments. His optimism had a different basis. It lay with the immense confidence Benjamin felt in the ability of the intellectual to discover and create streams in history, to rechannel the past in the cause of the present. This clearly was the nature of his intellectual commitment to socialism, and it strengthened rather than weakened with the passing years.

If Benjamin's confidence lay in intellectual activity rather than in any abstracted view of 'history' which was bound to win, he attached special importance to the intellectual products which the critic deals with, and particularly to the works of art of the past. The contemplation of works of art from the past remained justified for the energy and vitality of those works needed to be released afresh into each age. When he called the history of art 'a history of prophecies' and claimed that it could be interpreted 'only from the standpoint of the immediate and present moment', he was not only showing his confidence in the intellectual as the reader of prophecies but in those works 'with soul' (*beseelt*) which contained 'this dark, fermenting dimension of the future'.[34] Without breaking the materialism of his approach to the literature of the past, Benjamin had — like Bloch — preserved for art-works the ability to anticipate as well as reflect changes in the socio-economic base, and thus a special status.

On the surface, this may seem to undo the work of 'The Author as Producer' and to be a reversion to aesthetics after a period of political fervour. Critics have spoken in this connection of Benjamin's 'Janus face', looking longingly in two opposite directions. Yet the famous Benjamin-Adorno debate of the late 1930s shows Benjamin's positive appreciation of art to have had a far greater political consistency than that of Adorno. Adorno constantly refused to endorse any aesthetic position which took into consideration art's 'political effect on its audience'. He so disliked the mass-culture which he had encountered in America that he refused to admit any positive aspects in the mass reception of works of art, and for this reason refused to differentiate between the mass-art of socialism and that of fascism.[35] Artistic technique, in the limited sense of the artist's handling of the material of his craft, was the only dimension relevant to the discussion of the production of works of art, and their reception had no importance. Adorno was thus horrified when Benjamin dismissed all 'autonomous' art for art's sake as belonging to the realm of fascism. Benjamin, however, was convinced that it was possible 'to rescue art from its dependence on so-called talent and from the process of decay in which it is involved by associating it intimately with didactic, informational and political elements'.[36] He genuinely saw a rescue of art to lie in the process of its refunctioning. In Tretjakov he saw not the demise of the intellectual, but his rejuvenation. If faced with a choice between a hermetic, elite art and a mass-art which Adorno regarded as debased, Benjamin would always opt for the latter. Like Sartre, he insisted on the unity of the making and reception of art and believed that in both aspects art could act as a liberation of the productive capacities. This breadth of vision and this confidence, no less than the interest and insight of his works, assure him a place in the realignment of Marxist aesthetics which has gone on since his death. It was a feature of his historical situation that he could travel so little of that road except in theory.

NOTES

1. W. Benjamin, 'Fragment über Methodenfragen einer marxistischen Literatur-Analyse' in *Kursbuch* 20 (March 1970), p. 2.

2. *Einbahnstraße* in *Gesammelte Schriften*, ed. R. Tiedemann & H. Schweppenhäuser, vol. 4, 1 (Frankfurt am Main, 1972), pp. 100–01. Translated as *One-Way Street* by Edmund Jephcott (N.L.B., 1978). My translation here is coloured by Jephcott's.

3. Cf. Steiner's review of Benjamin-Scholem correspondence in *The Times Literary Supplement*, 27 June 1980.

4. Cf. Roland Barthes' comments on Brecht reception in the mid-1960s quoted in D. Lamb, *The Marxist Theory of Art* (Hassocks, 1978), p. 57.

5. The Benjamin numbers of *alternative* were 56–7 (October/December 1967) and 59–60 (April/June 1968). See also H. Lethen, *Neue Sachlichkeit, 1924–1932* (Stuttgart, 1970); H. Gallas *Marxistische Literaturtheorie* (Neuwied, 1971); M. Scharang, *Zur Emanzipation der Kunst* (Neuwied, 1971); H. Brüggemann, *Literarische Technik und soziale Revolution* (Reinbek, 1973).

6. For an account of the student generation's relationship to Benjamin's work see: A. Hillach, 'W. Benjamin: Korrektiv kritischer Theorie oder revolutionärer Handhabe?' W. Martin Ludke (ed.) *Literatur und Studentenbewegung* (Köln/Opladen, 1977), pp. 64–90.

7. 'Der Autor als Produzent' in W. Benjamin, *Versuche über Brecht* (Frankfurt, 1966), pp. 95–116. English translation by Anya Bostock in W. Benjamin, *Understanding Brecht* (N.L.B., 1977). Page references in this section are to the German edition, using my own translation. The speech was originally intended for the Institute for the Study of Fascism on 27 April 1934 in Paris.

8. Susan Buck-Morss, *The Origin of Negative Dialectics. Theodor W. Adorno, Walter Benjamin, and the Frankfurt Institute* (Hassocks, 1977), pp. 4–5. This is a small and obvious point, but my debt to Buck-Morss' study is general and considerable. Cf. for instance her very perceptive account of different theories of the avant-garde (pp. 30–33).

9. C. Caudwell, *Studies in a dying culture* (1938, rev. ed. London, 1957) p. 9. Caudwell was another welcome discovery of the German student generation.

10. Helmut Lethen has given a full critique of this literature, partly utilizing Benjamin's approach (*Neue Sachlichkeit*, passim).

11. See Raddatz's essays in *Merkur*, Vol. 27 (1973), pp. 1065–75 (the more vitriolic of the two) and Vol. 33 (1979), pp. 867–82.

12. Quoted by Buck-Morss, p. 137.

13. F. Raddatz, 'Die Kräfte des Rausches für die Revolution gewinnen' in *Merkur*, Vol. 33 (1979), p. 879. My own essay on Tretjakov saw more 'anti-intellectualism' in his position than I now regard as fair (Tretjakov in Berlin', in Keith Bullivant (ed.) *Culture and Society in the Weimar Republic* (Manchester, 1977, pp. 150–63).

14. This is the view of Susan Buck-Morss (p. 143).

15. V. I. Lenin, 'Party literature and party organization' (1905) in *Collected Works*, Vol. 10 (Moscow, 1960), p. 46.

16. F. Mehring, *Gesammelte Schriften*, Vol. 11 (Berlin, 1961), p. 139.

17. F. Mehring quoted by G. Fülberth, *Proletarische Partei und bürgerliche Literatur* (Neuwied, 1972), p. 43.

18. A footnote giving full details of the literature of the early years of Marxist aesthetics would take over the whole volume, but especially worthy of mention are P. Demetz, *Marx, Engels und die Dichter* (Frankfurt/Berlin, 1969), H. Gallas, *Marxistische Literaturtheorie* (Neuwied, 1971) and Rob Burns' excellent essay 'Theory and organisation of revolutionary working-class literature . . .' in *Culture and Society in the Weimar Republic,* pp. 122–49.

19. Cf. D. Craig, *Marxists on literature: an anthology* (Penguin Books, 1975) p. 23.

20. Anya Bostock's translation has 'literary technique' (*Understanding Brecht,* p. 87). Teaching-experience with this text suggests that it is just this phrase which is misleading to the English reader, and is taken usually to refer to technique only in the sense of interior 'style' and not to those external relations which are to be refunctioned.

21. R. Williams, *Marxism and Literature* (O.U.P., 1977), p. 52. Williams uses Benjamin's arguments directly on p. 103f.

22. Page references are to *Gesammelte Schriften,* Vol. 1, 2, pp. 471–508. An English translation by Harry Zahn is contained in W. Benjamin, *Illuminations* (Fontana, London, 1977).

23. Cf. A. Kaes, *Kino-Debatte* (Tübingen, 1978), pp. 1–35.

24. Benjamin was insistent on the inclusion of this parallel. (See the notes on the essay in *Gesammelte Schriften,* Vol. 1, 3, p. 991f.)

25. B. Balázs, *Der Geist des Films* (Halle, 1930), p. 217.

26. B. Brecht, *Über Realismus* (Frankfurt am Main, 1971), pp. 29–30. *Kuhle Wampe oder Wem gehört die Welt?* in B. Brecht, *Texte für Filme* (Frankfurt am Main, 1969), p. 129ff.

27. Cf. Louis James, *Fiction for the working-man* (Penguin, Harmondsworth, 1973), p. 12f.

28. In a letter to Adorno in December 1938 Benjamin claimed that the talking film was a deliberate attempt by the film-industry 'to torpedo the revolutionary primacy of the silent film' (quoted in *Gesammelte Schriften,* 1, 3, p. 1033).

29. R. Tiedemann, *Studien zur Philosophie Walter Benjamins* (Frankfurt am Main, 1965), p. 89ff. For the counter-argument see H. Lethen, *Neue Sachlichkeit,* pp. 134–8.

30. Unpublished summary, *Gesammelte Schriften,* 1, 3, p. 1050.

31. G. Benn, *Werke,* Vol. 1, p. 254.

32. Benjamin, 'Über den Begriff der Geschichte', vii: *Gesammelte Schriften,* Vol. 1, 2, p. 697.

33. Ibid. xi, p. 698.

34. Variant on the essay *Gesammelte Schriften,* 1, 3, p. 1046.

35. Cf. Buck-Morss, p. 34 and Lethen, p. 138. It is important to bear these differentiations in mind, since so much attention has focused on Adorno's criticisms of Benjamin for shortcomings in Marxism. English approaches can be found in E. Bloch *et al., Aesthetics and Politics* (N.L.B., 1977), pp. 100–9; and in *New Left Review's* introduction of the Adorno-Benjamin correspondence, no. 81 (Sept./Oct. 1973), p. 51f. Particularly interesting is the special Benjamin issue of *New German Critique* (No. 17, Spring 1979).

36. Variant on the essay, *Gesammelte Schriften,* 1, 3, p. 1051.